*Eternal Father,
I offer You the most precious Blood
of thy Divine Son, Jesus,
in union with the Masses said
throughout the world today,
for all the Holy Souls in Purgatory,
for sinners everywhere,
for sinners in the universal Church,
for those in my own home,
and in my family.*

Amen.

ST. GERTRUDE'S PRAYER FOR THE HOLY SOULS

The Month of
_____

DATE: _____

Today, have a Mass said for the soul of a family member or friend who has passed away. This can be through your own parish or through an order or national shrine via their website.

Morning Prayer for the Poor Souls:

Out of the depths I have cried to Thee O Lord! Lord, hear my voice. Let Thine ears be attentive to the voice of my supplication.
If Thou, O Lord, wilt mark iniquities, Lord, who shall stand it?
For with Thee there is mercy: and by reason of Thy law I have waited on Thee, O Lord! My soul hath relied on His word: my soul hath hoped in the Lord. From the morning watch even until night. Let Israel hope in the Lord. For with the Lord there is mercy; and with Him plentiful Redemption. And He will redeem Israel from all his iniquities.
Eternal rest give unto them, O Lord! And let perpetual light shine upon them. May they rest in peace. Amen.

Evening Prayer for the Poor Souls:

V. Lord, hear my prayer.
R. And let my cry come unto Thee.
Bless, O my God! the repose I am about to take, that, renewing my strength, I may be better enabled to serve Thee. Pour down Thy blessings, O Lord! on my parents, relations, friends, and enemies. Protect the Pope, our Bishop, and all the Pastors of Thy holy Church. Assist the poor and the afflicted, and those who are now in their last agony. Look with an eye of pity on the suffering souls in purgatory, particularly

_____
_____

_____

put an end to their torments and lead them forth into everlasting joy.

Eternal rest grant unto them and let perpetual light shine upon them. Amen.

DATE:

_____

Pray the Rosary today for the release of souls from Purgatory. Mystic saints have told us that the Blessed Mother herself comes to Purgatory to bring souls with her back to Heaven.

Morning Prayer for the Poor Souls:

Out of the depths I have cried to Thee O Lord! Lord, hear my voice. Let Thine ears be attentive to the voice of my supplication.
If Thou, O Lord, wilt mark iniquities, Lord, who shall stand it?
For with Thee there is mercy: and by reason of Thy law I have waited on Thee, O Lord! My soul hath relied on His word: my soul hath hoped in the Lord. From the morning watch even until night. Let Israel hope in the Lord. For with the Lord there is mercy; and with Him plentiful Redemption. And He will redeem Israel from all his iniquities.
Eternal rest give unto them, O Lord! And let perpetual light shine upon them. May they rest in peace. Amen.

Evening Prayer for the Poor Souls:

V. Lord, hear my prayer.
R. And let my cry come unto Thee.
Bless, O my God! the repose I am about to take, that, renewing my strength, I may be better enabled to serve Thee. Pour down Thy blessings, O Lord! on my parents, relations, friends, and enemies. Protect the Pope, our Bishop, and all the Pastors of Thy holy Church. Assist the poor and the afflicted, and those who are now in their last agony. Look with an eye of pity on the suffering souls in purgatory, particularly

_____

_____

_____

put an end to their torments and lead them forth into everlasting joy.

Eternal rest grant unto them and let perpetual light shine upon them. Amen.

DATE:

_____

Today, ask the Blessed Mother to apply your prayers and works to a poor soul who has no one to pray for them.

Morning Prayer for the Poor Souls:

Out of the depths I have cried to Thee O Lord! Lord, hear my voice. Let Thine ears be attentive to the voice of my supplication.
If Thou, O Lord, wilt mark iniquities, Lord, who shall stand it?
For with Thee there is mercy: and by reason of Thy law I have waited on Thee, O Lord! My soul hath relied on His word: my soul hath hoped in the Lord. From the morning watch even until night. Let Israel hope in the Lord. For with the Lord there is mercy; and with Him plentiful Redemption. And He will redeem Israel from all his iniquities.
Eternal rest give unto them, O Lord! And let perpetual light shine upon them. May they rest in peace. Amen.

Evening Prayer for the Poor Souls:

V. Lord, hear my prayer.
R. And let my cry come unto Thee.
Bless, O my God! the repose I am about to take, that, renewing my strength, I may be better enabled to serve Thee. Pour down Thy blessings, O Lord! on my parents, relations, friends, and enemies. Protect the Pope, our Bishop, and all the Pastors of Thy holy Church. Assist the poor and the afflicted, and those who are now in their last agony. Look with an eye of pity on the suffering souls in purgatory, particularly

_____

_____

put an end to their torments and lead them forth into everlasting joy.

Eternal rest grant unto them and let perpetual light shine upon them. Amen.

DATE:

_____

We all have a spiritual or physical affliction or burden that we suffer with daily. Today, dedicate your ailment-related suffering to the Poor souls.

Morning Prayer for the Poor Souls:

Out of the depths I have cried to Thee O Lord! Lord, hear my voice. Let Thine ears be attentive to the voice of my supplication.
If Thou, O Lord, wilt mark iniquities, Lord, who shall stand it?
For with Thee there is mercy: and by reason of Thy law I have waited on Thee, O Lord! My soul hath relied on His word: my soul hath hoped in the Lord. From the morning watch even until night. Let Israel hope in the Lord. For with the Lord there is mercy; and with Him plentiful Redemption. And He will redeem Israel from all his iniquities.
Eternal rest give unto them, O Lord! And let perpetual light shine upon them. May they rest in peace. Amen.

Evening Prayer for the Poor Souls:

V. Lord, hear my prayer.
R. And let my cry come unto Thee.
Bless, O my God! the repose I am about to take, that, renewing my strength, I may be better enabled to serve Thee. Pour down Thy blessings, O Lord! on my parents, relations, friends, and enemies. Protect the Pope, our Bishop, and all the Pastors of Thy holy Church. Assist the poor and the afflicted, and those who are now in their last agony. Look with an eye of pity on the suffering souls in purgatory, particularly

_____

_____

_____

put an end to their torments and lead them forth into everlasting joy.

Eternal rest grant unto them and let perpetual light shine upon them. Amen.

DATE:
_____

Today, visit or call someone elderly or alone and offer your work of mercy for the souls in Purgatory.

Morning Prayer for the Poor Souls:

Out of the depths I have cried to Thee O Lord! Lord, hear my voice. Let Thine ears be attentive to the voice of my supplication.
If Thou, O Lord, wilt mark iniquities, Lord, who shall stand it?
For with Thee there is mercy: and by reason of Thy law I have waited on Thee, O Lord! My soul hath relied on His word: my soul hath hoped in the Lord. From the morning watch even until night. Let Israel hope in the Lord. For with the Lord there is mercy; and with Him plentiful Redemption. And He will redeem Israel from all his iniquities.
Eternal rest give unto them, O Lord! And let perpetual light shine upon them. May they rest in peace. Amen.

Evening Prayer for the Poor Souls:

V. Lord, hear my prayer.
R. And let my cry come unto Thee.
Bless, O my God! the repose I am about to take, that, renewing my strength, I may be better enabled to serve Thee. Pour down Thy blessings, O Lord! on my parents, relations, friends, and enemies. Protect the Pope, our Bishop, and all the Pastors of Thy holy Church. Assist the poor and the afflicted, and those who are now in their last agony. Look with an eye of pity on the suffering souls in purgatory, particularly

_____

_____

_____

put an end to their torments and lead them forth into everlasting joy.

Eternal rest grant unto them and let perpetual light shine upon them. Amen.

DATE:

_____

During the course of the day today, pray for those you meet and strangers you see on street, asking God to apply your prayers for them to their future time in Purgatory.

Morning Prayer for the Poor Souls:

Out of the depths I have cried to Thee O Lord! Lord, hear my voice. Let Thine ears be attentive to the voice of my supplication.
If Thou, O Lord, wilt mark iniquities, Lord, who shall stand it?
For with Thee there is mercy: and by reason of Thy law I have waited on Thee, O Lord! My soul hath relied on His word: my soul hath hoped in the Lord. From the morning watch even until night. Let Israel hope in the Lord. For with the Lord there is mercy; and with Him plentiful Redemption. And He will redeem Israel from all his iniquities.
Eternal rest give unto them, O Lord! And let perpetual light shine upon them. May they rest in peace. Amen.

Evening Prayer for the Poor Souls:

V. Lord, hear my prayer.
R. And let my cry come unto Thee.
Bless, O my God! the repose I am about to take, that, renewing my strength, I may be better enabled to serve Thee. Pour down Thy blessings, O Lord! on my parents, relations, friends, and enemies. Protect the Pope, our Bishop, and all the Pastors of Thy holy Church. Assist the poor and the afflicted, and those who are now in their last agony. Look with an eye of pity on the suffering souls in purgatory, particularly

_____
_____

_____

put an end to their torments and lead them forth into everlasting joy.

Eternal rest grant unto them and let perpetual light shine upon them. Amen.

DATE:

_____

Today, ask the Blessed Mother to use your prayers for someone in Purgatory with no one to pray for them.

Morning Prayer for the Poor Souls:

Out of the depths I have cried to Thee O Lord! Lord, hear my voice. Let Thine ears be attentive to the voice of my supplication.
If Thou, O Lord, wilt mark iniquities, Lord, who shall stand it?
For with Thee there is mercy: and by reason of Thy law I have waited on Thee, O Lord! My soul hath relied on His word: my soul hath hoped in the Lord. From the morning watch even until night. Let Israel hope in the Lord. For with the Lord there is mercy; and with Him plentiful Redemption. And He will redeem Israel from all his iniquities.
Eternal rest give unto them, O Lord! And let perpetual light shine upon them. May they rest in peace. Amen.

Evening Prayer for the Poor Souls:

V. Lord, hear my prayer.
R. And let my cry come unto Thee.
Bless, O my God! the repose I am about to take, that, renewing my strength, I may be better enabled to serve Thee. Pour down Thy blessings, O Lord! on my parents, relations, friends, and enemies. Protect the Pope, our Bishop, and all the Pastors of Thy holy Church. Assist the poor and the afflicted, and those who are now in their last agony. Look with an eye of pity on the suffering souls in purgatory, particularly

_____

_____

_____

put an end to their torments and lead them forth into everlasting joy.

Eternal rest grant unto them and let perpetual light shine upon them. Amen.

DATE:
_____

Today, sprinkle holy water on the carpet of your home or outside your house as a comfort to the Poor Souls.

Morning Prayer for the Poor Souls:

Out of the depths I have cried to Thee O Lord! Lord, hear my voice. Let Thine ears be attentive to the voice of my supplication.
If Thou, O Lord, wilt mark iniquities, Lord, who shall stand it?
For with Thee there is mercy: and by reason of Thy law I have waited on Thee, O Lord! My soul hath relied on His word: my soul hath hoped in the Lord. From the morning watch even until night. Let Israel hope in the Lord. For with the Lord there is mercy; and with Him plentiful Redemption. And He will redeem Israel from all his iniquities.
Eternal rest give unto them, O Lord! And let perpetual light shine upon them. May they rest in peace. Amen.

Evening Prayer for the Poor Souls:

V. Lord, hear my prayer.
R. And let my cry come unto Thee.
Bless, O my God! the repose I am about to take, that, renewing my strength, I may be better enabled to serve Thee. Pour down Thy blessings, O Lord! on my parents, relations, friends, and enemies. Protect the Pope, our Bishop, and all the Pastors of Thy holy Church. Assist the poor and the afflicted, and those who are now in their last agony. Look with an eye of pity on the suffering souls in purgatory, particularly

_____
_____
_____

put an end to their torments and lead them forth into everlasting joy.

Eternal rest grant unto them and let perpetual light shine upon them. Amen.

DATE:

_____

Today, visit a church if you are able, and pray for the souls who are spending their Purgatorial time there. Catholic mystics have told us that God allows many souls to do so. If you cannot visit a church, think of a local church and pray for any souls who might be there.

Morning Prayer for the Poor Souls:

Out of the depths I have cried to Thee O Lord! Lord, hear my voice. Let Thine ears be attentive to the voice of my supplication.
If Thou, O Lord, wilt mark iniquities, Lord, who shall stand it?
For with Thee there is mercy: and by reason of Thy law I have waited on Thee, O Lord! My soul hath relied on His word: my soul hath hoped in the Lord. From the morning watch even until night. Let Israel hope in the Lord. For with the Lord there is mercy; and with Him plentiful Redemption. And He will redeem Israel from all his iniquities.
Eternal rest give unto them, O Lord! And let perpetual light shine upon them. May they rest in peace. Amen.

Evening Prayer for the Poor Souls:

V. Lord, hear my prayer.
R. And let my cry come unto Thee.
Bless, O my God! the repose I am about to take, that, renewing my strength, I may be better enabled to serve Thee. Pour down Thy blessings, O Lord! on my parents, relations, friends, and enemies. Protect the Pope, our Bishop, and all the Pastors of Thy holy Church. Assist the poor and the afflicted, and those who are now in their last agony. Look with an eye of pity on the suffering souls in purgatory, particularly

_____

_____

put an end to their torments and lead them forth into everlasting joy.

Eternal rest grant unto them and let perpetual light shine upon them. Amen.

DATE:

_____

Today, visit someone who is sick if you are able, and offer up this work of mercy for the Holy Souls. If you cannot, pray for those in your local hospital or nursing home.

Morning Prayer for the Poor Souls:

Out of the depths I have cried to Thee O Lord! Lord, hear my voice. Let Thine ears be attentive to the voice of my supplication.
If Thou, O Lord, wilt mark iniquities, Lord, who shall stand it?
For with Thee there is mercy: and by reason of Thy law I have waited on Thee, O Lord! My soul hath relied on His word: my soul hath hoped in the Lord. From the morning watch even until night. Let Israel hope in the Lord. For with the Lord there is mercy; and with Him plentiful Redemption. And He will redeem Israel from all his iniquities.
Eternal rest give unto them, O Lord! And let perpetual light shine upon them. May they rest in peace. Amen.

Evening Prayer for the Poor Souls:

V. Lord, hear my prayer.
R. And let my cry come unto Thee.
Bless, O my God! the repose I am about to take, that, renewing my strength, I may be better enabled to serve Thee. Pour down Thy blessings, O Lord! on my parents, relations, friends, and enemies. Protect the Pope, our Bishop, and all the Pastors of Thy holy Church. Assist the poor and the afflicted, and those who are now in their last agony. Look with an eye of pity on the suffering souls in purgatory, particularly

_____
_____

_____

put an end to their torments and lead them forth into everlasting joy.

Eternal rest grant unto them and let perpetual light shine upon them. Amen.

DATE:
_____

Today pray for the souls of all the atheists who have died.

Morning Prayer for the Poor Souls:

Out of the depths I have cried to Thee O Lord! Lord, hear my voice. Let Thine ears be attentive to the voice of my supplication.
If Thou, O Lord, wilt mark iniquities, Lord, who shall stand it?
For with Thee there is mercy: and by reason of Thy law I have waited on Thee, O Lord! My soul hath relied on His word: my soul hath hoped in the Lord. From the morning watch even until night. Let Israel hope in the Lord. For with the Lord there is mercy; and with Him plentiful Redemption. And He will redeem Israel from all his iniquities.
Eternal rest give unto them, O Lord! And let perpetual light shine upon them. May they rest in peace. Amen.

Evening Prayer for the Poor Souls:

V. Lord, hear my prayer.
R. And let my cry come unto Thee.
Bless, O my God! the repose I am about to take, that, renewing my strength, I may be better enabled to serve Thee. Pour down Thy blessings, O Lord! on my parents, relations, friends, and enemies. Protect the Pope, our Bishop, and all the Pastors of Thy holy Church. Assist the poor and the afflicted, and those who are now in their last agony. Look with an eye of pity on the suffering souls in purgatory, particularly

_____
_____
_____

put an end to their torments and lead them forth into everlasting joy.

Eternal rest grant unto them and let perpetual light shine upon them. Amen.

DATE:

_____

Today, read the obituaries in your local newspaper and pray for the souls who have died in the past several days.

Morning Prayer for the Poor Souls:

Out of the depths I have cried to Thee O Lord! Lord, hear my voice. Let Thine ears be attentive to the voice of my supplication.
If Thou, O Lord, wilt mark iniquities, Lord, who shall stand it?
For with Thee there is mercy: and by reason of Thy law I have waited on Thee, O Lord! My soul hath relied on His word: my soul hath hoped in the Lord. From the morning watch even until night. Let Israel hope in the Lord. For with the Lord there is mercy; and with Him plentiful Redemption. And He will redeem Israel from all his iniquities.
Eternal rest give unto them, O Lord! And let perpetual light shine upon them. May they rest in peace. Amen.

Evening Prayer for the Poor Souls:

V. Lord, hear my prayer.
R. And let my cry come unto Thee.
Bless, O my God! the repose I am about to take, that, renewing my strength, I may be better enabled to serve Thee. Pour down Thy blessings, O Lord! on my parents, relations, friends, and enemies. Protect the Pope, our Bishop, and all the Pastors of Thy holy Church. Assist the poor and the afflicted, and those who are now in their last agony. Look with an eye of pity on the suffering souls in purgatory, particularly

_____
_____
_____

put an end to their torments and lead them forth into everlasting joy.

Eternal rest grant unto them and let perpetual light shine upon them. Amen.

DATE:

_____

Spend some time in Eucharistic Adoration today for the Poor Souls. If you cannot travel to a church physically, watch live Adoration on EWTN, YouTube or Facebook.

Morning Prayer for the Poor Souls:

Out of the depths I have cried to Thee O Lord! Lord, hear my voice. Let Thine ears be attentive to the voice of my supplication.
If Thou, O Lord, wilt mark iniquities, Lord, who shall stand it?
For with Thee there is mercy: and by reason of Thy law I have waited on Thee, O Lord! My soul hath relied on His word: my soul hath hoped in the Lord. From the morning watch even until night. Let Israel hope in the Lord. For with the Lord there is mercy; and with Him plentiful Redemption. And He will redeem Israel from all his iniquities.
Eternal rest give unto them, O Lord! And let perpetual light shine upon them. May they rest in peace. Amen.

Evening Prayer for the Poor Souls:

V. Lord, hear my prayer.
R. And let my cry come unto Thee.
Bless, O my God! the repose I am about to take, that, renewing my strength, I may be better enabled to serve Thee. Pour down Thy blessings, O Lord! on my parents, relations, friends, and enemies. Protect the Pope, our Bishop, and all the Pastors of Thy holy Church. Assist the poor and the afflicted, and those who are now in their last agony. Look with an eye of pity on the suffering souls in purgatory, particularly

_____
_____
_____

put an end to their torments and lead them forth into everlasting joy.

Eternal rest grant unto them and let perpetual light shine upon them. Amen.

DATE:

_____

a drive today to a cemetery and pray for the souls of those interred there. If you cannot physically visit a cemetery, think of a cemetery in your city or town and pray for the souls of those buried there.

Morning Prayer for the Poor Souls:

Out of the depths I have cried to Thee O Lord! Lord, hear my voice. Let Thine ears be attentive to the voice of my supplication.
If Thou, O Lord, wilt mark iniquities, Lord, who shall stand it?
For with Thee there is mercy: and by reason of Thy law I have waited on Thee, O Lord! My soul hath relied on His word: my soul hath hoped in the Lord. From the morning watch even until night. Let Israel hope in the Lord. For with the Lord there is mercy; and with Him plentiful Redemption. And He will redeem Israel from all his iniquities.
Eternal rest give unto them, O Lord! And let perpetual light shine upon them. May they rest in peace. Amen.

Evening Prayer for the Poor Souls:

V. Lord, hear my prayer.
R. And let my cry come unto Thee.
Bless, O my God! the repose I am about to take, that, renewing my strength, I may be better enabled to serve Thee. Pour down Thy blessings, O Lord! on my parents, relations, friends, and enemies. Protect the Pope, our Bishop, and all the Pastors of Thy holy Church. Assist the poor and the afflicted, and those who are now in their last agony. Look with an eye of pity on the suffering souls in purgatory, particularly

_____
_____
_____

put an end to their torments and lead them forth into everlasting joy.

Eternal rest grant unto them and let perpetual light shine upon them. Amen.

DATE:

_____

Today, play some sacred music to comfort the Poor Souls. Mystic saints have told us that these small gestures provide great relief to their suffering.

Morning Prayer for the Poor Souls:

Out of the depths I have cried to Thee O Lord! Lord, hear my voice. Let Thine ears be attentive to the voice of my supplication.
If Thou, O Lord, wilt mark iniquities, Lord, who shall stand it?
For with Thee there is mercy: and by reason of Thy law I have waited on Thee, O Lord! My soul hath relied on His word: my soul hath hoped in the Lord. From the morning watch even until night. Let Israel hope in the Lord. For with the Lord there is mercy; and with Him plentiful Redemption. And He will redeem Israel from all his iniquities.
Eternal rest give unto them, O Lord! And let perpetual light shine upon them. May they rest in peace. Amen.

Evening Prayer for the Poor Souls:

V. Lord, hear my prayer.
R. And let my cry come unto Thee.
Bless, O my God! the repose I am about to take, that, renewing my strength, I may be better enabled to serve Thee. Pour down Thy blessings, O Lord! on my parents, relations, friends, and enemies. Protect the Pope, our Bishop, and all the Pastors of Thy holy Church. Assist the poor and the afflicted, and those who are now in their last agony. Look with an eye of pity on the suffering souls in purgatory, particularly

_____

_____

_____

put an end to their torments and lead them forth into everlasting joy.

Eternal rest grant unto them and let perpetual light shine upon them. Amen.

DATE:

_____

Today, make reparation to the Sacred Heart of Jesus for the souls in Purgatory who offended His most precious Heart with the following: Adorable Heart of Jesus, glowing with love for us and inflamed with zeal for our salvation. O Heart that understands the misery to which our sins have brought us, infinitely rich in mercy to heal the wounds of our souls, behold me humbly kneeling before You to express the sorrow that fills my heart for the coldness and indifference with which I have so long returned the numberless benefits which You have bestowed upon me.

Morning Prayer for the Poor Souls:

Out of the depths I have cried to Thee O Lord! Lord, hear my voice. Let Thine ears be attentive to the voice of my supplication. If Thou, O Lord, wilt mark iniquities, Lord, who shall stand it? For with Thee there is mercy: and by reason of Thy law I have waited on Thee, O Lord! My soul hath relied on His word: my soul hath hoped in the Lord. From the morning watch even until night. Let Israel hope in the Lord. For with the Lord there is mercy; and with Him plentiful Redemption. And He will redeem Israel from all his iniquities. Eternal rest give unto them, O Lord! And let perpetual light shine upon them. May they rest in peace. Amen.

Evening Prayer for the Poor Souls:

V. Lord, hear my prayer.
R. And let my cry come unto Thee.
Bless, O my God! the repose I am about to take, that, renewing my strength, I may be better enabled to serve Thee. Pour down Thy blessings, O Lord! on my parents, relations, friends, and enemies. Protect the Pope, our Bishop, and all the Pastors of Thy holy Church. Assist the poor and the afflicted, and those who are now in their last agony. Look with an eye of pity on the suffering souls in purgatory, particularly

_____

put an end to their torments and lead them forth into everlasting joy.

Eternal rest grant unto them and let perpetual light shine upon them. Amen.

DATE:
_____

Start a Mass Collection jar or envelope today for the Holy Souls. Add money to it as you are able, and when you have enough for a donation, have a Mass said for a soul in Purgatory.

Morning Prayer for the Poor Souls:

Out of the depths I have cried to Thee O Lord! Lord, hear my voice. Let Thine ears be attentive to the voice of my supplication.
If Thou, O Lord, wilt mark iniquities, Lord, who shall stand it?
For with Thee there is mercy: and by reason of Thy law I have waited on Thee, O Lord! My soul hath relied on His word: my soul hath hoped in the Lord. From the morning watch even until night. Let Israel hope in the Lord. For with the Lord there is mercy; and with Him plentiful Redemption. And He will redeem Israel from all his iniquities.
Eternal rest give unto them, O Lord! And let perpetual light shine upon them. May they rest in peace. Amen.

Evening Prayer for the Poor Souls:

V. Lord, hear my prayer.
R. And let my cry come unto Thee.
Bless, O my God! the repose I am about to take, that, renewing my strength, I may be better enabled to serve Thee. Pour down Thy blessings, O Lord! on my parents, relations, friends, and enemies. Protect the Pope, our Bishop, and all the Pastors of Thy holy Church. Assist the poor and the afflicted, and those who are now in their last agony. Look with an eye of pity on the suffering souls in purgatory, particularly

_____
_____
_____

put an end to their torments and lead them forth into everlasting joy.

Eternal rest grant unto them and let perpetual light shine upon them. Amen.

DATE:

_____

Go without a meal or snack today if possible, for the benefit of the Holy Souls. If you are in ill health, give up a special treat instead.

Morning Prayer for the Poor Souls:

Out of the depths I have cried to Thee O Lord! Lord, hear my voice. Let Thine ears be attentive to the voice of my supplication.
If Thou, O Lord, wilt mark iniquities, Lord, who shall stand it?
For with Thee there is mercy: and by reason of Thy law I have waited on Thee, O Lord! My soul hath relied on His word: my soul hath hoped in the Lord. From the morning watch even until night. Let Israel hope in the Lord. For with the Lord there is mercy; and with Him plentiful Redemption. And He will redeem Israel from all his iniquities.
Eternal rest give unto them, O Lord! And let perpetual light shine upon them. May they rest in peace. Amen.

Evening Prayer for the Poor Souls:

V. Lord, hear my prayer.
R. And let my cry come unto Thee.
Bless, O my God! the repose I am about to take, that, renewing my strength, I may be better enabled to serve Thee. Pour down Thy blessings, O Lord! on my parents, relations, friends, and enemies. Protect the Pope, our Bishop, and all the Pastors of Thy holy Church. Assist the poor and the afflicted, and those who are now in their last agony. Look with an eye of pity on the suffering souls in purgatory, particularly

_____
_____

_____

put an end to their torments and lead them forth into everlasting joy.

Eternal rest grant unto them and let perpetual light shine upon them. Amen.

DATE:

_____

Today, say a Divine Mercy chaplet for the Poor Souls.

Morning Prayer for the Poor Souls:

Out of the depths I have cried to Thee O Lord! Lord, hear my voice. Let Thine ears be attentive to the voice of my supplication.
If Thou, O Lord, wilt mark iniquities, Lord, who shall stand it?
For with Thee there is mercy: and by reason of Thy law I have waited on Thee, O Lord! My soul hath relied on His word: my soul hath hoped in the Lord. From the morning watch even until night. Let Israel hope in the Lord. For with the Lord there is mercy; and with Him plentiful Redemption. And He will redeem Israel from all his iniquities.
Eternal rest give unto them, O Lord! And let perpetual light shine upon them. May they rest in peace. Amen.

Evening Prayer for the Poor Souls:

V. Lord, hear my prayer.
R. And let my cry come unto Thee.
Bless, O my God! the repose I am about to take, that, renewing my strength, I may be better enabled to serve Thee. Pour down Thy blessings, O Lord! on my parents, relations, friends, and enemies. Protect the Pope, our Bishop, and all the Pastors of Thy holy Church. Assist the poor and the afflicted, and those who are now in their last agony. Look with an eye of pity on the suffering souls in purgatory, particularly

_____

_____

_____

put an end to their torments and lead them forth into everlasting joy.

Eternal rest grant unto them and let perpetual light shine upon them. Amen.

DATE: _____

Pray today for the souls of priests and religious in Purgatory.

Morning Prayer for the Poor Souls:

Out of the depths I have cried to Thee O Lord! Lord, hear my voice. Let Thine ears be attentive to the voice of my supplication.
If Thou, O Lord, wilt mark iniquities, Lord, who shall stand it?
For with Thee there is mercy: and by reason of Thy law I have waited on Thee, O Lord! My soul hath relied on His word: my soul hath hoped in the Lord. From the morning watch even until night. Let Israel hope in the Lord. For with the Lord there is mercy; and with Him plentiful Redemption. And He will redeem Israel from all his iniquities.
Eternal rest give unto them, O Lord! And let perpetual light shine upon them. May they rest in peace. Amen.

Evening Prayer for the Poor Souls:

V. Lord, hear my prayer.
R. And let my cry come unto Thee.
Bless, O my God! the repose I am about to take, that, renewing my strength, I may be better enabled to serve Thee. Pour down Thy blessings, O Lord! on my parents, relations, friends, and enemies. Protect the Pope, our Bishop, and all the Pastors of Thy holy Church. Assist the poor and the afflicted, and those who are now in their last agony. Look with an eye of pity on the suffering souls in purgatory, particularly

_____
_____
_____

put an end to their torments and lead them forth into everlasting joy.

Eternal rest grant unto them and let perpetual light shine upon them. Amen.

DATE: _____

While you are going about your day today, remember your friends and colleagues who have passed away over the years, asking God to release them from Purgatory.

Morning Prayer for the Poor Souls:

Out of the depths I have cried to Thee O Lord! Lord, hear my voice. Let Thine ears be attentive to the voice of my supplication.
If Thou, O Lord, wilt mark iniquities, Lord, who shall stand it?
For with Thee there is mercy: and by reason of Thy law I have waited on Thee, O Lord! My soul hath relied on His word: my soul hath hoped in the Lord. From the morning watch even until night. Let Israel hope in the Lord. For with the Lord there is mercy; and with Him plentiful Redemption. And He will redeem Israel from all his iniquities.
Eternal rest give unto them, O Lord! And let perpetual light shine upon them. May they rest in peace. Amen.

Evening Prayer for the Poor Souls:

V. Lord, hear my prayer.
R. And let my cry come unto Thee.
Bless, O my God! the repose I am about to take, that, renewing my strength, I may be better enabled to serve Thee. Pour down Thy blessings, O Lord! on my parents, relations, friends, and enemies. Protect the Pope, our Bishop, and all the Pastors of Thy holy Church. Assist the poor and the afflicted, and those who are now in their last agony. Look with an eye of pity on the suffering souls in purgatory, particularly

put an end to their torments and lead them forth into everlasting joy.

Eternal rest grant unto them and let perpetual light shine upon them. Amen.

DATE: _____

Pray today for the dead who heard the Gospel but rejected it. May they be spared Hell and be released from Purgatory to be with Jesus.

Morning Prayer for the Poor Souls:

Out of the depths I have cried to Thee O Lord! Lord, hear my voice. Let Thine ears be attentive to the voice of my supplication.
If Thou, O Lord, wilt mark iniquities, Lord, who shall stand it?
For with Thee there is mercy: and by reason of Thy law I have waited on Thee, O Lord! My soul hath relied on His word: my soul hath hoped in the Lord. From the morning watch even until night. Let Israel hope in the Lord. For with the Lord there is mercy; and with Him plentiful Redemption. And He will redeem Israel from all his iniquities.
Eternal rest give unto them, O Lord! And let perpetual light shine upon them. May they rest in peace. Amen.

Evening Prayer for the Poor Souls:

V. Lord, hear my prayer.
R. And let my cry come unto Thee.
Bless, O my God! the repose I am about to take, that, renewing my strength, I may be better enabled to serve Thee. Pour down Thy blessings, O Lord! on my parents, relations, friends, and enemies. Protect the Pope, our Bishop, and all the Pastors of Thy holy Church. Assist the poor and the afflicted, and those who are now in their last agony. Look with an eye of pity on the suffering souls in purgatory, particularly

_____

_____

_____

put an end to their torments and lead them forth into everlasting joy.

Eternal rest grant unto them and let perpetual light shine upon them. Amen.

DATE: _____

Today, spend some time reading devotional literature aloud for the comfort of the Poor Souls.

Morning Prayer for the Poor Souls:

Out of the depths I have cried to Thee O Lord! Lord, hear my voice. Let Thine ears be attentive to the voice of my supplication.
If Thou, O Lord, wilt mark iniquities, Lord, who shall stand it?
For with Thee there is mercy: and by reason of Thy law I have waited on Thee, O Lord! My soul hath relied on His word: my soul hath hoped in the Lord. From the morning watch even until night. Let Israel hope in the Lord. For with the Lord there is mercy; and with Him plentiful Redemption. And He will redeem Israel from all his iniquities.
Eternal rest give unto them, O Lord! And let perpetual light shine upon them. May they rest in peace. Amen.

Evening Prayer for the Poor Souls:

V. Lord, hear my prayer.
R. And let my cry come unto Thee.
Bless, O my God! the repose I am about to take, that, renewing my strength, I may be better enabled to serve Thee. Pour down Thy blessings, O Lord! on my parents, relations, friends, and enemies. Protect the Pope, our Bishop, and all the Pastors of Thy holy Church. Assist the poor and the afflicted, and those who are now in their last agony. Look with an eye of pity on the suffering souls in purgatory, particularly

_____
_____
_____

put an end to their torments and lead them forth into everlasting joy.

Eternal rest grant unto them and let perpetual light shine upon them. Amen.

DATE: _____

Today make the Stations of the Cross for the benefit of the Holy Souls in Purgatory.

Morning Prayer for the Poor Souls:

Out of the depths I have cried to Thee O Lord! Lord, hear my voice. Let Thine ears be attentive to the voice of my supplication.
If Thou, O Lord, wilt mark iniquities, Lord, who shall stand it?
For with Thee there is mercy: and by reason of Thy law I have waited on Thee, O Lord! My soul hath relied on His word: my soul hath hoped in the Lord. From the morning watch even until night. Let Israel hope in the Lord. For with the Lord there is mercy; and with Him plentiful Redemption. And He will redeem Israel from all his iniquities.
Eternal rest give unto them, O Lord! And let perpetual light shine upon them. May they rest in peace. Amen.

Evening Prayer for the Poor Souls:

V. Lord, hear my prayer.
R. And let my cry come unto Thee.
Bless, O my God! the repose I am about to take, that, renewing my strength, I may be better enabled to serve Thee. Pour down Thy blessings, O Lord! on my parents, relations, friends, and enemies. Protect the Pope, our Bishop, and all the Pastors of Thy holy Church. Assist the poor and the afflicted, and those who are now in their last agony. Look with an eye of pity on the suffering souls in purgatory, particularly

_____

_____

_____

put an end to their torments and lead them forth into everlasting joy.

Eternal rest grant unto them and let perpetual light shine upon them. Amen.

DATE: _____

Pray today for the souls of all Jewish people who have died.

Morning Prayer for the Poor Souls:

Out of the depths I have cried to Thee O Lord! Lord, hear my voice. Let Thine ears be attentive to the voice of my supplication.
If Thou, O Lord, wilt mark iniquities, Lord, who shall stand it?
For with Thee there is mercy: and by reason of Thy law I have waited on Thee, O Lord! My soul hath relied on His word: my soul hath hoped in the Lord. From the morning watch even until night. Let Israel hope in the Lord. For with the Lord there is mercy; and with Him plentiful Redemption. And He will redeem Israel from all his iniquities.
Eternal rest give unto them, O Lord! And let perpetual light shine upon them. May they rest in peace. Amen.

Evening Prayer for the Poor Souls:

V. Lord, hear my prayer.
R. And let my cry come unto Thee.
Bless, O my God! the repose I am about to take, that, renewing my strength, I may be better enabled to serve Thee. Pour down Thy blessings, O Lord! on my parents, relations, friends, and enemies. Protect the Pope, our Bishop, and all the Pastors of Thy holy Church. Assist the poor and the afflicted, and those who are now in their last agony. Look with an eye of pity on the suffering souls in purgatory, particularly

_____
_____
_____

put an end to their torments and lead them forth into everlasting joy.

Eternal rest grant unto them and let perpetual light shine upon them. Amen.

DATE: _____

Today, pray for the souls of persecutors of Christians who have died.

Morning Prayer for the Poor Souls:

Out of the depths I have cried to Thee O Lord! Lord, hear my voice. Let Thine ears be attentive to the voice of my supplication.
If Thou, O Lord, wilt mark iniquities, Lord, who shall stand it?
For with Thee there is mercy: and by reason of Thy law I have waited on Thee, O Lord! My soul hath relied on His word: my soul hath hoped in the Lord. From the morning watch even until night. Let Israel hope in the Lord. For with the Lord there is mercy; and with Him plentiful Redemption. And He will redeem Israel from all his iniquities.
Eternal rest give unto them, O Lord! And let perpetual light shine upon them. May they rest in peace. Amen.

Evening Prayer for the Poor Souls:

V. Lord, hear my prayer.
R. And let my cry come unto Thee.
Bless, O my God! the repose I am about to take, that, renewing my strength, I may be better enabled to serve Thee. Pour down Thy blessings, O Lord! on my parents, relations, friends, and enemies. Protect the Pope, our Bishop, and all the Pastors of Thy holy Church. Assist the poor and the afflicted, and those who are now in their last agony. Look with an eye of pity on the suffering souls in purgatory, particularly

_____
_____

_____

put an end to their torments and lead them forth into everlasting joy.

Eternal rest grant unto them and let perpetual light shine upon them. Amen.

DATE: _____

Light a blessed candle today in remembrance of the Holy Souls.

Morning Prayer for the Poor Souls:

Out of the depths I have cried to Thee O Lord! Lord, hear my voice. Let Thine ears be attentive to the voice of my supplication.
If Thou, O Lord, wilt mark iniquities, Lord, who shall stand it?
For with Thee there is mercy: and by reason of Thy law I have waited on Thee, O Lord! My soul hath relied on His word: my soul hath hoped in the Lord. From the morning watch even until night. Let Israel hope in the Lord. For with the Lord there is mercy; and with Him plentiful Redemption. And He will redeem Israel from all his iniquities.
Eternal rest give unto them, O Lord! And let perpetual light shine upon them. May they rest in peace. Amen.

Evening Prayer for the Poor Souls:

V. Lord, hear my prayer.
R. And let my cry come unto Thee.
Bless, O my God! the repose I am about to take, that, renewing my strength, I may be better enabled to serve Thee. Pour down Thy blessings, O Lord! on my parents, relations, friends, and enemies. Protect the Pope, our Bishop, and all the Pastors of Thy holy Church. Assist the poor and the afflicted, and those who are now in their last agony. Look with an eye of pity on the suffering souls in purgatory, particularly

_____

_____

_____

put an end to their torments and lead them forth into everlasting joy.

Eternal rest grant unto them and let perpetual light shine upon them. Amen.

DATE: _____

Begin a Novena today for the benefit of the Poor Souls. St. Alphonsus Liguori wrote a powerful one just for the Holy Souls, which may be found online, but any Novena will be appreciated.

Morning Prayer for the Poor Souls:

Out of the depths I have cried to Thee O Lord! Lord, hear my voice. Let Thine ears be attentive to the voice of my supplication.
If Thou, O Lord, wilt mark iniquities, Lord, who shall stand it?
For with Thee there is mercy: and by reason of Thy law I have waited on Thee, O Lord! My soul hath relied on His word: my soul hath hoped in the Lord. From the morning watch even until night. Let Israel hope in the Lord. For with the Lord there is mercy; and with Him plentiful Redemption. And He will redeem Israel from all his iniquities.
Eternal rest give unto them, O Lord! And let perpetual light shine upon them. May they rest in peace. Amen.

Evening Prayer for the Poor Souls:

V. Lord, hear my prayer.
R. And let my cry come unto Thee.
Bless, O my God! the repose I am about to take, that, renewing my strength, I may be better enabled to serve Thee. Pour down Thy blessings, O Lord! on my parents, relations, friends, and enemies. Protect the Pope, our Bishop, and all the Pastors of Thy holy Church. Assist the poor and the afflicted, and those who are now in their last agony. Look with an eye of pity on the suffering souls in purgatory, particularly

_____

_____

_____

put an end to their torments and lead them forth into everlasting joy.

Eternal rest grant unto them and let perpetual light shine upon them. Amen.

DATE: _____

Give alms to the poor today to benefit the souls in Purgatory. We are told that giving alms is of great benefit to suffering souls.

Morning Prayer for the Poor Souls:

Out of the depths I have cried to Thee O Lord! Lord, hear my voice. Let Thine ears be attentive to the voice of my supplication.
If Thou, O Lord, wilt mark iniquities, Lord, who shall stand it?
For with Thee there is mercy: and by reason of Thy law I have waited on Thee, O Lord! My soul hath relied on His word: my soul hath hoped in the Lord. From the morning watch even until night. Let Israel hope in the Lord. For with the Lord there is mercy; and with Him plentiful Redemption. And He will redeem Israel from all his iniquities.
Eternal rest give unto them, O Lord! And let perpetual light shine upon them. May they rest in peace. Amen.

Evening Prayer for the Poor Souls:

V. Lord, hear my prayer.
R. And let my cry come unto Thee.
Bless, O my God! the repose I am about to take, that, renewing my strength, I may be better enabled to serve Thee. Pour down Thy blessings, O Lord! on my parents, relations, friends, and enemies. Protect the Pope, our Bishop, and all the Pastors of Thy holy Church. Assist the poor and the afflicted, and those who are now in their last agony. Look with an eye of pity on the suffering souls in purgatory, particularly

_____

_____

_____

put an end to their torments and lead them forth into everlasting joy.

Eternal rest grant unto them and let perpetual light shine upon them. Amen.

DATE: _____

Read aloud today from the Acts of the Apostles to comfort the Holy Souls. The Good News of Jesus' salvation is of great relief to their suffering.

Morning Prayer for the Poor Souls:

Out of the depths I have cried to Thee O Lord! Lord, hear my voice. Let Thine ears be attentive to the voice of my supplication.
If Thou, O Lord, wilt mark iniquities, Lord, who shall stand it?
For with Thee there is mercy: and by reason of Thy law I have waited on Thee, O Lord! My soul hath relied on His word: my soul hath hoped in the Lord. From the morning watch even until night. Let Israel hope in the Lord. For with the Lord there is mercy; and with Him plentiful Redemption. And He will redeem Israel from all his iniquities.
Eternal rest give unto them, O Lord! And let perpetual light shine upon them. May they rest in peace. Amen.

Evening Prayer for the Poor Souls:

V. Lord, hear my prayer.
R. And let my cry come unto Thee.
Bless, O my God! the repose I am about to take, that, renewing my strength, I may be better enabled to serve Thee. Pour down Thy blessings, O Lord! on my parents, relations, friends, and enemies. Protect the Pope, our Bishop, and all the Pastors of Thy holy Church. Assist the poor and the afflicted, and those who are now in their last agony. Look with an eye of pity on the suffering souls in purgatory, particularly

_____

_____

_____

put an end to their torments and lead them forth into everlasting joy.

Eternal rest grant unto them and let perpetual light shine upon them. Amen.

DATE: _____

Today, ask the saints known as intercessors for the dead to pray with you for their release, including St. Nicholas of Tolentino, St. Gertrude the Great, St. Catherine of Genoa, St. Padre Pio, St. Philip Neri, St. John Macías, St. Faustina Kowalska, St. Joseph and, of course, the Blessed Mother.

Morning Prayer for the Poor Souls:

Out of the depths I have cried to Thee O Lord! Lord, hear my voice. Let Thine ears be attentive to the voice of my supplication.
If Thou, O Lord, wilt mark iniquities, Lord, who shall stand it?
For with Thee there is mercy: and by reason of Thy law I have waited on Thee, O Lord! My soul hath relied on His word: my soul hath hoped in the Lord. From the morning watch even until night. Let Israel hope in the Lord. For with the Lord there is mercy; and with Him plentiful Redemption. And He will redeem Israel from all his iniquities.
Eternal rest give unto them, O Lord! And let perpetual light shine upon them. May they rest in peace. Amen.

Evening Prayer for the Poor Souls:

V. Lord, hear my prayer.
R. And let my cry come unto Thee.
Bless, O my God! the repose I am about to take, that, renewing my strength, I may be better enabled to serve Thee. Pour down Thy blessings, O Lord! on my parents, relations, friends, and enemies. Protect the Pope, our Bishop, and all the Pastors of Thy holy Church. Assist the poor and the afflicted, and those who are now in their last agony. Look with an eye of pity on the suffering souls in purgatory, particularly

_____
_____

_____

put an end to their torments and lead them forth into everlasting joy.

Eternal rest grant unto them and let perpetual light shine upon them. Amen.

DATE: _____

Today, have a Mass said for the soul of a family member or friend who has passed away. This can be through your own parish or through an order or national shrine via their website.

Morning Prayer for the Poor Souls:

Out of the depths I have cried to Thee O Lord! Lord, hear my voice. Let Thine ears be attentive to the voice of my supplication.
If Thou, O Lord, wilt mark iniquities, Lord, who shall stand it?
For with Thee there is mercy: and by reason of Thy law I have waited on Thee, O Lord! My soul hath relied on His word: my soul hath hoped in the Lord. From the morning watch even until night. Let Israel hope in the Lord. For with the Lord there is mercy; and with Him plentiful Redemption. And He will redeem Israel from all his iniquities.
Eternal rest give unto them, O Lord! And let perpetual light shine upon them. May they rest in peace. Amen.

Evening Prayer for the Poor Souls:

V. Lord, hear my prayer.
R. And let my cry come unto Thee.
Bless, O my God! the repose I am about to take, that, renewing my strength, I may be better enabled to serve Thee. Pour down Thy blessings, O Lord! on my parents, relations, friends, and enemies. Protect the Pope, our Bishop, and all the Pastors of Thy holy Church. Assist the poor and the afflicted, and those who are now in their last agony. Look with an eye of pity on the suffering souls in purgatory, particularly

_____
_____
_____

put an end to their torments and lead them forth into everlasting joy.

Eternal rest grant unto them and let perpetual light shine upon them. Amen.

DATE:

_____

Pray the Rosary today for the release of souls from Purgatory. Mystic saints have told us that the Blessed Mother herself comes to Purgatory to bring souls with her back to Heaven.

Morning Prayer for the Poor Souls:

Out of the depths I have cried to Thee O Lord! Lord, hear my voice. Let Thine ears be attentive to the voice of my supplication.
If Thou, O Lord, wilt mark iniquities, Lord, who shall stand it?
For with Thee there is mercy: and by reason of Thy law I have waited on Thee, O Lord! My soul hath relied on His word: my soul hath hoped in the Lord. From the morning watch even until night. Let Israel hope in the Lord. For with the Lord there is mercy; and with Him plentiful Redemption. And He will redeem Israel from all his iniquities.
Eternal rest give unto them, O Lord! And let perpetual light shine upon them. May they rest in peace. Amen.

Evening Prayer for the Poor Souls:

V. Lord, hear my prayer.
R. And let my cry come unto Thee.
Bless, O my God! the repose I am about to take, that, renewing my strength, I may be better enabled to serve Thee. Pour down Thy blessings, O Lord! on my parents, relations, friends, and enemies. Protect the Pope, our Bishop, and all the Pastors of Thy holy Church. Assist the poor and the afflicted, and those who are now in their last agony. Look with an eye of pity on the suffering souls in purgatory, particularly

_____
_____
_____

put an end to their torments and lead them forth into everlasting joy.

Eternal rest grant unto them and let perpetual light shine upon them. Amen.

DATE: _____

Today, ask the Blessed Mother to apply your prayers and works to a poor soul who has no one to pray for them.

Morning Prayer for the Poor Souls:

Out of the depths I have cried to Thee O Lord! Lord, hear my voice. Let Thine ears be attentive to the voice of my supplication.
If Thou, O Lord, wilt mark iniquities, Lord, who shall stand it?
For with Thee there is mercy: and by reason of Thy law I have waited on Thee, O Lord! My soul hath relied on His word: my soul hath hoped in the Lord. From the morning watch even until night. Let Israel hope in the Lord. For with the Lord there is mercy; and with Him plentiful Redemption. And He will redeem Israel from all his iniquities.
Eternal rest give unto them, O Lord! And let perpetual light shine upon them. May they rest in peace. Amen.

Evening Prayer for the Poor Souls:

V. Lord, hear my prayer.
R. And let my cry come unto Thee.
Bless, O my God! the repose I am about to take, that, renewing my strength, I may be better enabled to serve Thee. Pour down Thy blessings, O Lord! on my parents, relations, friends, and enemies. Protect the Pope, our Bishop, and all the Pastors of Thy holy Church. Assist the poor and the afflicted, and those who are now in their last agony. Look with an eye of pity on the suffering souls in purgatory, particularly

_____
_____

_____

put an end to their torments and lead them forth into everlasting joy.

Eternal rest grant unto them and let perpetual light shine upon them. Amen.

DATE:
_____

We all have a spiritual or physical affliction or burden that we suffer with daily. Today, dedicate your ailment-related suffering to the Poor souls.

Morning Prayer for the Poor Souls:

Out of the depths I have cried to Thee O Lord! Lord, hear my voice. Let Thine ears be attentive to the voice of my supplication.
If Thou, O Lord, wilt mark iniquities, Lord, who shall stand it?
For with Thee there is mercy: and by reason of Thy law I have waited on Thee, O Lord! My soul hath relied on His word: my soul hath hoped in the Lord. From the morning watch even until night. Let Israel hope in the Lord. For with the Lord there is mercy; and with Him plentiful Redemption. And He will redeem Israel from all his iniquities.
Eternal rest give unto them, O Lord! And let perpetual light shine upon them. May they rest in peace. Amen.

Evening Prayer for the Poor Souls:

V. Lord, hear my prayer.
R. And let my cry come unto Thee.
Bless, O my God! the repose I am about to take, that, renewing my strength, I may be better enabled to serve Thee. Pour down Thy blessings, O Lord! on my parents, relations, friends, and enemies. Protect the Pope, our Bishop, and all the Pastors of Thy holy Church. Assist the poor and the afflicted, and those who are now in their last agony. Look with an eye of pity on the suffering souls in purgatory, particularly

_____
_____
_____

put an end to their torments and lead them forth into everlasting joy.

Eternal rest grant unto them and let perpetual light shine upon them. Amen.

DATE:

_____

Today, visit or call someone elderly or alone and offer your work of mercy for the souls in Purgatory.

Morning Prayer for the Poor Souls:

Out of the depths I have cried to Thee O Lord! Lord, hear my voice. Let Thine ears be attentive to the voice of my supplication.
If Thou, O Lord, wilt mark iniquities, Lord, who shall stand it?
For with Thee there is mercy: and by reason of Thy law I have waited on Thee, O Lord! My soul hath relied on His word: my soul hath hoped in the Lord. From the morning watch even until night. Let Israel hope in the Lord. For with the Lord there is mercy; and with Him plentiful Redemption. And He will redeem Israel from all his iniquities.
Eternal rest give unto them, O Lord! And let perpetual light shine upon them. May they rest in peace. Amen.

Evening Prayer for the Poor Souls:

V. Lord, hear my prayer.
R. And let my cry come unto Thee.
Bless, O my God! the repose I am about to take, that, renewing my strength, I may be better enabled to serve Thee. Pour down Thy blessings, O Lord! on my parents, relations, friends, and enemies. Protect the Pope, our Bishop, and all the Pastors of Thy holy Church. Assist the poor and the afflicted, and those who are now in their last agony. Look with an eye of pity on the suffering souls in purgatory, particularly

_____

_____

_____

put an end to their torments and lead them forth into everlasting joy.

Eternal rest grant unto them and let perpetual light shine upon them. Amen.

DATE:

_____

During the course of the day today, pray for those you meet and strangers you see on street, asking God to apply your prayers for them to their future time in Purgatory.

Morning Prayer for the Poor Souls:

Out of the depths I have cried to Thee O Lord! Lord, hear my voice. Let Thine ears be attentive to the voice of my supplication.
If Thou, O Lord, wilt mark iniquities, Lord, who shall stand it?
For with Thee there is mercy: and by reason of Thy law I have waited on Thee, O Lord! My soul hath relied on His word: my soul hath hoped in the Lord. From the morning watch even until night. Let Israel hope in the Lord. For with the Lord there is mercy; and with Him plentiful Redemption. And He will redeem Israel from all his iniquities.
Eternal rest give unto them, O Lord! And let perpetual light shine upon them. May they rest in peace. Amen.

Evening Prayer for the Poor Souls:

V. Lord, hear my prayer.
R. And let my cry come unto Thee.
Bless, O my God! the repose I am about to take, that, renewing my strength, I may be better enabled to serve Thee. Pour down Thy blessings, O Lord! on my parents, relations, friends, and enemies. Protect the Pope, our Bishop, and all the Pastors of Thy holy Church. Assist the poor and the afflicted, and those who are now in their last agony. Look with an eye of pity on the suffering souls in purgatory, particularly

_____

_____

_____

put an end to their torments and lead them forth into everlasting joy.

Eternal rest grant unto them and let perpetual light shine upon them. Amen.

DATE:

_____

Today, ask the Blessed Mother to use your prayers for someone in Purgatory with no one to pray for them.

Morning Prayer for the Poor Souls:

Out of the depths I have cried to Thee O Lord! Lord, hear my voice. Let Thine ears be attentive to the voice of my supplication.
If Thou, O Lord, wilt mark iniquities, Lord, who shall stand it?
For with Thee there is mercy: and by reason of Thy law I have waited on Thee, O Lord! My soul hath relied on His word: my soul hath hoped in the Lord. From the morning watch even until night. Let Israel hope in the Lord. For with the Lord there is mercy; and with Him plentiful Redemption. And He will redeem Israel from all his iniquities.
Eternal rest give unto them, O Lord! And let perpetual light shine upon them. May they rest in peace. Amen.

Evening Prayer for the Poor Souls:

V. Lord, hear my prayer.
R. And let my cry come unto Thee.
Bless, O my God! the repose I am about to take, that, renewing my strength, I may be better enabled to serve Thee. Pour down Thy blessings, O Lord! on my parents, relations, friends, and enemies. Protect the Pope, our Bishop, and all the Pastors of Thy holy Church. Assist the poor and the afflicted, and those who are now in their last agony. Look with an eye of pity on the suffering souls in purgatory, particularly

_____

_____

_____

put an end to their torments and lead them forth into everlasting joy.

Eternal rest grant unto them and let perpetual light shine upon them. Amen.

DATE:

_____

Today, sprinkle holy water on the carpet of your home or outside your house as a comfort to the Poor Souls.

Morning Prayer for the Poor Souls:

Out of the depths I have cried to Thee O Lord! Lord, hear my voice. Let Thine ears be attentive to the voice of my supplication.
If Thou, O Lord, wilt mark iniquities, Lord, who shall stand it?
For with Thee there is mercy: and by reason of Thy law I have waited on Thee, O Lord! My soul hath relied on His word: my soul hath hoped in the Lord. From the morning watch even until night. Let Israel hope in the Lord. For with the Lord there is mercy; and with Him plentiful Redemption. And He will redeem Israel from all his iniquities.
Eternal rest give unto them, O Lord! And let perpetual light shine upon them. May they rest in peace. Amen.

Evening Prayer for the Poor Souls:

V. Lord, hear my prayer.
R. And let my cry come unto Thee.
Bless, O my God! the repose I am about to take, that, renewing my strength, I may be better enabled to serve Thee. Pour down Thy blessings, O Lord! on my parents, relations, friends, and enemies. Protect the Pope, our Bishop, and all the Pastors of Thy holy Church. Assist the poor and the afflicted, and those who are now in their last agony. Look with an eye of pity on the suffering souls in purgatory, particularly

_____

_____

_____

put an end to their torments and lead them forth into everlasting joy.

Eternal rest grant unto them and let perpetual light shine upon them. Amen.

DATE:

_____

Today, visit a church if you are able, and pray for the souls who are spending their Purgatorial time there. Catholic mystics have told us that God allows many souls to do so. If you cannot visit a church, think of a local church and pray for any souls who might be there.

Morning Prayer for the Poor Souls:

Out of the depths I have cried to Thee O Lord! Lord, hear my voice. Let Thine ears be attentive to the voice of my supplication.
If Thou, O Lord, wilt mark iniquities, Lord, who shall stand it?
For with Thee there is mercy: and by reason of Thy law I have waited on Thee, O Lord! My soul hath relied on His word: my soul hath hoped in the Lord. From the morning watch even until night. Let Israel hope in the Lord. For with the Lord there is mercy; and with Him plentiful Redemption. And He will redeem Israel from all his iniquities.
Eternal rest give unto them, O Lord! And let perpetual light shine upon them. May they rest in peace. Amen.

Evening Prayer for the Poor Souls:

V. Lord, hear my prayer.
R. And let my cry come unto Thee.
Bless, O my God! the repose I am about to take, that, renewing my strength, I may be better enabled to serve Thee. Pour down Thy blessings, O Lord! on my parents, relations, friends, and enemies. Protect the Pope, our Bishop, and all the Pastors of Thy holy Church. Assist the poor and the afflicted, and those who are now in their last agony. Look with an eye of pity on the suffering souls in purgatory, particularly

_____

_____

put an end to their torments and lead them forth into everlasting joy.

Eternal rest grant unto them and let perpetual light shine upon them. Amen.

DATE:

_____

Today, visit someone who is sick if you are able, and offer up this work of mercy for the Holy Souls. If you cannot, pray for those in your local hospital or nursing home.

Morning Prayer for the Poor Souls:

Out of the depths I have cried to Thee O Lord! Lord, hear my voice. Let Thine ears be attentive to the voice of my supplication.
If Thou, O Lord, wilt mark iniquities, Lord, who shall stand it?
For with Thee there is mercy: and by reason of Thy law I have waited on Thee, O Lord! My soul hath relied on His word: my soul hath hoped in the Lord. From the morning watch even until night. Let Israel hope in the Lord. For with the Lord there is mercy; and with Him plentiful Redemption. And He will redeem Israel from all his iniquities.
Eternal rest give unto them, O Lord! And let perpetual light shine upon them. May they rest in peace. Amen.

Evening Prayer for the Poor Souls:

V. Lord, hear my prayer.
R. And let my cry come unto Thee.
Bless, O my God! the repose I am about to take, that, renewing my strength, I may be better enabled to serve Thee. Pour down Thy blessings, O Lord! on my parents, relations, friends, and enemies. Protect the Pope, our Bishop, and all the Pastors of Thy holy Church. Assist the poor and the afflicted, and those who are now in their last agony. Look with an eye of pity on the suffering souls in purgatory, particularly

_____

_____

_____

put an end to their torments and lead them forth into everlasting joy.

Eternal rest grant unto them and let perpetual light shine upon them. Amen.

DATE:

_____

Today pray for the souls of all the atheists who have died.

Morning Prayer for the Poor Souls:

Out of the depths I have cried to Thee O Lord! Lord, hear my voice. Let Thine ears be attentive to the voice of my supplication.
If Thou, O Lord, wilt mark iniquities, Lord, who shall stand it?
For with Thee there is mercy: and by reason of Thy law I have waited on Thee, O Lord! My soul hath relied on His word: my soul hath hoped in the Lord. From the morning watch even until night. Let Israel hope in the Lord. For with the Lord there is mercy; and with Him plentiful Redemption. And He will redeem Israel from all his iniquities.
Eternal rest give unto them, O Lord! And let perpetual light shine upon them. May they rest in peace. Amen.

Evening Prayer for the Poor Souls:

V. Lord, hear my prayer.
R. And let my cry come unto Thee.
Bless, O my God! the repose I am about to take, that, renewing my strength, I may be better enabled to serve Thee. Pour down Thy blessings, O Lord! on my parents, relations, friends, and enemies. Protect the Pope, our Bishop, and all the Pastors of Thy holy Church. Assist the poor and the afflicted, and those who are now in their last agony. Look with an eye of pity on the suffering souls in purgatory, particularly

_____

_____

_____

put an end to their torments and lead them forth into everlasting joy.

Eternal rest grant unto them and let perpetual light shine upon them. Amen.

DATE:
_____

Today, read the obituaries in your local newspaper and pray for the souls who have died in the past several days.

Morning Prayer for the Poor Souls:

Out of the depths I have cried to Thee O Lord! Lord, hear my voice. Let Thine ears be attentive to the voice of my supplication.
If Thou, O Lord, wilt mark iniquities, Lord, who shall stand it?
For with Thee there is mercy: and by reason of Thy law I have waited on Thee, O Lord! My soul hath relied on His word: my soul hath hoped in the Lord. From the morning watch even until night. Let Israel hope in the Lord. For with the Lord there is mercy; and with Him plentiful Redemption. And He will redeem Israel from all his iniquities.
Eternal rest give unto them, O Lord! And let perpetual light shine upon them. May they rest in peace. Amen.

Evening Prayer for the Poor Souls:

V. Lord, hear my prayer.
R. And let my cry come unto Thee.
Bless, O my God! the repose I am about to take, that, renewing my strength, I may be better enabled to serve Thee. Pour down Thy blessings, O Lord! on my parents, relations, friends, and enemies. Protect the Pope, our Bishop, and all the Pastors of Thy holy Church. Assist the poor and the afflicted, and those who are now in their last agony. Look with an eye of pity on the suffering souls in purgatory, particularly

_____
_____

_____

put an end to their torments and lead them forth into everlasting joy.

Eternal rest grant unto them and let perpetual light shine upon them. Amen.

DATE:

_____

Spend some time in Eucharistic Adoration today for the Poor Souls. If you cannot travel to a church physically, watch live Adoration on EWTN, YouTube or Facebook.

Morning Prayer for the Poor Souls:

Out of the depths I have cried to Thee O Lord! Lord, hear my voice. Let Thine ears be attentive to the voice of my supplication.
If Thou, O Lord, wilt mark iniquities, Lord, who shall stand it?
For with Thee there is mercy: and by reason of Thy law I have waited on Thee, O Lord! My soul hath relied on His word: my soul hath hoped in the Lord. From the morning watch even until night. Let Israel hope in the Lord. For with the Lord there is mercy; and with Him plentiful Redemption. And He will redeem Israel from all his iniquities.
Eternal rest give unto them, O Lord! And let perpetual light shine upon them. May they rest in peace. Amen.

Evening Prayer for the Poor Souls:

V. Lord, hear my prayer.
R. And let my cry come unto Thee.
Bless, O my God! the repose I am about to take, that, renewing my strength, I may be better enabled to serve Thee. Pour down Thy blessings, O Lord! on my parents, relations, friends, and enemies. Protect the Pope, our Bishop, and all the Pastors of Thy holy Church. Assist the poor and the afflicted, and those who are now in their last agony. Look with an eye of pity on the suffering souls in purgatory, particularly

_____
_____
_____

put an end to their torments and lead them forth into everlasting joy.

Eternal rest grant unto them and let perpetual light shine upon them. Amen.

DATE:
_____

a drive today to a cemetery and pray for the souls of those interred there. If you cannot physically visit a cemetery, think of a cemetery in your city or town and pray for the souls of those buried there.

Morning Prayer for the Poor Souls:

Out of the depths I have cried to Thee O Lord! Lord, hear my voice. Let Thine ears be attentive to the voice of my supplication.
If Thou, O Lord, wilt mark iniquities, Lord, who shall stand it?
For with Thee there is mercy: and by reason of Thy law I have waited on Thee, O Lord! My soul hath relied on His word: my soul hath hoped in the Lord. From the morning watch even until night. Let Israel hope in the Lord. For with the Lord there is mercy; and with Him plentiful Redemption. And He will redeem Israel from all his iniquities.
Eternal rest give unto them, O Lord! And let perpetual light shine upon them. May they rest in peace. Amen.

Evening Prayer for the Poor Souls:

V. Lord, hear my prayer.
R. And let my cry come unto Thee.
Bless, O my God! the repose I am about to take, that, renewing my strength, I may be better enabled to serve Thee. Pour down Thy blessings, O Lord! on my parents, relations, friends, and enemies. Protect the Pope, our Bishop, and all the Pastors of Thy holy Church. Assist the poor and the afflicted, and those who are now in their last agony. Look with an eye of pity on the suffering souls in purgatory, particularly

_____
_____

_____

put an end to their torments and lead them forth into everlasting joy.

Eternal rest grant unto them and let perpetual light shine upon them. Amen.

DATE:
_____

Today, play some sacred music to comfort the Poor Souls. Mystic saints have told us that these small gestures provide great relief to their suffering.

Morning Prayer for the Poor Souls:

Out of the depths I have cried to Thee O Lord! Lord, hear my voice. Let Thine ears be attentive to the voice of my supplication.
If Thou, O Lord, wilt mark iniquities, Lord, who shall stand it?
For with Thee there is mercy: and by reason of Thy law I have waited on Thee, O Lord! My soul hath relied on His word: my soul hath hoped in the Lord. From the morning watch even until night. Let Israel hope in the Lord. For with the Lord there is mercy; and with Him plentiful Redemption. And He will redeem Israel from all his iniquities.
Eternal rest give unto them, O Lord! And let perpetual light shine upon them. May they rest in peace. Amen.

Evening Prayer for the Poor Souls:

V. Lord, hear my prayer.
R. And let my cry come unto Thee.
Bless, O my God! the repose I am about to take, that, renewing my strength, I may be better enabled to serve Thee. Pour down Thy blessings, O Lord! on my parents, relations, friends, and enemies. Protect the Pope, our Bishop, and all the Pastors of Thy holy Church. Assist the poor and the afflicted, and those who are now in their last agony. Look with an eye of pity on the suffering souls in purgatory, particularly

_____
_____
_____

put an end to their torments and lead them forth into everlasting joy.

Eternal rest grant unto them and let perpetual light shine upon them. Amen.

DATE:

_____

Today, make reparation to the Sacred Heart of Jesus for the souls in Purgatory who offended His most precious Heart with the following: Adorable Heart of Jesus, glowing with love for us and inflamed with zeal for our salvation. O Heart that understands the misery to which our sins have brought us, infinitely rich in mercy to heal the wounds of our souls, behold me humbly kneeling before You to express the sorrow that fills my heart for the coldness and indifference with which I have so long returned the numberless benefits which You have bestowed upon me.

Morning Prayer for the Poor Souls:

Out of the depths I have cried to Thee O Lord! Lord, hear my voice. Let Thine ears be attentive to the voice of my supplication. If Thou, O Lord, wilt mark iniquities, Lord, who shall stand it? For with Thee there is mercy: and by reason of Thy law I have waited on Thee, O Lord! My soul hath relied on His word: my soul hath hoped in the Lord. From the morning watch even until night. Let Israel hope in the Lord. For with the Lord there is mercy; and with Him plentiful Redemption. And He will redeem Israel from all his iniquities. Eternal rest give unto them, O Lord! And let perpetual light shine upon them. May they rest in peace. Amen.

Evening Prayer for the Poor Souls:

V. Lord, hear my prayer.
R. And let my cry come unto Thee.
Bless, O my God! the repose I am about to take, that, renewing my strength, I may be better enabled to serve Thee. Pour down Thy blessings, O Lord! on my parents, relations, friends, and enemies. Protect the Pope, our Bishop, and all the Pastors of Thy holy Church. Assist the poor and the afflicted, and those who are now in their last agony. Look with an eye of pity on the suffering souls in purgatory, particularly

_____

put an end to their torments and lead them forth into everlasting joy.

Eternal rest grant unto them and let perpetual light shine upon them. Amen.

DATE:
_____

Start a Mass Collection jar or envelope today for the Holy Souls. Add money to it as you are able, and when you have enough for a donation, have a Mass said for a soul in Purgatory.

Morning Prayer for the Poor Souls:

Out of the depths I have cried to Thee O Lord! Lord, hear my voice. Let Thine ears be attentive to the voice of my supplication.
If Thou, O Lord, wilt mark iniquities, Lord, who shall stand it?
For with Thee there is mercy: and by reason of Thy law I have waited on Thee, O Lord! My soul hath relied on His word: my soul hath hoped in the Lord. From the morning watch even until night. Let Israel hope in the Lord. For with the Lord there is mercy; and with Him plentiful Redemption. And He will redeem Israel from all his iniquities.
Eternal rest give unto them, O Lord! And let perpetual light shine upon them. May they rest in peace. Amen.

Evening Prayer for the Poor Souls:

V. Lord, hear my prayer.
R. And let my cry come unto Thee.
Bless, O my God! the repose I am about to take, that, renewing my strength, I may be better enabled to serve Thee. Pour down Thy blessings, O Lord! on my parents, relations, friends, and enemies. Protect the Pope, our Bishop, and all the Pastors of Thy holy Church. Assist the poor and the afflicted, and those who are now in their last agony. Look with an eye of pity on the suffering souls in purgatory, particularly

_____
_____
_____

put an end to their torments and lead them forth into everlasting joy.

Eternal rest grant unto them and let perpetual light shine upon them. Amen.

DATE:
_____

Go without a meal or snack today if possible, for the benefit of the Holy Souls. If you are in ill health, give up a special treat instead.

Morning Prayer for the Poor Souls:

Out of the depths I have cried to Thee O Lord! Lord, hear my voice. Let Thine ears be attentive to the voice of my supplication.
If Thou, O Lord, wilt mark iniquities, Lord, who shall stand it?
For with Thee there is mercy: and by reason of Thy law I have waited on Thee, O Lord! My soul hath relied on His word: my soul hath hoped in the Lord. From the morning watch even until night. Let Israel hope in the Lord. For with the Lord there is mercy; and with Him plentiful Redemption. And He will redeem Israel from all his iniquities.
Eternal rest give unto them, O Lord! And let perpetual light shine upon them. May they rest in peace. Amen.

Evening Prayer for the Poor Souls:

V. Lord, hear my prayer.
R. And let my cry come unto Thee.
Bless, O my God! the repose I am about to take, that, renewing my strength, I may be better enabled to serve Thee. Pour down Thy blessings, O Lord! on my parents, relations, friends, and enemies. Protect the Pope, our Bishop, and all the Pastors of Thy holy Church. Assist the poor and the afflicted, and those who are now in their last agony. Look with an eye of pity on the suffering souls in purgatory, particularly

_____
_____
_____

put an end to their torments and lead them forth into everlasting joy.

Eternal rest grant unto them and let perpetual light shine upon them. Amen.

DATE:

_____

Today, say a Divine Mercy chaplet for the Poor Souls.

Morning Prayer for the Poor Souls:

Out of the depths I have cried to Thee O Lord! Lord, hear my voice. Let Thine ears be attentive to the voice of my supplication.
If Thou, O Lord, wilt mark iniquities, Lord, who shall stand it?
For with Thee there is mercy: and by reason of Thy law I have waited on Thee, O Lord! My soul hath relied on His word: my soul hath hoped in the Lord. From the morning watch even until night. Let Israel hope in the Lord. For with the Lord there is mercy; and with Him plentiful Redemption. And He will redeem Israel from all his iniquities.
Eternal rest give unto them, O Lord! And let perpetual light shine upon them. May they rest in peace. Amen.

Evening Prayer for the Poor Souls:

V. Lord, hear my prayer.
R. And let my cry come unto Thee.
Bless, O my God! the repose I am about to take, that, renewing my strength, I may be better enabled to serve Thee. Pour down Thy blessings, O Lord! on my parents, relations, friends, and enemies. Protect the Pope, our Bishop, and all the Pastors of Thy holy Church. Assist the poor and the afflicted, and those who are now in their last agony. Look with an eye of pity on the suffering souls in purgatory, particularly

_____

_____

_____

put an end to their torments and lead them forth into everlasting joy.

Eternal rest grant unto them and let perpetual light shine upon them. Amen.

DATE: _____

Pray today for the souls of priests and religious in Purgatory.

Morning Prayer for the Poor Souls:

Out of the depths I have cried to Thee O Lord! Lord, hear my voice. Let Thine ears be attentive to the voice of my supplication.
If Thou, O Lord, wilt mark iniquities, Lord, who shall stand it?
For with Thee there is mercy: and by reason of Thy law I have waited on Thee, O Lord! My soul hath relied on His word: my soul hath hoped in the Lord. From the morning watch even until night. Let Israel hope in the Lord. For with the Lord there is mercy; and with Him plentiful Redemption. And He will redeem Israel from all his iniquities.
Eternal rest give unto them, O Lord! And let perpetual light shine upon them. May they rest in peace. Amen.

Evening Prayer for the Poor Souls:

V. Lord, hear my prayer.
R. And let my cry come unto Thee.
Bless, O my God! the repose I am about to take, that, renewing my strength, I may be better enabled to serve Thee. Pour down Thy blessings, O Lord! on my parents, relations, friends, and enemies. Protect the Pope, our Bishop, and all the Pastors of Thy holy Church. Assist the poor and the afflicted, and those who are now in their last agony. Look with an eye of pity on the suffering souls in purgatory, particularly

_____

_____

_____

put an end to their torments and lead them forth into everlasting joy.

Eternal rest grant unto them, and let perpetual light shine upon them. Amen.

DATE: _____

While you are going about your day today, remember your friends and colleagues who have passed away over the years, asking God to release them from Purgatory.

Morning Prayer for the Poor Souls:

Out of the depths I have cried to Thee O Lord! Lord, hear my voice. Let Thine ears be attentive to the voice of my supplication.
If Thou, O Lord, wilt mark iniquities, Lord, who shall stand it?
For with Thee there is mercy: and by reason of Thy law I have waited on Thee, O Lord! My soul hath relied on His word: my soul hath hoped in the Lord. From the morning watch even until night. Let Israel hope in the Lord. For with the Lord there is mercy; and with Him plentiful Redemption. And He will redeem Israel from all his iniquities.
Eternal rest give unto them, O Lord! And let perpetual light shine upon them. May they rest in peace. Amen.

Evening Prayer for the Poor Souls:

V. Lord, hear my prayer.
R. And let my cry come unto Thee.
Bless, O my God! the repose I am about to take, that, renewing my strength, I may be better enabled to serve Thee. Pour down Thy blessings, O Lord! on my parents, relations, friends, and enemies. Protect the Pope, our Bishop, and all the Pastors of Thy holy Church. Assist the poor and the afflicted, and those who are now in their last agony. Look with an eye of pity on the suffering souls in purgatory, particularly

put an end to their torments and lead them forth into everlasting joy.

Eternal rest grant unto them, and let perpetual light shine upon them. Amen.

DATE: _____

Pray today for the dead who heard the Gospel but rejected it. May they be spared Hell and be released from Purgatory to be with Jesus.

*Morning Prayer for the Poor Souls***:**

Out of the depths I have cried to Thee O Lord! Lord, hear my voice. Let Thine ears be attentive to the voice of my supplication.
If Thou, O Lord, wilt mark iniquities, Lord, who shall stand it?
For with Thee there is mercy: and by reason of Thy law I have waited on Thee, O Lord! My soul hath relied on His word: my soul hath hoped in the Lord. From the morning watch even until night. Let Israel hope in the Lord. For with the Lord there is mercy; and with Him plentiful Redemption. And He will redeem Israel from all his iniquities.
Eternal rest give unto them, O Lord! And let perpetual light shine upon them. May they rest in peace. Amen.

Evening Prayer for the Poor Souls:

V. Lord, hear my prayer.
R. And let my cry come unto Thee.
Bless, O my God! the repose I am about to take, that, renewing my strength, I may be better enabled to serve Thee. Pour down Thy blessings, O Lord! on my parents, relations, friends, and enemies. Protect the Pope, our Bishop, and all the Pastors of Thy holy Church. Assist the poor and the afflicted, and those who are now in their last agony. Look with an eye of pity on the suffering souls in purgatory, particularly

_____
_____
_____

put an end to their torments and lead them forth into everlasting joy.

Eternal rest grant unto them and let perpetual light shine upon them. Amen.

DATE: _____

Today, spend some time reading devotional literature aloud for the comfort of the Poor Souls.

Morning Prayer for the Poor Souls:

Out of the depths I have cried to Thee O Lord! Lord, hear my voice. Let Thine ears be attentive to the voice of my supplication.
If Thou, O Lord, wilt mark iniquities, Lord, who shall stand it?
For with Thee there is mercy: and by reason of Thy law I have waited on Thee, O Lord! My soul hath relied on His word: my soul hath hoped in the Lord. From the morning watch even until night. Let Israel hope in the Lord. For with the Lord there is mercy; and with Him plentiful Redemption. And He will redeem Israel from all his iniquities.
Eternal rest give unto them, O Lord! And let perpetual light shine upon them. May they rest in peace. Amen.

Evening Prayer for the Poor Souls:

V. Lord, hear my prayer.
R. And let my cry come unto Thee.
Bless, O my God! the repose I am about to take, that, renewing my strength, I may be better enabled to serve Thee. Pour down Thy blessings, O Lord! on my parents, relations, friends, and enemies. Protect the Pope, our Bishop, and all the Pastors of Thy holy Church. Assist the poor and the afflicted, and those who are now in their last agony. Look with an eye of pity on the suffering souls in purgatory, particularly

_____
_____
_____

put an end to their torments and lead them forth into everlasting joy.

Eternal rest grant unto them and let perpetual light shine upon them. Amen.

DATE: _____

Today make the Stations of the Cross for the benefit of the Holy Souls in Purgatory.

Morning Prayer for the Poor Souls:

Out of the depths I have cried to Thee O Lord! Lord, hear my voice. Let Thine ears be attentive to the voice of my supplication.
If Thou, O Lord, wilt mark iniquities, Lord, who shall stand it?
For with Thee there is mercy: and by reason of Thy law I have waited on Thee, O Lord! My soul hath relied on His word: my soul hath hoped in the Lord. From the morning watch even until night. Let Israel hope in the Lord. For with the Lord there is mercy; and with Him plentiful Redemption. And He will redeem Israel from all his iniquities.
Eternal rest give unto them, O Lord! And let perpetual light shine upon them. May they rest in peace. Amen.

Evening Prayer for the Poor Souls:

V. Lord, hear my prayer.
R. And let my cry come unto Thee.
Bless, O my God! the repose I am about to take, that, renewing my strength, I may be better enabled to serve Thee. Pour down Thy blessings, O Lord! on my parents, relations, friends, and enemies. Protect the Pope, our Bishop, and all the Pastors of Thy holy Church. Assist the poor and the afflicted, and those who are now in their last agony. Look with an eye of pity on the suffering souls in purgatory, particularly

_____
_____

_____

put an end to their torments and lead them forth into everlasting joy.

Eternal rest grant unto them and let perpetual light shine upon them. Amen.

DATE: _____

Pray today for the souls of all Jewish people who have died.

Morning Prayer for the Poor Souls:

Out of the depths I have cried to Thee O Lord! Lord, hear my voice. Let Thine ears be attentive to the voice of my supplication.
If Thou, O Lord, wilt mark iniquities, Lord, who shall stand it?
For with Thee there is mercy: and by reason of Thy law I have waited on Thee, O Lord! My soul hath relied on His word: my soul hath hoped in the Lord. From the morning watch even until night. Let Israel hope in the Lord. For with the Lord there is mercy; and with Him plentiful Redemption. And He will redeem Israel from all his iniquities.
Eternal rest give unto them, O Lord! And let perpetual light shine upon them. May they rest in peace. Amen.

Evening Prayer for the Poor Souls:

V. Lord, hear my prayer.
R. And let my cry come unto Thee.
Bless, O my God! the repose I am about to take, that, renewing my strength, I may be better enabled to serve Thee. Pour down Thy blessings, O Lord! on my parents, relations, friends, and enemies. Protect the Pope, our Bishop, and all the Pastors of Thy holy Church. Assist the poor and the afflicted, and those who are now in their last agony. Look with an eye of pity on the suffering souls in purgatory, particularly

_____
_____
_____

put an end to their torments and lead them forth into everlasting joy.

Eternal rest grant unto them and let perpetual light shine upon them. Amen.

DATE: _____

Today, pray for the souls of persecutors of Christians who have died.

Morning Prayer for the Poor Souls:

Out of the depths I have cried to Thee O Lord! Lord, hear my voice. Let Thine ears be attentive to the voice of my supplication.
If Thou, O Lord, wilt mark iniquities, Lord, who shall stand it?
For with Thee there is mercy: and by reason of Thy law I have waited on Thee, O Lord! My soul hath relied on His word: my soul hath hoped in the Lord. From the morning watch even until night. Let Israel hope in the Lord. For with the Lord there is mercy; and with Him plentiful Redemption. And He will redeem Israel from all his iniquities.
Eternal rest give unto them, O Lord! And let perpetual light shine upon them. May they rest in peace. Amen.

Evening Prayer for the Poor Souls:

V. Lord, hear my prayer.
R. And let my cry come unto Thee.
Bless, O my God! the repose I am about to take, that, renewing my strength, I may be better enabled to serve Thee. Pour down Thy blessings, O Lord! on my parents, relations, friends, and enemies. Protect the Pope, our Bishop, and all the Pastors of Thy holy Church. Assist the poor and the afflicted, and those who are now in their last agony. Look with an eye of pity on the suffering souls in purgatory, particularly

_____

_____

_____

put an end to their torments and lead them forth into everlasting joy.

Eternal rest grant unto them and let perpetual light shine upon them. Amen.

DATE: _____

Light a blessed candle today in remembrance of the Holy Souls.

Morning Prayer for the Poor Souls:

Out of the depths I have cried to Thee O Lord! Lord, hear my voice. Let Thine ears be attentive to the voice of my supplication.
If Thou, O Lord, wilt mark iniquities, Lord, who shall stand it?
For with Thee there is mercy: and by reason of Thy law I have waited on Thee, O Lord! My soul hath relied on His word: my soul hath hoped in the Lord. From the morning watch even until night. Let Israel hope in the Lord. For with the Lord there is mercy; and with Him plentiful Redemption. And He will redeem Israel from all his iniquities.
Eternal rest give unto them, O Lord! And let perpetual light shine upon them. May they rest in peace. Amen.

Evening Prayer for the Poor Souls:

V. Lord, hear my prayer.
R. And let my cry come unto Thee.
Bless, O my God! the repose I am about to take, that, renewing my strength, I may be better enabled to serve Thee. Pour down Thy blessings, O Lord! on my parents, relations, friends, and enemies. Protect the Pope, our Bishop, and all the Pastors of Thy holy Church. Assist the poor and the afflicted, and those who are now in their last agony. Look with an eye of pity on the suffering souls in purgatory, particularly

_____

_____

_____

put an end to their torments and lead them forth into everlasting joy.

Eternal rest grant unto them and let perpetual light shine upon them. Amen.

DATE: _____

Begin a Novena today for the benefit of the Poor Souls. St. Alphonsus Liguori wrote a powerful one just for the Holy Souls, which may be found online, but any Novena will be appreciated.

Morning Prayer for the Poor Souls:

Out of the depths I have cried to Thee O Lord! Lord, hear my voice. Let Thine ears be attentive to the voice of my supplication.
If Thou, O Lord, wilt mark iniquities, Lord, who shall stand it?
For with Thee there is mercy: and by reason of Thy law I have waited on Thee, O Lord! My soul hath relied on His word: my soul hath hoped in the Lord. From the morning watch even until night. Let Israel hope in the Lord. For with the Lord there is mercy; and with Him plentiful Redemption. And He will redeem Israel from all his iniquities.
Eternal rest give unto them, O Lord! And let perpetual light shine upon them. May they rest in peace. Amen.

Evening Prayer for the Poor Souls:

V. Lord, hear my prayer.
R. And let my cry come unto Thee.
Bless, O my God! the repose I am about to take, that, renewing my strength, I may be better enabled to serve Thee. Pour down Thy blessings, O Lord! on my parents, relations, friends, and enemies. Protect the Pope, our Bishop, and all the Pastors of Thy holy Church. Assist the poor and the afflicted, and those who are now in their last agony. Look with an eye of pity on the suffering souls in purgatory, particularly

_____
_____
_____

put an end to their torments and lead them forth into everlasting joy.

Eternal rest grant unto them and let perpetual light shine upon them. Amen.

DATE: _____

Give alms to the poor today to benefit the souls in Purgatory. We are told that giving alms is of great benefit to suffering souls.

Morning Prayer for the Poor Souls:

Out of the depths I have cried to Thee O Lord! Lord, hear my voice. Let Thine ears be attentive to the voice of my supplication.
If Thou, O Lord, wilt mark iniquities, Lord, who shall stand it?
For with Thee there is mercy: and by reason of Thy law I have waited on Thee, O Lord! My soul hath relied on His word: my soul hath hoped in the Lord. From the morning watch even until night. Let Israel hope in the Lord. For with the Lord there is mercy; and with Him plentiful Redemption. And He will redeem Israel from all his iniquities.
Eternal rest give unto them, O Lord! And let perpetual light shine upon them. May they rest in peace. Amen.

Evening Prayer for the Poor Souls:

V. Lord, hear my prayer.
R. And let my cry come unto Thee.
Bless, O my God! the repose I am about to take, that, renewing my strength, I may be better enabled to serve Thee. Pour down Thy blessings, O Lord! on my parents, relations, friends, and enemies. Protect the Pope, our Bishop, and all the Pastors of Thy holy Church. Assist the poor and the afflicted, and those who are now in their last agony. Look with an eye of pity on the suffering souls in purgatory, particularly

_____

_____

_____

put an end to their torments and lead them forth into everlasting joy.

Eternal rest grant unto them and let perpetual light shine upon them. Amen.

DATE: _____

Read aloud today from the Acts of the Apostles to comfort the Holy Souls. The Good News of Jesus' salvation is of great relief to their suffering.

Morning Prayer for the Poor Souls:

Out of the depths I have cried to Thee O Lord! Lord, hear my voice. Let Thine ears be attentive to the voice of my supplication.
If Thou, O Lord, wilt mark iniquities, Lord, who shall stand it?
For with Thee there is mercy: and by reason of Thy law I have waited on Thee, O Lord! My soul hath relied on His word: my soul hath hoped in the Lord. From the morning watch even until night. Let Israel hope in the Lord. For with the Lord there is mercy; and with Him plentiful Redemption. And He will redeem Israel from all his iniquities.
Eternal rest give unto them, O Lord! And let perpetual light shine upon them. May they rest in peace. Amen.

Evening Prayer for the Poor Souls:

V. Lord, hear my prayer.
R. And let my cry come unto Thee.
Bless, O my God! the repose I am about to take, that, renewing my strength, I may be better enabled to serve Thee. Pour down Thy blessings, O Lord! on my parents, relations, friends, and enemies. Protect the Pope, our Bishop, and all the Pastors of Thy holy Church. Assist the poor and the afflicted, and those who are now in their last agony. Look with an eye of pity on the suffering souls in purgatory, particularly

_____
_____
_____

put an end to their torments and lead them forth into everlasting joy.

Eternal rest grant unto them and let perpetual light shine upon them. Amen.

DATE: _____

Today, ask the saints known as intercessors for the dead to pray with you for their release, including St. Nicholas of Tolentino, St. Gertrude the Great, St. Catherine of Genoa, St. Padre Pio, St. Philip Neri, St. John Macías, St. Faustina Kowalska, St. Joseph and, of course, the Blessed Mother.

Morning Prayer for the Poor Souls:

Out of the depths I have cried to Thee O Lord! Lord, hear my voice. Let Thine ears be attentive to the voice of my supplication.
If Thou, O Lord, wilt mark iniquities, Lord, who shall stand it?
For with Thee there is mercy: and by reason of Thy law I have waited on Thee, O Lord! My soul hath relied on His word: my soul hath hoped in the Lord. From the morning watch even until night. Let Israel hope in the Lord. For with the Lord there is mercy; and with Him plentiful Redemption. And He will redeem Israel from all his iniquities.
Eternal rest give unto them, O Lord! And let perpetual light shine upon them. May they rest in peace. Amen.

Evening Prayer for the Poor Souls:

V. Lord, hear my prayer.
R. And let my cry come unto Thee.
Bless, O my God! the repose I am about to take, that, renewing my strength, I may be better enabled to serve Thee. Pour down Thy blessings, O Lord! on my parents, relations, friends, and enemies. Protect the Pope, our Bishop, and all the Pastors of Thy holy Church. Assist the poor and the afflicted, and those who are now in their last agony. Look with an eye of pity on the suffering souls in purgatory, particularly

_____
_____
_____

put an end to their torments and lead them forth into everlasting joy.

Eternal rest grant unto them and let perpetual light shine upon them. Amen.

DATE: _____

Today, have a Mass said for the soul of a family member or friend who has passed away. This can be through your own parish or through an order or national shrine via their website.

Morning Prayer for the Poor Souls:

Out of the depths I have cried to Thee O Lord! Lord, hear my voice. Let Thine ears be attentive to the voice of my supplication.
If Thou, O Lord, wilt mark iniquities, Lord, who shall stand it?
For with Thee there is mercy: and by reason of Thy law I have waited on Thee, O Lord! My soul hath relied on His word: my soul hath hoped in the Lord. From the morning watch even until night. Let Israel hope in the Lord. For with the Lord there is mercy; and with Him plentiful Redemption. And He will redeem Israel from all his iniquities.
Eternal rest give unto them, O Lord! And let perpetual light shine upon them. May they rest in peace. Amen.

Evening Prayer for the Poor Souls:

V. Lord, hear my prayer.
R. And let my cry come unto Thee.
Bless, O my God! the repose I am about to take, that, renewing my strength, I may be better enabled to serve Thee. Pour down Thy blessings, O Lord! on my parents, relations, friends, and enemies. Protect the Pope, our Bishop, and all the Pastors of Thy holy Church. Assist the poor and the afflicted, and those who are now in their last agony. Look with an eye of pity on the suffering souls in purgatory, particularly

_____

_____

_____

put an end to their torments and lead them forth into everlasting joy.

Eternal rest grant unto them and let perpetual light shine upon them. Amen.

DATE:
_____

Pray the Rosary today for the release of souls from Purgatory. Mystic saints have told us that the Blessed Mother herself comes to Purgatory to bring souls with her back to Heaven.

Morning Prayer for the Poor Souls:

Out of the depths I have cried to Thee O Lord! Lord, hear my voice. Let Thine ears be attentive to the voice of my supplication.
If Thou, O Lord, wilt mark iniquities, Lord, who shall stand it?
For with Thee there is mercy: and by reason of Thy law I have waited on Thee, O Lord! My soul hath relied on His word: my soul hath hoped in the Lord. From the morning watch even until night. Let Israel hope in the Lord. For with the Lord there is mercy; and with Him plentiful Redemption. And He will redeem Israel from all his iniquities.
Eternal rest give unto them, O Lord! And let perpetual light shine upon them. May they rest in peace. Amen.

Evening Prayer for the Poor Souls:

V. Lord, hear my prayer.
R. And let my cry come unto Thee.
Bless, O my God! the repose I am about to take, that, renewing my strength, I may be better enabled to serve Thee. Pour down Thy blessings, O Lord! on my parents, relations, friends, and enemies. Protect the Pope, our Bishop, and all the Pastors of Thy holy Church. Assist the poor and the afflicted, and those who are now in their last agony. Look with an eye of pity on the suffering souls in purgatory, particularly

_____
_____

_____

put an end to their torments and lead them forth into everlasting joy.

Eternal rest grant unto them and let perpetual light shine upon them. Amen.

DATE:

_____

Today, ask the Blessed Mother to apply your prayers and works to a poor soul who has no one to pray for them.

Morning Prayer for the Poor Souls:

Out of the depths I have cried to Thee O Lord! Lord, hear my voice. Let Thine ears be attentive to the voice of my supplication.
If Thou, O Lord, wilt mark iniquities, Lord, who shall stand it?
For with Thee there is mercy: and by reason of Thy law I have waited on Thee, O Lord! My soul hath relied on His word: my soul hath hoped in the Lord. From the morning watch even until night. Let Israel hope in the Lord. For with the Lord there is mercy; and with Him plentiful Redemption. And He will redeem Israel from all his iniquities.
Eternal rest give unto them, O Lord! And let perpetual light shine upon them. May they rest in peace. Amen.

Evening Prayer for the Poor Souls:

V. Lord, hear my prayer.
R. And let my cry come unto Thee.
Bless, O my God! the repose I am about to take, that, renewing my strength, I may be better enabled to serve Thee. Pour down Thy blessings, O Lord! on my parents, relations, friends, and enemies. Protect the Pope, our Bishop, and all the Pastors of Thy holy Church. Assist the poor and the afflicted, and those who are now in their last agony. Look with an eye of pity on the suffering souls in purgatory, particularly

_____
_____

_____

put an end to their torments and lead them forth into everlasting joy.

Eternal rest grant unto them and let perpetual light shine upon them. Amen.

DATE:
_____

We all have a spiritual or physical affliction or burden that we suffer with daily. Today, dedicate your ailment-related suffering to the Poor souls.

Morning Prayer for the Poor Souls:

Out of the depths I have cried to Thee O Lord! Lord, hear my voice. Let Thine ears be attentive to the voice of my supplication.
If Thou, O Lord, wilt mark iniquities, Lord, who shall stand it?
For with Thee there is mercy: and by reason of Thy law I have waited on Thee, O Lord! My soul hath relied on His word: my soul hath hoped in the Lord. From the morning watch even until night. Let Israel hope in the Lord. For with the Lord there is mercy; and with Him plentiful Redemption. And He will redeem Israel from all his iniquities.
Eternal rest give unto them, O Lord! And let perpetual light shine upon them. May they rest in peace. Amen.

Evening Prayer for the Poor Souls:

V. Lord, hear my prayer.
R. And let my cry come unto Thee.
Bless, O my God! the repose I am about to take, that, renewing my strength, I may be better enabled to serve Thee. Pour down Thy blessings, O Lord! on my parents, relations, friends, and enemies. Protect the Pope, our Bishop, and all the Pastors of Thy holy Church. Assist the poor and the afflicted, and those who are now in their last agony. Look with an eye of pity on the suffering souls in purgatory, particularly

_____
_____
_____

put an end to their torments and lead them forth into everlasting joy.

Eternal rest grant unto them and let perpetual light shine upon them. Amen.

DATE:
_____

Today, visit or call someone elderly or alone and offer your work of mercy for the souls in Purgatory.

Morning Prayer for the Poor Souls:

Out of the depths I have cried to Thee O Lord! Lord, hear my voice. Let Thine ears be attentive to the voice of my supplication.
If Thou, O Lord, wilt mark iniquities, Lord, who shall stand it?
For with Thee there is mercy: and by reason of Thy law I have waited on Thee, O Lord! My soul hath relied on His word: my soul hath hoped in the Lord. From the morning watch even until night. Let Israel hope in the Lord. For with the Lord there is mercy; and with Him plentiful Redemption. And He will redeem Israel from all his iniquities.
Eternal rest give unto them, O Lord! And let perpetual light shine upon them. May they rest in peace. Amen.

Evening Prayer for the Poor Souls:

V. Lord, hear my prayer.
R. And let my cry come unto Thee.
Bless, O my God! the repose I am about to take, that, renewing my strength, I may be better enabled to serve Thee. Pour down Thy blessings, O Lord! on my parents, relations, friends, and enemies. Protect the Pope, our Bishop, and all the Pastors of Thy holy Church. Assist the poor and the afflicted, and those who are now in their last agony. Look with an eye of pity on the suffering souls in purgatory, particularly

_____
_____
_____

put an end to their torments and lead them forth into everlasting joy.

Eternal rest grant unto them and let perpetual light shine upon them. Amen.

DATE:
_____

During the course of the day today, pray for those you meet and strangers you see on street, asking God to apply your prayers for them to their future time in Purgatory.

Morning Prayer for the Poor Souls:

Out of the depths I have cried to Thee O Lord! Lord, hear my voice. Let Thine ears be attentive to the voice of my supplication.
If Thou, O Lord, wilt mark iniquities, Lord, who shall stand it?
For with Thee there is mercy: and by reason of Thy law I have waited on Thee, O Lord! My soul hath relied on His word: my soul hath hoped in the Lord. From the morning watch even until night. Let Israel hope in the Lord. For with the Lord there is mercy; and with Him plentiful Redemption. And He will redeem Israel from all his iniquities.
Eternal rest give unto them, O Lord! And let perpetual light shine upon them. May they rest in peace. Amen.

Evening Prayer for the Poor Souls:

V. Lord, hear my prayer.
R. And let my cry come unto Thee.
Bless, O my God! the repose I am about to take, that, renewing my strength, I may be better enabled to serve Thee. Pour down Thy blessings, O Lord! on my parents, relations, friends, and enemies. Protect the Pope, our Bishop, and all the Pastors of Thy holy Church. Assist the poor and the afflicted, and those who are now in their last agony. Look with an eye of pity on the suffering souls in purgatory, particularly

_____
_____
_____

put an end to their torments and lead them forth into everlasting joy.

Eternal rest grant unto them and let perpetual light shine upon them. Amen.

DATE:

_____

Today, ask the Blessed Mother to use your prayers for someone in Purgatory with no one to pray for them.

Morning Prayer for the Poor Souls:

Out of the depths I have cried to Thee O Lord! Lord, hear my voice. Let Thine ears be attentive to the voice of my supplication.
If Thou, O Lord, wilt mark iniquities, Lord, who shall stand it?
For with Thee there is mercy: and by reason of Thy law I have waited on Thee, O Lord! My soul hath relied on His word: my soul hath hoped in the Lord. From the morning watch even until night. Let Israel hope in the Lord. For with the Lord there is mercy; and with Him plentiful Redemption. And He will redeem Israel from all his iniquities.
Eternal rest give unto them, O Lord! And let perpetual light shine upon them. May they rest in peace. Amen.

Evening Prayer for the Poor Souls:

V. Lord, hear my prayer.
R. And let my cry come unto Thee.
Bless, O my God! the repose I am about to take, that, renewing my strength, I may be better enabled to serve Thee. Pour down Thy blessings, O Lord! on my parents, relations, friends, and enemies. Protect the Pope, our Bishop, and all the Pastors of Thy holy Church. Assist the poor and the afflicted, and those who are now in their last agony. Look with an eye of pity on the suffering souls in purgatory, particularly

_____
_____
_____

put an end to their torments and lead them forth into everlasting joy.

Eternal rest grant unto them and let perpetual light shine upon them. Amen.

DATE:

_____

Today, sprinkle holy water on the carpet of your home or outside your house as a comfort to the Poor Souls.

Morning Prayer for the Poor Souls:

Out of the depths I have cried to Thee O Lord! Lord, hear my voice. Let Thine ears be attentive to the voice of my supplication.
If Thou, O Lord, wilt mark iniquities, Lord, who shall stand it?
For with Thee there is mercy: and by reason of Thy law I have waited on Thee, O Lord! My soul hath relied on His word: my soul hath hoped in the Lord. From the morning watch even until night. Let Israel hope in the Lord. For with the Lord there is mercy; and with Him plentiful Redemption. And He will redeem Israel from all his iniquities.
Eternal rest give unto them, O Lord! And let perpetual light shine upon them. May they rest in peace. Amen.

Evening Prayer for the Poor Souls:

V. Lord, hear my prayer.
R. And let my cry come unto Thee.
Bless, O my God! the repose I am about to take, that, renewing my strength, I may be better enabled to serve Thee. Pour down Thy blessings, O Lord! on my parents, relations, friends, and enemies. Protect the Pope, our Bishop, and all the Pastors of Thy holy Church. Assist the poor and the afflicted, and those who are now in their last agony. Look with an eye of pity on the suffering souls in purgatory, particularly

_____

_____

_____

put an end to their torments and lead them forth into everlasting joy.

Eternal rest grant unto them and let perpetual light shine upon them. Amen.

DATE:

_____

Today, visit a church if you are able, and pray for the souls who are spending their Purgatorial time there. Catholic mystics have told us that God allows many souls to do so. If you cannot visit a church, think of a local church and pray for any souls who might be there.

Morning Prayer for the Poor Souls:

Out of the depths I have cried to Thee O Lord! Lord, hear my voice. Let Thine ears be attentive to the voice of my supplication.
If Thou, O Lord, wilt mark iniquities, Lord, who shall stand it?
For with Thee there is mercy: and by reason of Thy law I have waited on Thee, O Lord! My soul hath relied on His word: my soul hath hoped in the Lord. From the morning watch even until night. Let Israel hope in the Lord. For with the Lord there is mercy; and with Him plentiful Redemption. And He will redeem Israel from all his iniquities.
Eternal rest give unto them, O Lord! And let perpetual light shine upon them. May they rest in peace. Amen.

Evening Prayer for the Poor Souls:

V. Lord, hear my prayer.
R. And let my cry come unto Thee.
Bless, O my God! the repose I am about to take, that, renewing my strength, I may be better enabled to serve Thee. Pour down Thy blessings, O Lord! on my parents, relations, friends, and enemies. Protect the Pope, our Bishop, and all the Pastors of Thy holy Church. Assist the poor and the afflicted, and those who are now in their last agony. Look with an eye of pity on the suffering souls in purgatory, particularly

_____

_____

put an end to their torments and lead them forth into everlasting joy.

Eternal rest grant unto them and let perpetual light shine upon them. Amen.

DATE:
_____

Today, visit someone who is sick if you are able, and offer up this work of mercy for the Holy Souls. If you cannot, pray for those in your local hospital or nursing home.

Morning Prayer for the Poor Souls:

Out of the depths I have cried to Thee O Lord! Lord, hear my voice. Let Thine ears be attentive to the voice of my supplication.
If Thou, O Lord, wilt mark iniquities, Lord, who shall stand it?
For with Thee there is mercy: and by reason of Thy law I have waited on Thee, O Lord! My soul hath relied on His word: my soul hath hoped in the Lord. From the morning watch even until night. Let Israel hope in the Lord. For with the Lord there is mercy; and with Him plentiful Redemption. And He will redeem Israel from all his iniquities.
Eternal rest give unto them, O Lord! And let perpetual light shine upon them. May they rest in peace. Amen.

Evening Prayer for the Poor Souls:

V. Lord, hear my prayer.
R. And let my cry come unto Thee.
Bless, O my God! the repose I am about to take, that, renewing my strength, I may be better enabled to serve Thee. Pour down Thy blessings, O Lord! on my parents, relations, friends, and enemies. Protect the Pope, our Bishop, and all the Pastors of Thy holy Church. Assist the poor and the afflicted, and those who are now in their last agony. Look with an eye of pity on the suffering souls in purgatory, particularly

_____
_____
_____

put an end to their torments and lead them forth into everlasting joy.

Eternal rest grant unto them and let perpetual light shine upon them. Amen.

DATE:

_____

Today pray for the souls of all the atheists who have died.

Morning Prayer for the Poor Souls:

Out of the depths I have cried to Thee O Lord! Lord, hear my voice. Let Thine ears be attentive to the voice of my supplication.
If Thou, O Lord, wilt mark iniquities, Lord, who shall stand it?
For with Thee there is mercy: and by reason of Thy law I have waited on Thee, O Lord! My soul hath relied on His word: my soul hath hoped in the Lord. From the morning watch even until night. Let Israel hope in the Lord. For with the Lord there is mercy; and with Him plentiful Redemption. And He will redeem Israel from all his iniquities.
Eternal rest give unto them, O Lord! And let perpetual light shine upon them. May they rest in peace. Amen.

Evening Prayer for the Poor Souls:

V. Lord, hear my prayer.
R. And let my cry come unto Thee.
Bless, O my God! the repose I am about to take, that, renewing my strength, I may be better enabled to serve Thee. Pour down Thy blessings, O Lord! on my parents, relations, friends, and enemies. Protect the Pope, our Bishop, and all the Pastors of Thy holy Church. Assist the poor and the afflicted, and those who are now in their last agony. Look with an eye of pity on the suffering souls in purgatory, particularly

_____

_____

_____

put an end to their torments and lead them forth into everlasting joy.

Eternal rest grant unto them and let perpetual light shine upon them. Amen.

DATE:

_____

Today, read the obituaries in your local newspaper and pray for the souls who have died in the past several days.

Morning Prayer for the Poor Souls:

Out of the depths I have cried to Thee O Lord! Lord, hear my voice. Let Thine ears be attentive to the voice of my supplication.
If Thou, O Lord, wilt mark iniquities, Lord, who shall stand it?
For with Thee there is mercy: and by reason of Thy law I have waited on Thee, O Lord! My soul hath relied on His word: my soul hath hoped in the Lord. From the morning watch even until night. Let Israel hope in the Lord. For with the Lord there is mercy; and with Him plentiful Redemption. And He will redeem Israel from all his iniquities.
Eternal rest give unto them, O Lord! And let perpetual light shine upon them. May they rest in peace. Amen.

Evening Prayer for the Poor Souls:

V. Lord, hear my prayer.
R. And let my cry come unto Thee.
Bless, O my God! the repose I am about to take, that, renewing my strength, I may be better enabled to serve Thee. Pour down Thy blessings, O Lord! on my parents, relations, friends, and enemies. Protect the Pope, our Bishop, and all the Pastors of Thy holy Church. Assist the poor and the afflicted, and those who are now in their last agony. Look with an eye of pity on the suffering souls in purgatory, particularly

_____
_____
_____

put an end to their torments and lead them forth into everlasting joy.

Eternal rest grant unto them and let perpetual light shine upon them. Amen.

DATE:

_____

Spend some time in Eucharistic Adoration today for the Poor Souls. If you cannot travel to a church physically, watch live Adoration on EWTN, YouTube or Facebook.

Morning Prayer for the Poor Souls:

Out of the depths I have cried to Thee O Lord! Lord, hear my voice. Let Thine ears be attentive to the voice of my supplication.
If Thou, O Lord, wilt mark iniquities, Lord, who shall stand it?
For with Thee there is mercy: and by reason of Thy law I have waited on Thee, O Lord! My soul hath relied on His word: my soul hath hoped in the Lord. From the morning watch even until night. Let Israel hope in the Lord. For with the Lord there is mercy; and with Him plentiful Redemption. And He will redeem Israel from all his iniquities.
Eternal rest give unto them, O Lord! And let perpetual light shine upon them. May they rest in peace. Amen.

Evening Prayer for the Poor Souls:

V. Lord, hear my prayer.
R. And let my cry come unto Thee.
Bless, O my God! the repose I am about to take, that, renewing my strength, I may be better enabled to serve Thee. Pour down Thy blessings, O Lord! on my parents, relations, friends, and enemies. Protect the Pope, our Bishop, and all the Pastors of Thy holy Church. Assist the poor and the afflicted, and those who are now in their last agony. Look with an eye of pity on the suffering souls in purgatory, particularly

_____
_____
_____

put an end to their torments and lead them forth into everlasting joy.

Eternal rest grant unto them and let perpetual light shine upon them. Amen.

DATE:

_____

a drive today to a cemetery and pray for the souls of those interred there. If you cannot physically visit a cemetery, think of a cemetery in your city or town and pray for the souls of those buried there.

Morning Prayer for the Poor Souls:

Out of the depths I have cried to Thee O Lord! Lord, hear my voice. Let Thine ears be attentive to the voice of my supplication.
If Thou, O Lord, wilt mark iniquities, Lord, who shall stand it?
For with Thee there is mercy: and by reason of Thy law I have waited on Thee, O Lord! My soul hath relied on His word: my soul hath hoped in the Lord. From the morning watch even until night. Let Israel hope in the Lord. For with the Lord there is mercy; and with Him plentiful Redemption. And He will redeem Israel from all his iniquities.
Eternal rest give unto them, O Lord! And let perpetual light shine upon them. May they rest in peace. Amen.

Evening Prayer for the Poor Souls:

V. Lord, hear my prayer.
R. And let my cry come unto Thee.
Bless, O my God! the repose I am about to take, that, renewing my strength, I may be better enabled to serve Thee. Pour down Thy blessings, O Lord! on my parents, relations, friends, and enemies. Protect the Pope, our Bishop, and all the Pastors of Thy holy Church. Assist the poor and the afflicted, and those who are now in their last agony. Look with an eye of pity on the suffering souls in purgatory, particularly

_____
_____
_____

put an end to their torments and lead them forth into everlasting joy.

Eternal rest grant unto them and let perpetual light shine upon them. Amen.

DATE:

_____

Today, play some sacred music to comfort the Poor Souls. Mystic saints have told us that these small gestures provide great relief to their suffering.

Morning Prayer for the Poor Souls:

Out of the depths I have cried to Thee O Lord! Lord, hear my voice. Let Thine ears be attentive to the voice of my supplication.
If Thou, O Lord, wilt mark iniquities, Lord, who shall stand it?
For with Thee there is mercy: and by reason of Thy law I have waited on Thee, O Lord! My soul hath relied on His word: my soul hath hoped in the Lord. From the morning watch even until night. Let Israel hope in the Lord. For with the Lord there is mercy; and with Him plentiful Redemption. And He will redeem Israel from all his iniquities.
Eternal rest give unto them, O Lord! And let perpetual light shine upon them. May they rest in peace. Amen.

Evening Prayer for the Poor Souls:

V. Lord, hear my prayer.
R. And let my cry come unto Thee.
Bless, O my God! the repose I am about to take, that, renewing my strength, I may be better enabled to serve Thee. Pour down Thy blessings, O Lord! on my parents, relations, friends, and enemies. Protect the Pope, our Bishop, and all the Pastors of Thy holy Church. Assist the poor and the afflicted, and those who are now in their last agony. Look with an eye of pity on the suffering souls in purgatory, particularly

_____

_____

_____

put an end to their torments and lead them forth into everlasting joy.

Eternal rest grant unto them and let perpetual light shine upon them. Amen.

DATE:

Today, make reparation to the Sacred Heart of Jesus for the souls in Purgatory who offended His most precious Heart with the following: Adorable Heart of Jesus, glowing with love for us and inflamed with zeal for our salvation. O Heart that understands the misery to which our sins have brought us, infinitely rich in mercy to heal the wounds of our souls, behold me humbly kneeling before You to express the sorrow that fills my heart for the coldness and indifference with which I have so long returned the numberless benefits which You have bestowed upon me.

Morning Prayer for the Poor Souls:

Out of the depths I have cried to Thee O Lord! Lord, hear my voice. Let Thine ears be attentive to the voice of my supplication. If Thou, O Lord, wilt mark iniquities, Lord, who shall stand it? For with Thee there is mercy: and by reason of Thy law I have waited on Thee, O Lord! My soul hath relied on His word: my soul hath hoped in the Lord. From the morning watch even until night. Let Israel hope in the Lord. For with the Lord there is mercy; and with Him plentiful Redemption. And He will redeem Israel from all his iniquities. Eternal rest give unto them, O Lord! And let perpetual light shine upon them. May they rest in peace. Amen.

Evening Prayer for the Poor Souls:

V. Lord, hear my prayer.
R. And let my cry come unto Thee.
Bless, O my God! the repose I am about to take, that, renewing my strength, I may be better enabled to serve Thee. Pour down Thy blessings, O Lord! on my parents, relations, friends, and enemies. Protect the Pope, our Bishop, and all the Pastors of Thy holy Church. Assist the poor and the afflicted, and those who are now in their last agony. Look with an eye of pity on the suffering souls in purgatory, particularly

---

put an end to their torments and lead them forth into everlasting joy.

Eternal rest grant unto them and let perpetual light shine upon them. Amen.

DATE:
_____

Start a Mass Collection jar or envelope today for the Holy Souls. Add money to it as you are able, and when you have enough for a donation, have a Mass said for a soul in Purgatory.

Morning Prayer for the Poor Souls:

Out of the depths I have cried to Thee O Lord! Lord, hear my voice. Let Thine ears be attentive to the voice of my supplication.
If Thou, O Lord, wilt mark iniquities, Lord, who shall stand it?
For with Thee there is mercy: and by reason of Thy law I have waited on Thee, O Lord! My soul hath relied on His word: my soul hath hoped in the Lord. From the morning watch even until night. Let Israel hope in the Lord. For with the Lord there is mercy; and with Him plentiful Redemption. And He will redeem Israel from all his iniquities.
Eternal rest give unto them, O Lord! And let perpetual light shine upon them. May they rest in peace. Amen.

Evening Prayer for the Poor Souls:

V. Lord, hear my prayer.
R. And let my cry come unto Thee.
Bless, O my God! the repose I am about to take, that, renewing my strength, I may be better enabled to serve Thee. Pour down Thy blessings, O Lord! on my parents, relations, friends, and enemies. Protect the Pope, our Bishop, and all the Pastors of Thy holy Church. Assist the poor and the afflicted, and those who are now in their last agony. Look with an eye of pity on the suffering souls in purgatory, particularly

_____
_____
_____

put an end to their torments and lead them forth into everlasting joy.

Eternal rest grant unto them and let perpetual light shine upon them. Amen.

DATE:
_____

Go without a meal or snack today if possible, for the benefit of the Holy Souls. If you are in ill health, give up a special treat instead.

Morning Prayer for the Poor Souls:

Out of the depths I have cried to Thee O Lord! Lord, hear my voice. Let Thine ears be attentive to the voice of my supplication.
If Thou, O Lord, wilt mark iniquities, Lord, who shall stand it?
For with Thee there is mercy: and by reason of Thy law I have waited on Thee, O Lord! My soul hath relied on His word: my soul hath hoped in the Lord. From the morning watch even until night. Let Israel hope in the Lord. For with the Lord there is mercy; and with Him plentiful Redemption. And He will redeem Israel from all his iniquities.
Eternal rest give unto them, O Lord! And let perpetual light shine upon them. May they rest in peace. Amen.

Evening Prayer for the Poor Souls:

V. Lord, hear my prayer.
R. And let my cry come unto Thee.
Bless, O my God! the repose I am about to take, that, renewing my strength, I may be better enabled to serve Thee. Pour down Thy blessings, O Lord! on my parents, relations, friends, and enemies. Protect the Pope, our Bishop, and all the Pastors of Thy holy Church. Assist the poor and the afflicted, and those who are now in their last agony. Look with an eye of pity on the suffering souls in purgatory, particularly

_____
_____
_____

put an end to their torments and lead them forth into everlasting joy.

Eternal rest grant unto them and let perpetual light shine upon them. Amen.

DATE:

_____

Today, say a Divine Mercy chaplet for the Poor Souls.

Morning Prayer for the Poor Souls:

Out of the depths I have cried to Thee O Lord! Lord, hear my voice. Let Thine ears be attentive to the voice of my supplication.
If Thou, O Lord, wilt mark iniquities, Lord, who shall stand it?
For with Thee there is mercy: and by reason of Thy law I have waited on Thee, O Lord! My soul hath relied on His word: my soul hath hoped in the Lord. From the morning watch even until night. Let Israel hope in the Lord. For with the Lord there is mercy; and with Him plentiful Redemption. And He will redeem Israel from all his iniquities.
Eternal rest give unto them, O Lord! And let perpetual light shine upon them. May they rest in peace. Amen.

Evening Prayer for the Poor Souls:

V. Lord, hear my prayer.
R. And let my cry come unto Thee.
Bless, O my God! the repose I am about to take, that, renewing my strength, I may be better enabled to serve Thee. Pour down Thy blessings, O Lord! on my parents, relations, friends, and enemies. Protect the Pope, our Bishop, and all the Pastors of Thy holy Church. Assist the poor and the afflicted, and those who are now in their last agony. Look with an eye of pity on the suffering souls in purgatory, particularly

_____

_____

_____

put an end to their torments and lead them forth into everlasting joy.

Eternal rest grant unto them and let perpetual light shine upon them. Amen.

DATE: _____

Pray today for the souls of priests and religious in Purgatory.

Morning Prayer for the Poor Souls:

Out of the depths I have cried to Thee O Lord! Lord, hear my voice. Let Thine ears be attentive to the voice of my supplication.
If Thou, O Lord, wilt mark iniquities, Lord, who shall stand it?
For with Thee there is mercy: and by reason of Thy law I have waited on Thee, O Lord! My soul hath relied on His word: my soul hath hoped in the Lord. From the morning watch even until night. Let Israel hope in the Lord. For with the Lord there is mercy; and with Him plentiful Redemption. And He will redeem Israel from all his iniquities.
Eternal rest give unto them, O Lord! And let perpetual light shine upon them. May they rest in peace. Amen.

Evening Prayer for the Poor Souls:

V. Lord, hear my prayer.
R. And let my cry come unto Thee.
Bless, O my God! the repose I am about to take, that, renewing my strength, I may be better enabled to serve Thee. Pour down Thy blessings, O Lord! on my parents, relations, friends, and enemies. Protect the Pope, our Bishop, and all the Pastors of Thy holy Church. Assist the poor and the afflicted, and those who are now in their last agony. Look with an eye of pity on the suffering souls in purgatory, particularly

_____

_____

_____

put an end to their torments and lead them forth into everlasting joy.

Eternal rest grant unto them and let perpetual light shine upon them. Amen.

DATE: _____

While you are going about your day today, remember your friends and colleagues who have passed away over the years, asking God to release them from Purgatory.

Morning Prayer for the Poor Souls:

Out of the depths I have cried to Thee O Lord! Lord, hear my voice. Let Thine ears be attentive to the voice of my supplication.
If Thou, O Lord, wilt mark iniquities, Lord, who shall stand it?
For with Thee there is mercy: and by reason of Thy law I have waited on Thee, O Lord! My soul hath relied on His word: my soul hath hoped in the Lord. From the morning watch even until night. Let Israel hope in the Lord. For with the Lord there is mercy; and with Him plentiful Redemption. And He will redeem Israel from all his iniquities.
Eternal rest give unto them, O Lord! And let perpetual light shine upon them. May they rest in peace. Amen.

Evening Prayer for the Poor Souls:

V. Lord, hear my prayer.
R. And let my cry come unto Thee.
Bless, O my God! the repose I am about to take, that, renewing my strength, I may be better enabled to serve Thee. Pour down Thy blessings, O Lord! on my parents, relations, friends, and enemies. Protect the Pope, our Bishop, and all the Pastors of Thy holy Church. Assist the poor and the afflicted, and those who are now in their last agony. Look with an eye of pity on the suffering souls in purgatory, particularly

put an end to their torments and lead them forth into everlasting joy.

Eternal rest grant unto them and let perpetual light shine upon them. Amen.

DATE: _____

Pray today for the dead who heard the Gospel but rejected it. May they be spared Hell and be released from Purgatory to be with Jesus.

Morning Prayer for the Poor Souls:

Out of the depths I have cried to Thee O Lord! Lord, hear my voice. Let Thine ears be attentive to the voice of my supplication.
If Thou, O Lord, wilt mark iniquities, Lord, who shall stand it?
For with Thee there is mercy: and by reason of Thy law I have waited on Thee, O Lord! My soul hath relied on His word: my soul hath hoped in the Lord. From the morning watch even until night. Let Israel hope in the Lord. For with the Lord there is mercy; and with Him plentiful Redemption. And He will redeem Israel from all his iniquities.
Eternal rest give unto them, O Lord! And let perpetual light shine upon them. May they rest in peace. Amen.

Evening Prayer for the Poor Souls:

V. Lord, hear my prayer.
R. And let my cry come unto Thee.
Bless, O my God! the repose I am about to take, that, renewing my strength, I may be better enabled to serve Thee. Pour down Thy blessings, O Lord! on my parents, relations, friends, and enemies. Protect the Pope, our Bishop, and all the Pastors of Thy holy Church. Assist the poor and the afflicted, and those who are now in their last agony. Look with an eye of pity on the suffering souls in purgatory, particularly

_____

_____

_____

put an end to their torments and lead them forth into everlasting joy.

Eternal rest grant unto them and let perpetual light shine upon them. Amen.

DATE: _____

Today, spend some time reading devotional literature aloud for the comfort of the Poor Souls.

Morning Prayer for the Poor Souls:

Out of the depths I have cried to Thee O Lord! Lord, hear my voice. Let Thine ears be attentive to the voice of my supplication.
If Thou, O Lord, wilt mark iniquities, Lord, who shall stand it?
For with Thee there is mercy: and by reason of Thy law I have waited on Thee, O Lord! My soul hath relied on His word: my soul hath hoped in the Lord. From the morning watch even until night. Let Israel hope in the Lord. For with the Lord there is mercy; and with Him plentiful Redemption. And He will redeem Israel from all his iniquities.
Eternal rest give unto them, O Lord! And let perpetual light shine upon them. May they rest in peace. Amen.

Evening Prayer for the Poor Souls:

V. Lord, hear my prayer.
R. And let my cry come unto Thee.
Bless, O my God! the repose I am about to take, that, renewing my strength, I may be better enabled to serve Thee. Pour down Thy blessings, O Lord! on my parents, relations, friends, and enemies. Protect the Pope, our Bishop, and all the Pastors of Thy holy Church. Assist the poor and the afflicted, and those who are now in their last agony. Look with an eye of pity on the suffering souls in purgatory, particularly

_____
_____
_____

put an end to their torments and lead them forth into everlasting joy.

Eternal rest grant unto them and let perpetual light shine upon them. Amen.

DATE: _____

Today make the Stations of the Cross for the benefit of the Holy Souls in Purgatory.

Morning Prayer for the Poor Souls:

Out of the depths I have cried to Thee O Lord! Lord, hear my voice. Let Thine ears be attentive to the voice of my supplication.
If Thou, O Lord, wilt mark iniquities, Lord, who shall stand it?
For with Thee there is mercy: and by reason of Thy law I have waited on Thee, O Lord! My soul hath relied on His word: my soul hath hoped in the Lord. From the morning watch even until night. Let Israel hope in the Lord. For with the Lord there is mercy; and with Him plentiful Redemption. And He will redeem Israel from all his iniquities.
Eternal rest give unto them, O Lord! And let perpetual light shine upon them. May they rest in peace. Amen.

Evening Prayer for the Poor Souls:

V. Lord, hear my prayer.
R. And let my cry come unto Thee.
Bless, O my God! the repose I am about to take, that, renewing my strength, I may be better enabled to serve Thee. Pour down Thy blessings, O Lord! on my parents, relations, friends, and enemies. Protect the Pope, our Bishop, and all the Pastors of Thy holy Church. Assist the poor and the afflicted, and those who are now in their last agony. Look with an eye of pity on the suffering souls in purgatory, particularly

_____

_____

_____

put an end to their torments and lead them forth into everlasting joy.

Eternal rest grant unto them and let perpetual light shine upon them. Amen.

DATE: _____

Pray today for the souls of all Jewish people who have died.

Morning Prayer for the Poor Souls:

Out of the depths I have cried to Thee O Lord! Lord, hear my voice. Let Thine ears be attentive to the voice of my supplication.
If Thou, O Lord, wilt mark iniquities, Lord, who shall stand it?
For with Thee there is mercy: and by reason of Thy law I have waited on Thee, O Lord! My soul hath relied on His word: my soul hath hoped in the Lord. From the morning watch even until night. Let Israel hope in the Lord. For with the Lord there is mercy; and with Him plentiful Redemption. And He will redeem Israel from all his iniquities.
Eternal rest give unto them, O Lord! And let perpetual light shine upon them. May they rest in peace. Amen.

Evening Prayer for the Poor Souls:

V. Lord, hear my prayer.
R. And let my cry come unto Thee.
Bless, O my God! the repose I am about to take, that, renewing my strength, I may be better enabled to serve Thee. Pour down Thy blessings, O Lord! on my parents, relations, friends, and enemies. Protect the Pope, our Bishop, and all the Pastors of Thy holy Church. Assist the poor and the afflicted, and those who are now in their last agony. Look with an eye of pity on the suffering souls in purgatory, particularly

_____
_____

_____

put an end to their torments and lead them forth into everlasting joy.

Eternal rest grant unto them and let perpetual light shine upon them. Amen.

DATE: _____

Today, pray for the souls of persecutors of Christians who have died.

Morning Prayer for the Poor Souls:

Out of the depths I have cried to Thee O Lord! Lord, hear my voice. Let Thine ears be attentive to the voice of my supplication.
If Thou, O Lord, wilt mark iniquities, Lord, who shall stand it?
For with Thee there is mercy: and by reason of Thy law I have waited on Thee, O Lord! My soul hath relied on His word: my soul hath hoped in the Lord. From the morning watch even until night. Let Israel hope in the Lord. For with the Lord there is mercy; and with Him plentiful Redemption. And He will redeem Israel from all his iniquities.
Eternal rest give unto them, O Lord! And let perpetual light shine upon them. May they rest in peace. Amen.

Evening Prayer for the Poor Souls:

V. Lord, hear my prayer.
R. And let my cry come unto Thee.
Bless, O my God! the repose I am about to take, that, renewing my strength, I may be better enabled to serve Thee. Pour down Thy blessings, O Lord! on my parents, relations, friends, and enemies. Protect the Pope, our Bishop, and all the Pastors of Thy holy Church. Assist the poor and the afflicted, and those who are now in their last agony. Look with an eye of pity on the suffering souls in purgatory, particularly

_____
_____

_____

put an end to their torments and lead them forth into everlasting joy.

Eternal rest grant unto them and let perpetual light shine upon them. Amen.

DATE: _____

Light a blessed candle today in remembrance of the Holy Souls.

Morning Prayer for the Poor Souls:

Out of the depths I have cried to Thee O Lord! Lord, hear my voice. Let Thine ears be attentive to the voice of my supplication.
If Thou, O Lord, wilt mark iniquities, Lord, who shall stand it?
For with Thee there is mercy: and by reason of Thy law I have waited on Thee, O Lord! My soul hath relied on His word: my soul hath hoped in the Lord. From the morning watch even until night. Let Israel hope in the Lord. For with the Lord there is mercy; and with Him plentiful Redemption. And He will redeem Israel from all his iniquities.
Eternal rest give unto them, O Lord! And let perpetual light shine upon them. May they rest in peace. Amen.

Evening Prayer for the Poor Souls:

V. Lord, hear my prayer.
R. And let my cry come unto Thee.
Bless, O my God! the repose I am about to take, that, renewing my strength, I may be better enabled to serve Thee. Pour down Thy blessings, O Lord! on my parents, relations, friends, and enemies. Protect the Pope, our Bishop, and all the Pastors of Thy holy Church. Assist the poor and the afflicted, and those who are now in their last agony. Look with an eye of pity on the suffering souls in purgatory, particularly

_____

_____

_____

put an end to their torments and lead them forth into everlasting joy.

Eternal rest grant unto them, and let perpetual light shine upon them. Amen.

DATE: _____

Begin a Novena today for the benefit of the Poor Souls. St. Alphonsus Liguori wrote a powerful one just for the Holy Souls, which may be found online, but any Novena will be appreciated.

Morning Prayer for the Poor Souls:

Out of the depths I have cried to Thee O Lord! Lord, hear my voice. Let Thine ears be attentive to the voice of my supplication.
If Thou, O Lord, wilt mark iniquities, Lord, who shall stand it?
For with Thee there is mercy: and by reason of Thy law I have waited on Thee, O Lord! My soul hath relied on His word: my soul hath hoped in the Lord. From the morning watch even until night. Let Israel hope in the Lord. For with the Lord there is mercy; and with Him plentiful Redemption. And He will redeem Israel from all his iniquities.
Eternal rest give unto them, O Lord! And let perpetual light shine upon them. May they rest in peace. Amen.

Evening Prayer for the Poor Souls:

V. Lord, hear my prayer.
R. And let my cry come unto Thee.
Bless, O my God! the repose I am about to take, that, renewing my strength, I may be better enabled to serve Thee. Pour down Thy blessings, O Lord! on my parents, relations, friends, and enemies. Protect the Pope, our Bishop, and all the Pastors of Thy holy Church. Assist the poor and the afflicted, and those who are now in their last agony. Look with an eye of pity on the suffering souls in purgatory, particularly

_____

_____

_____

put an end to their torments and lead them forth into everlasting joy.

Eternal rest grant unto them, and let perpetual light shine upon them. Amen.

DATE: _____

Give alms to the poor today to benefit the souls in Purgatory. We are told that giving alms is of great benefit to suffering souls.

Morning Prayer for the Poor Souls:

Out of the depths I have cried to Thee O Lord! Lord, hear my voice. Let Thine ears be attentive to the voice of my supplication.
If Thou, O Lord, wilt mark iniquities, Lord, who shall stand it?
For with Thee there is mercy: and by reason of Thy law I have waited on Thee, O Lord! My soul hath relied on His word: my soul hath hoped in the Lord. From the morning watch even until night. Let Israel hope in the Lord. For with the Lord there is mercy; and with Him plentiful Redemption. And He will redeem Israel from all his iniquities.
Eternal rest give unto them, O Lord! And let perpetual light shine upon them. May they rest in peace. Amen.

Evening Prayer for the Poor Souls:

V. Lord, hear my prayer.
R. And let my cry come unto Thee.
Bless, O my God! the repose I am about to take, that, renewing my strength, I may be better enabled to serve Thee. Pour down Thy blessings, O Lord! on my parents, relations, friends, and enemies. Protect the Pope, our Bishop, and all the Pastors of Thy holy Church. Assist the poor and the afflicted, and those who are now in their last agony. Look with an eye of pity on the suffering souls in purgatory, particularly

_____

_____

_____

put an end to their torments and lead them forth into everlasting joy.

Eternal rest grant unto them, and let perpetual light shine upon them. Amen.

DATE: _____

Read aloud today from the Acts of the Apostles to comfort the Holy Souls. The Good News of Jesus' salvation is of great relief to their suffering.

Morning Prayer for the Poor Souls:

Out of the depths I have cried to Thee O Lord! Lord, hear my voice. Let Thine ears be attentive to the voice of my supplication.
If Thou, O Lord, wilt mark iniquities, Lord, who shall stand it?
For with Thee there is mercy: and by reason of Thy law I have waited on Thee, O Lord! My soul hath relied on His word: my soul hath hoped in the Lord. From the morning watch even until night. Let Israel hope in the Lord. For with the Lord there is mercy; and with Him plentiful Redemption. And He will redeem Israel from all his iniquities.
Eternal rest give unto them, O Lord! And let perpetual light shine upon them. May they rest in peace. Amen.

Evening Prayer for the Poor Souls:

V. Lord, hear my prayer.
R. And let my cry come unto Thee.
Bless, O my God! the repose I am about to take, that, renewing my strength, I may be better enabled to serve Thee. Pour down Thy blessings, O Lord! on my parents, relations, friends, and enemies. Protect the Pope, our Bishop, and all the Pastors of Thy holy Church. Assist the poor and the afflicted, and those who are now in their last agony. Look with an eye of pity on the suffering souls in purgatory, particularly

_____

_____

_____

put an end to their torments and lead them forth into everlasting joy.

Eternal rest grant unto them, and let perpetual light shine upon them. Amen.

DATE: _____

Today, ask the saints known as intercessors for the dead to pray with you for their release, including St. Nicholas of Tolentino, St. Gertrude the Great, St. Catherine of Genoa, St. Padre Pio, St. Philip Neri, St. John Macías, St. Faustina Kowalska, St. Joseph and, of course, the Blessed Mother.

Morning Prayer for the Poor Souls:

Out of the depths I have cried to Thee O Lord! Lord, hear my voice. Let Thine ears be attentive to the voice of my supplication.
If Thou, O Lord, wilt mark iniquities, Lord, who shall stand it?
For with Thee there is mercy: and by reason of Thy law I have waited on Thee, O Lord! My soul hath relied on His word: my soul hath hoped in the Lord. From the morning watch even until night. Let Israel hope in the Lord. For with the Lord there is mercy; and with Him plentiful Redemption. And He will redeem Israel from all his iniquities.
Eternal rest give unto them, O Lord! And let perpetual light shine upon them. May they rest in peace. Amen.

Evening Prayer for the Poor Souls:

V. Lord, hear my prayer.
R. And let my cry come unto Thee.
Bless, O my God! the repose I am about to take, that, renewing my strength, I may be better enabled to serve Thee. Pour down Thy blessings, O Lord! on my parents, relations, friends, and enemies. Protect the Pope, our Bishop, and all the Pastors of Thy holy Church. Assist the poor and the afflicted, and those who are now in their last agony. Look with an eye of pity on the suffering souls in purgatory, particularly

_____
_____
_____

put an end to their torments and lead them forth into everlasting joy.

Eternal rest grant unto them, and let perpetual light shine upon them. Amen.

The Month of
_____

DATE: _____

Today, have a Mass said for the soul of a family member or friend who has passed away. This can be through your own parish or through an order or national shrine via their website.

Morning Prayer for the Poor Souls:

Out of the depths I have cried to Thee O Lord! Lord, hear my voice. Let Thine ears be attentive to the voice of my supplication.
If Thou, O Lord, wilt mark iniquities, Lord, who shall stand it?
For with Thee there is mercy: and by reason of Thy law I have waited on Thee, O Lord! My soul hath relied on His word: my soul hath hoped in the Lord. From the morning watch even until night. Let Israel hope in the Lord. For with the Lord there is mercy; and with Him plentiful Redemption. And He will redeem Israel from all his iniquities.
Eternal rest give unto them, O Lord! And let perpetual light shine upon them. May they rest in peace. Amen.

Evening Prayer for the Poor Souls:

V. Lord, hear my prayer.
R. And let my cry come unto Thee.
Bless, O my God! the repose I am about to take, that, renewing my strength, I may be better enabled to serve Thee. Pour down Thy blessings, O Lord! on my parents, relations, friends, and enemies. Protect the Pope, our Bishop, and all the Pastors of Thy holy Church. Assist the poor and the afflicted, and those who are now in their last agony. Look with an eye of pity on the suffering souls in purgatory, particularly

_____

_____

_____

put an end to their torments and lead them forth into everlasting joy.

Eternal rest grant unto them, and let perpetual light shine upon them. Amen.

DATE:
_____

Pray the Rosary today for the release of souls from Purgatory. Mystic saints have told us that the Blessed Mother herself comes to Purgatory to bring souls with her back to Heaven.

Morning Prayer for the Poor Souls:

Out of the depths I have cried to Thee O Lord! Lord, hear my voice. Let Thine ears be attentive to the voice of my supplication.
If Thou, O Lord, wilt mark iniquities, Lord, who shall stand it?
For with Thee there is mercy: and by reason of Thy law I have waited on Thee, O Lord! My soul hath relied on His word: my soul hath hoped in the Lord. From the morning watch even until night. Let Israel hope in the Lord. For with the Lord there is mercy; and with Him plentiful Redemption. And He will redeem Israel from all his iniquities.
Eternal rest give unto them, O Lord! And let perpetual light shine upon them. May they rest in peace. Amen.

Evening Prayer for the Poor Souls:

V. Lord, hear my prayer.
R. And let my cry come unto Thee.
Bless, O my God! the repose I am about to take, that, renewing my strength, I may be better enabled to serve Thee. Pour down Thy blessings, O Lord! on my parents, relations, friends, and enemies. Protect the Pope, our Bishop, and all the Pastors of Thy holy Church. Assist the poor and the afflicted, and those who are now in their last agony. Look with an eye of pity on the suffering souls in purgatory, particularly

_____
_____
_____

put an end to their torments and lead them forth into everlasting joy.

Eternal rest grant unto them, and let perpetual light shine upon them. Amen.

DATE:

_____

Today, ask the Blessed Mother to apply your prayers and works to a poor soul who has no one to pray for them.

Morning Prayer for the Poor Souls:

Out of the depths I have cried to Thee O Lord! Lord, hear my voice. Let Thine ears be attentive to the voice of my supplication.
If Thou, O Lord, wilt mark iniquities, Lord, who shall stand it?
For with Thee there is mercy: and by reason of Thy law I have waited on Thee, O Lord! My soul hath relied on His word: my soul hath hoped in the Lord. From the morning watch even until night. Let Israel hope in the Lord. For with the Lord there is mercy; and with Him plentiful Redemption. And He will redeem Israel from all his iniquities.
Eternal rest give unto them, O Lord! And let perpetual light shine upon them. May they rest in peace. Amen.

Evening Prayer for the Poor Souls:

V. Lord, hear my prayer.
R. And let my cry come unto Thee.
Bless, O my God! the repose I am about to take, that, renewing my strength, I may be better enabled to serve Thee. Pour down Thy blessings, O Lord! on my parents, relations, friends, and enemies. Protect the Pope, our Bishop, and all the Pastors of Thy holy Church. Assist the poor and the afflicted, and those who are now in their last agony. Look with an eye of pity on the suffering souls in purgatory, particularly

_____
_____
_____

put an end to their torments and lead them forth into everlasting joy.

Eternal rest grant unto them, and let perpetual light shine upon them. Amen.

DATE:

_____

We all have a spiritual or physical affliction or burden that we suffer with daily. Today, dedicate your ailment-related suffering to the Poor souls.

Morning Prayer for the Poor Souls:

Out of the depths I have cried to Thee O Lord! Lord, hear my voice. Let Thine ears be attentive to the voice of my supplication.
If Thou, O Lord, wilt mark iniquities, Lord, who shall stand it?
For with Thee there is mercy: and by reason of Thy law I have waited on Thee, O Lord! My soul hath relied on His word: my soul hath hoped in the Lord. From the morning watch even until night. Let Israel hope in the Lord. For with the Lord there is mercy; and with Him plentiful Redemption. And He will redeem Israel from all his iniquities.
Eternal rest give unto them, O Lord! And let perpetual light shine upon them. May they rest in peace. Amen.

Evening Prayer for the Poor Souls:

V. Lord, hear my prayer.
R. And let my cry come unto Thee.
Bless, O my God! the repose I am about to take, that, renewing my strength, I may be better enabled to serve Thee. Pour down Thy blessings, O Lord! on my parents, relations, friends, and enemies. Protect the Pope, our Bishop, and all the Pastors of Thy holy Church. Assist the poor and the afflicted, and those who are now in their last agony. Look with an eye of pity on the suffering souls in purgatory, particularly

_____

_____

_____

put an end to their torments and lead them forth into everlasting joy.

Eternal rest grant unto them, and let perpetual light shine upon them. Amen.

DATE: _____

Today, visit or call someone elderly or alone and offer your work of mercy for the souls in Purgatory.

Morning Prayer for the Poor Souls:

Out of the depths I have cried to Thee O Lord! Lord, hear my voice. Let Thine ears be attentive to the voice of my supplication.
If Thou, O Lord, wilt mark iniquities, Lord, who shall stand it?
For with Thee there is mercy: and by reason of Thy law I have waited on Thee, O Lord! My soul hath relied on His word: my soul hath hoped in the Lord. From the morning watch even until night. Let Israel hope in the Lord. For with the Lord there is mercy; and with Him plentiful Redemption. And He will redeem Israel from all his iniquities.
Eternal rest give unto them, O Lord! And let perpetual light shine upon them. May they rest in peace. Amen.

Evening Prayer for the Poor Souls:

V. Lord, hear my prayer.
R. And let my cry come unto Thee.
Bless, O my God! the repose I am about to take, that, renewing my strength, I may be better enabled to serve Thee. Pour down Thy blessings, O Lord! on my parents, relations, friends, and enemies. Protect the Pope, our Bishop, and all the Pastors of Thy holy Church. Assist the poor and the afflicted, and those who are now in their last agony. Look with an eye of pity on the suffering souls in purgatory, particularly

_____

_____

put an end to their torments and lead them forth into everlasting joy.

Eternal rest grant unto them, and let perpetual light shine upon them. Amen.

DATE:
_____

During the course of the day today, pray for those you meet and strangers you see on street, asking God to apply your prayers for them to their future time in Purgatory.

Morning Prayer for the Poor Souls:

Out of the depths I have cried to Thee O Lord! Lord, hear my voice. Let Thine ears be attentive to the voice of my supplication.
If Thou, O Lord, wilt mark iniquities, Lord, who shall stand it?
For with Thee there is mercy: and by reason of Thy law I have waited on Thee, O Lord! My soul hath relied on His word: my soul hath hoped in the Lord. From the morning watch even until night. Let Israel hope in the Lord. For with the Lord there is mercy; and with Him plentiful Redemption. And He will redeem Israel from all his iniquities.
Eternal rest give unto them, O Lord! And let perpetual light shine upon them. May they rest in peace. Amen.

Evening Prayer for the Poor Souls:

V. Lord, hear my prayer.
R. And let my cry come unto Thee.
Bless, O my God! the repose I am about to take, that, renewing my strength, I may be better enabled to serve Thee. Pour down Thy blessings, O Lord! on my parents, relations, friends, and enemies. Protect the Pope, our Bishop, and all the Pastors of Thy holy Church. Assist the poor and the afflicted, and those who are now in their last agony. Look with an eye of pity on the suffering souls in purgatory, particularly

_____
_____

_____

put an end to their torments and lead them forth into everlasting joy.

Eternal rest grant unto them, and let perpetual light shine upon them. Amen.

DATE:

_____

Today, ask the Blessed Mother to use your prayers for someone in Purgatory with no one to pray for them.

Morning Prayer for the Poor Souls:

Out of the depths I have cried to Thee O Lord! Lord, hear my voice. Let Thine ears be attentive to the voice of my supplication.
If Thou, O Lord, wilt mark iniquities, Lord, who shall stand it?
For with Thee there is mercy: and by reason of Thy law I have waited on Thee, O Lord! My soul hath relied on His word: my soul hath hoped in the Lord. From the morning watch even until night. Let Israel hope in the Lord. For with the Lord there is mercy; and with Him plentiful Redemption. And He will redeem Israel from all his iniquities.
Eternal rest give unto them, O Lord! And let perpetual light shine upon them. May they rest in peace. Amen.

Evening Prayer for the Poor Souls:

V. Lord, hear my prayer.
R. And let my cry come unto Thee.
Bless, O my God! the repose I am about to take, that, renewing my strength, I may be better enabled to serve Thee. Pour down Thy blessings, O Lord! on my parents, relations, friends, and enemies. Protect the Pope, our Bishop, and all the Pastors of Thy holy Church. Assist the poor and the afflicted, and those who are now in their last agony. Look with an eye of pity on the suffering souls in purgatory, particularly

_____

_____

_____

put an end to their torments and lead them forth into everlasting joy.

Eternal rest grant unto them, and let perpetual light shine upon them. Amen.

DATE:
_____

Today, sprinkle holy water on the carpet of your home or outside your house as a comfort to the Poor Souls.

Morning Prayer for the Poor Souls:

Out of the depths I have cried to Thee O Lord! Lord, hear my voice. Let Thine ears be attentive to the voice of my supplication.
If Thou, O Lord, wilt mark iniquities, Lord, who shall stand it?
For with Thee there is mercy: and by reason of Thy law I have waited on Thee, O Lord! My soul hath relied on His word: my soul hath hoped in the Lord. From the morning watch even until night. Let Israel hope in the Lord. For with the Lord there is mercy; and with Him plentiful Redemption. And He will redeem Israel from all his iniquities.
Eternal rest give unto them, O Lord! And let perpetual light shine upon them. May they rest in peace. Amen.

Evening Prayer for the Poor Souls:

V. Lord, hear my prayer.
R. And let my cry come unto Thee.
Bless, O my God! the repose I am about to take, that, renewing my strength, I may be better enabled to serve Thee. Pour down Thy blessings, O Lord! on my parents, relations, friends, and enemies. Protect the Pope, our Bishop, and all the Pastors of Thy holy Church. Assist the poor and the afflicted, and those who are now in their last agony. Look with an eye of pity on the suffering souls in purgatory, particularly

_____

_____

_____

put an end to their torments and lead them forth into everlasting joy.

Eternal rest grant unto them, and let perpetual light shine upon them. Amen.

DATE:
_____

Today, visit a church if you are able, and pray for the souls who are spending their Purgatorial time there. Catholic mystics have told us that God allows many souls to do so. If you cannot visit a church, think of a local church and pray for any souls who might be there.

Morning Prayer for the Poor Souls:

Out of the depths I have cried to Thee O Lord! Lord, hear my voice. Let Thine ears be attentive to the voice of my supplication.
If Thou, O Lord, wilt mark iniquities, Lord, who shall stand it?
For with Thee there is mercy: and by reason of Thy law I have waited on Thee, O Lord! My soul hath relied on His word: my soul hath hoped in the Lord. From the morning watch even until night. Let Israel hope in the Lord. For with the Lord there is mercy; and with Him plentiful Redemption. And He will redeem Israel from all his iniquities.
Eternal rest give unto them, O Lord! And let perpetual light shine upon them. May they rest in peace. Amen.

Evening Prayer for the Poor Souls:

V. Lord, hear my prayer.
R. And let my cry come unto Thee.
Bless, O my God! the repose I am about to take, that, renewing my strength, I may be better enabled to serve Thee. Pour down Thy blessings, O Lord! on my parents, relations, friends, and enemies. Protect the Pope, our Bishop, and all the Pastors of Thy holy Church. Assist the poor and the afflicted, and those who are now in their last agony. Look with an eye of pity on the suffering souls in purgatory, particularly

_____
_____

put an end to their torments and lead them forth into everlasting joy.

Eternal rest grant unto them, and let perpetual light shine upon them. Amen.

DATE:

_____

Today, visit someone who is sick if you are able, and offer up this work of mercy for the Holy Souls. If you cannot, pray for those in your local hospital or nursing home.

Morning Prayer for the Poor Souls:

Out of the depths I have cried to Thee O Lord! Lord, hear my voice. Let Thine ears be attentive to the voice of my supplication.
If Thou, O Lord, wilt mark iniquities, Lord, who shall stand it?
For with Thee there is mercy: and by reason of Thy law I have waited on Thee, O Lord! My soul hath relied on His word: my soul hath hoped in the Lord. From the morning watch even until night. Let Israel hope in the Lord. For with the Lord there is mercy; and with Him plentiful Redemption. And He will redeem Israel from all his iniquities.
Eternal rest give unto them, O Lord! And let perpetual light shine upon them. May they rest in peace. Amen.

Evening Prayer for the Poor Souls:

V. Lord, hear my prayer.
R. And let my cry come unto Thee.
Bless, O my God! the repose I am about to take, that, renewing my strength, I may be better enabled to serve Thee. Pour down Thy blessings, O Lord! on my parents, relations, friends, and enemies. Protect the Pope, our Bishop, and all the Pastors of Thy holy Church. Assist the poor and the afflicted, and those who are now in their last agony. Look with an eye of pity on the suffering souls in purgatory, particularly

_____

_____

_____

put an end to their torments and lead them forth into everlasting joy.

Eternal rest grant unto them, and let perpetual light shine upon them. Amen.

DATE:

_____

Today pray for the souls of all the atheists who have died.

Morning Prayer for the Poor Souls:

Out of the depths I have cried to Thee O Lord! Lord, hear my voice. Let Thine ears be attentive to the voice of my supplication.
If Thou, O Lord, wilt mark iniquities, Lord, who shall stand it?
For with Thee there is mercy: and by reason of Thy law I have waited on Thee, O Lord! My soul hath relied on His word: my soul hath hoped in the Lord. From the morning watch even until night. Let Israel hope in the Lord. For with the Lord there is mercy; and with Him plentiful Redemption. And He will redeem Israel from all his iniquities.
Eternal rest give unto them, O Lord! And let perpetual light shine upon them. May they rest in peace. Amen.

Evening Prayer for the Poor Souls:

V. Lord, hear my prayer.
R. And let my cry come unto Thee.
Bless, O my God! the repose I am about to take, that, renewing my strength, I may be better enabled to serve Thee. Pour down Thy blessings, O Lord! on my parents, relations, friends, and enemies. Protect the Pope, our Bishop, and all the Pastors of Thy holy Church. Assist the poor and the afflicted, and those who are now in their last agony. Look with an eye of pity on the suffering souls in purgatory, particularly

_____

_____

_____

put an end to their torments and lead them forth into everlasting joy.

Eternal rest grant unto them, and let perpetual light shine upon them. Amen.

DATE:

_____

Today, read the obituaries in your local newspaper and pray for the souls who have died in the past several days.

Morning Prayer for the Poor Souls:

Out of the depths I have cried to Thee O Lord! Lord, hear my voice. Let Thine ears be attentive to the voice of my supplication.
If Thou, O Lord, wilt mark iniquities, Lord, who shall stand it?
For with Thee there is mercy: and by reason of Thy law I have waited on Thee, O Lord! My soul hath relied on His word: my soul hath hoped in the Lord. From the morning watch even until night. Let Israel hope in the Lord. For with the Lord there is mercy; and with Him plentiful Redemption. And He will redeem Israel from all his iniquities.
Eternal rest give unto them, O Lord! And let perpetual light shine upon them. May they rest in peace. Amen.

Evening Prayer for the Poor Souls:

V. Lord, hear my prayer.
R. And let my cry come unto Thee.
Bless, O my God! the repose I am about to take, that, renewing my strength, I may be better enabled to serve Thee. Pour down Thy blessings, O Lord! on my parents, relations, friends, and enemies. Protect the Pope, our Bishop, and all the Pastors of Thy holy Church. Assist the poor and the afflicted, and those who are now in their last agony. Look with an eye of pity on the suffering souls in purgatory, particularly

_____
_____

_____

put an end to their torments and lead them forth into everlasting joy.

Eternal rest grant unto them, and let perpetual light shine upon them. Amen.

DATE: _____

Spend some time in Eucharistic Adoration today for the Poor Souls. If you cannot travel to a church physically, watch live Adoration on EWTN, YouTube or Facebook.

Morning Prayer for the Poor Souls:

Out of the depths I have cried to Thee O Lord! Lord, hear my voice. Let Thine ears be attentive to the voice of my supplication.
If Thou, O Lord, wilt mark iniquities, Lord, who shall stand it?
For with Thee there is mercy: and by reason of Thy law I have waited on Thee, O Lord! My soul hath relied on His word: my soul hath hoped in the Lord. From the morning watch even until night. Let Israel hope in the Lord. For with the Lord there is mercy; and with Him plentiful Redemption. And He will redeem Israel from all his iniquities.
Eternal rest give unto them, O Lord! And let perpetual light shine upon them. May they rest in peace. Amen.

Evening Prayer for the Poor Souls:

V. Lord, hear my prayer.
R. And let my cry come unto Thee.
Bless, O my God! the repose I am about to take, that, renewing my strength, I may be better enabled to serve Thee. Pour down Thy blessings, O Lord! on my parents, relations, friends, and enemies. Protect the Pope, our Bishop, and all the Pastors of Thy holy Church. Assist the poor and the afflicted, and those who are now in their last agony. Look with an eye of pity on the suffering souls in purgatory, particularly

_____

_____

_____

put an end to their torments and lead them forth into everlasting joy.

Eternal rest grant unto them, and let perpetual light shine upon them. Amen.

DATE:
_____

a drive today to a cemetery and pray for the souls of those interred there. If you cannot physically visit a cemetery, think of a cemetery in your city or town and pray for the souls of those buried there.

Morning Prayer for the Poor Souls:

Out of the depths I have cried to Thee O Lord! Lord, hear my voice. Let Thine ears be attentive to the voice of my supplication.
If Thou, O Lord, wilt mark iniquities, Lord, who shall stand it?
For with Thee there is mercy: and by reason of Thy law I have waited on Thee, O Lord! My soul hath relied on His word: my soul hath hoped in the Lord. From the morning watch even until night. Let Israel hope in the Lord. For with the Lord there is mercy; and with Him plentiful Redemption. And He will redeem Israel from all his iniquities.
Eternal rest give unto them, O Lord! And let perpetual light shine upon them. May they rest in peace. Amen.

Evening Prayer for the Poor Souls:

V. Lord, hear my prayer.
R. And let my cry come unto Thee.
Bless, O my God! the repose I am about to take, that, renewing my strength, I may be better enabled to serve Thee. Pour down Thy blessings, O Lord! on my parents, relations, friends, and enemies. Protect the Pope, our Bishop, and all the Pastors of Thy holy Church. Assist the poor and the afflicted, and those who are now in their last agony. Look with an eye of pity on the suffering souls in purgatory, particularly

_____
_____
_____

put an end to their torments and lead them forth into everlasting joy.

Eternal rest grant unto them, and let perpetual light shine upon them. Amen.

DATE:
_____

Today, play some sacred music to comfort the Poor Souls. Mystic saints have told us that these small gestures provide great relief to their suffering.

Morning Prayer for the Poor Souls:

Out of the depths I have cried to Thee O Lord! Lord, hear my voice. Let Thine ears be attentive to the voice of my supplication.
If Thou, O Lord, wilt mark iniquities, Lord, who shall stand it?
For with Thee there is mercy: and by reason of Thy law I have waited on Thee, O Lord! My soul hath relied on His word: my soul hath hoped in the Lord. From the morning watch even until night. Let Israel hope in the Lord. For with the Lord there is mercy; and with Him plentiful Redemption. And He will redeem Israel from all his iniquities.
Eternal rest give unto them, O Lord! And let perpetual light shine upon them. May they rest in peace. Amen.

Evening Prayer for the Poor Souls:

V. Lord, hear my prayer.
R. And let my cry come unto Thee.
Bless, O my God! the repose I am about to take, that, renewing my strength, I may be better enabled to serve Thee. Pour down Thy blessings, O Lord! on my parents, relations, friends, and enemies. Protect the Pope, our Bishop, and all the Pastors of Thy holy Church. Assist the poor and the afflicted, and those who are now in their last agony. Look with an eye of pity on the suffering souls in purgatory, particularly

_____
_____
_____

put an end to their torments and lead them forth into everlasting joy.

Eternal rest grant unto them, and let perpetual light shine upon them. Amen.

DATE:

_____

Today, make reparation to the Sacred Heart of Jesus for the souls in Purgatory who offended His most precious Heart with the following: Adorable Heart of Jesus, glowing with love for us and inflamed with zeal for our salvation. O Heart that understands the misery to which our sins have brought us, infinitely rich in mercy to heal the wounds of our souls, behold me humbly kneeling before You to express the sorrow that fills my heart for the coldness and indifference with which I have so long returned the numberless benefits which You have bestowed upon me.

Morning Prayer for the Poor Souls:

Out of the depths I have cried to Thee O Lord! Lord, hear my voice. Let Thine ears be attentive to the voice of my supplication. If Thou, O Lord, wilt mark iniquities, Lord, who shall stand it? For with Thee there is mercy: and by reason of Thy law I have waited on Thee, O Lord! My soul hath relied on His word: my soul hath hoped in the Lord. From the morning watch even until night. Let Israel hope in the Lord. For with the Lord there is mercy; and with Him plentiful Redemption. And He will redeem Israel from all his iniquities. Eternal rest give unto them, O Lord! And let perpetual light shine upon them. May they rest in peace. Amen.

Evening Prayer for the Poor Souls:

V. Lord, hear my prayer.
R. And let my cry come unto Thee.
Bless, O my God! the repose I am about to take, that, renewing my strength, I may be better enabled to serve Thee. Pour down Thy blessings, O Lord! on my parents, relations, friends, and enemies. Protect the Pope, our Bishop, and all the Pastors of Thy holy Church. Assist the poor and the afflicted, and those who are now in their last agony. Look with an eye of pity on the suffering souls in purgatory, particularly

_____

put an end to their torments and lead them forth into everlasting joy.

Eternal rest grant unto them, and let perpetual light shine upon them. Amen.

DATE:
_____

Start a Mass Collection jar or envelope today for the Holy Souls. Add money to it as you are able, and when you have enough for a donation, have a Mass said for a soul in Purgatory.

Morning Prayer for the Poor Souls:

Out of the depths I have cried to Thee O Lord! Lord, hear my voice. Let Thine ears be attentive to the voice of my supplication.
If Thou, O Lord, wilt mark iniquities, Lord, who shall stand it?
For with Thee there is mercy: and by reason of Thy law I have waited on Thee, O Lord! My soul hath relied on His word: my soul hath hoped in the Lord. From the morning watch even until night. Let Israel hope in the Lord. For with the Lord there is mercy; and with Him plentiful Redemption. And He will redeem Israel from all his iniquities.
Eternal rest give unto them, O Lord! And let perpetual light shine upon them. May they rest in peace. Amen.

Evening Prayer for the Poor Souls:

V. Lord, hear my prayer.
R. And let my cry come unto Thee.
Bless, O my God! the repose I am about to take, that, renewing my strength, I may be better enabled to serve Thee. Pour down Thy blessings, O Lord! on my parents, relations, friends, and enemies. Protect the Pope, our Bishop, and all the Pastors of Thy holy Church. Assist the poor and the afflicted, and those who are now in their last agony. Look with an eye of pity on the suffering souls in purgatory, particularly

_____
_____
_____

put an end to their torments and lead them forth into everlasting joy.

Eternal rest grant unto them, and let perpetual light shine upon them. Amen.

DATE:
_____

Go without a meal or snack today if possible, for the benefit of the Holy Souls. If you are in ill health, give up a special treat instead.

Morning Prayer for the Poor Souls:

Out of the depths I have cried to Thee O Lord! Lord, hear my voice. Let Thine ears be attentive to the voice of my supplication.
If Thou, O Lord, wilt mark iniquities, Lord, who shall stand it?
For with Thee there is mercy: and by reason of Thy law I have waited on Thee, O Lord! My soul hath relied on His word: my soul hath hoped in the Lord. From the morning watch even until night. Let Israel hope in the Lord. For with the Lord there is mercy; and with Him plentiful Redemption. And He will redeem Israel from all his iniquities.
Eternal rest give unto them, O Lord! And let perpetual light shine upon them. May they rest in peace. Amen.

Evening Prayer for the Poor Souls:

V. Lord, hear my prayer.
R. And let my cry come unto Thee.
Bless, O my God! the repose I am about to take, that, renewing my strength, I may be better enabled to serve Thee. Pour down Thy blessings, O Lord! on my parents, relations, friends, and enemies. Protect the Pope, our Bishop, and all the Pastors of Thy holy Church. Assist the poor and the afflicted, and those who are now in their last agony. Look with an eye of pity on the suffering souls in purgatory, particularly

_____
_____
_____

put an end to their torments and lead them forth into everlasting joy.

Eternal rest grant unto them, and let perpetual light shine upon them. Amen.

DATE:
_____

Today, say a Divine Mercy chaplet for the Poor Souls.

Morning Prayer for the Poor Souls:

Out of the depths I have cried to Thee O Lord! Lord, hear my voice. Let Thine ears be attentive to the voice of my supplication.
If Thou, O Lord, wilt mark iniquities, Lord, who shall stand it?
For with Thee there is mercy: and by reason of Thy law I have waited on Thee, O Lord! My soul hath relied on His word: my soul hath hoped in the Lord. From the morning watch even until night. Let Israel hope in the Lord. For with the Lord there is mercy; and with Him plentiful Redemption. And He will redeem Israel from all his iniquities.
Eternal rest give unto them, O Lord! And let perpetual light shine upon them. May they rest in peace. Amen.

Evening Prayer for the Poor Souls:

V. Lord, hear my prayer.
R. And let my cry come unto Thee.
Bless, O my God! the repose I am about to take, that, renewing my strength, I may be better enabled to serve Thee. Pour down Thy blessings, O Lord! on my parents, relations, friends, and enemies. Protect the Pope, our Bishop, and all the Pastors of Thy holy Church. Assist the poor and the afflicted, and those who are now in their last agony. Look with an eye of pity on the suffering souls in purgatory, particularly

_____

_____

_____

put an end to their torments and lead them forth into everlasting joy.

Eternal rest grant unto them, and let perpetual light shine upon them. Amen.

DATE: _____

Pray today for the souls of priests and religious in Purgatory.

Morning Prayer for the Poor Souls:

Out of the depths I have cried to Thee O Lord! Lord, hear my voice. Let Thine ears be attentive to the voice of my supplication.
If Thou, O Lord, wilt mark iniquities, Lord, who shall stand it?
For with Thee there is mercy: and by reason of Thy law I have waited on Thee, O Lord! My soul hath relied on His word: my soul hath hoped in the Lord. From the morning watch even until night. Let Israel hope in the Lord. For with the Lord there is mercy; and with Him plentiful Redemption. And He will redeem Israel from all his iniquities.
Eternal rest give unto them, O Lord! And let perpetual light shine upon them. May they rest in peace. Amen.

Evening Prayer for the Poor Souls:

V. Lord, hear my prayer.
R. And let my cry come unto Thee.
Bless, O my God! the repose I am about to take, that, renewing my strength, I may be better enabled to serve Thee. Pour down Thy blessings, O Lord! on my parents, relations, friends, and enemies. Protect the Pope, our Bishop, and all the Pastors of Thy holy Church. Assist the poor and the afflicted, and those who are now in their last agony. Look with an eye of pity on the suffering souls in purgatory, particularly

_____

_____

_____

put an end to their torments and lead them forth into everlasting joy.

Eternal rest grant unto them, and let perpetual light shine upon them. Amen.

DATE: _____

While you are going about your day today, remember your friends and colleagues who have passed away over the years, asking God to release them from Purgatory.

Morning Prayer for the Poor Souls:

Out of the depths I have cried to Thee O Lord! Lord, hear my voice. Let Thine ears be attentive to the voice of my supplication.
If Thou, O Lord, wilt mark iniquities, Lord, who shall stand it?
For with Thee there is mercy: and by reason of Thy law I have waited on Thee, O Lord! My soul hath relied on His word: my soul hath hoped in the Lord. From the morning watch even until night. Let Israel hope in the Lord. For with the Lord there is mercy; and with Him plentiful Redemption. And He will redeem Israel from all his iniquities.
Eternal rest give unto them, O Lord! And let perpetual light shine upon them. May they rest in peace. Amen.

Evening Prayer for the Poor Souls:

V. Lord, hear my prayer.
R. And let my cry come unto Thee.
Bless, O my God! the repose I am about to take, that, renewing my strength, I may be better enabled to serve Thee. Pour down Thy blessings, O Lord! on my parents, relations, friends, and enemies. Protect the Pope, our Bishop, and all the Pastors of Thy holy Church. Assist the poor and the afflicted, and those who are now in their last agony. Look with an eye of pity on the suffering souls in purgatory, particularly

put an end to their torments and lead them forth into everlasting joy.

Eternal rest grant unto them, and let perpetual light shine upon them. Amen.

DATE: _____

Pray today for the dead who heard the Gospel but rejected it. May they be spared Hell and be released from Purgatory to be with Jesus.

Morning Prayer for the Poor Souls:

Out of the depths I have cried to Thee O Lord! Lord, hear my voice. Let Thine ears be attentive to the voice of my supplication.
If Thou, O Lord, wilt mark iniquities, Lord, who shall stand it?
For with Thee there is mercy: and by reason of Thy law I have waited on Thee, O Lord! My soul hath relied on His word: my soul hath hoped in the Lord. From the morning watch even until night. Let Israel hope in the Lord. For with the Lord there is mercy; and with Him plentiful Redemption. And He will redeem Israel from all his iniquities.
Eternal rest give unto them, O Lord! And let perpetual light shine upon them. May they rest in peace. Amen.

Evening Prayer for the Poor Souls:

V. Lord, hear my prayer.
R. And let my cry come unto Thee.
Bless, O my God! the repose I am about to take, that, renewing my strength, I may be better enabled to serve Thee. Pour down Thy blessings, O Lord! on my parents, relations, friends, and enemies. Protect the Pope, our Bishop, and all the Pastors of Thy holy Church. Assist the poor and the afflicted, and those who are now in their last agony. Look with an eye of pity on the suffering souls in purgatory, particularly

_____

_____

_____

put an end to their torments and lead them forth into everlasting joy.

Eternal rest grant unto them, and let perpetual light shine upon them. Amen.

DATE: _____

Today, spend some time reading devotional literature aloud for the comfort of the Poor Souls.

Morning Prayer for the Poor Souls:

Out of the depths I have cried to Thee O Lord! Lord, hear my voice. Let Thine ears be attentive to the voice of my supplication.
If Thou, O Lord, wilt mark iniquities, Lord, who shall stand it?
For with Thee there is mercy: and by reason of Thy law I have waited on Thee, O Lord! My soul hath relied on His word: my soul hath hoped in the Lord. From the morning watch even until night. Let Israel hope in the Lord. For with the Lord there is mercy; and with Him plentiful Redemption. And He will redeem Israel from all his iniquities.
Eternal rest give unto them, O Lord! And let perpetual light shine upon them. May they rest in peace. Amen.

Evening Prayer for the Poor Souls:

V. Lord, hear my prayer.
R. And let my cry come unto Thee.
Bless, O my God! the repose I am about to take, that, renewing my strength, I may be better enabled to serve Thee. Pour down Thy blessings, O Lord! on my parents, relations, friends, and enemies. Protect the Pope, our Bishop, and all the Pastors of Thy holy Church. Assist the poor and the afflicted, and those who are now in their last agony. Look with an eye of pity on the suffering souls in purgatory, particularly

_____

_____

put an end to their torments and lead them forth into everlasting joy.

Eternal rest grant unto them, and let perpetual light shine upon them. Amen.

DATE: _____

Today make the Stations of the Cross for the benefit of the Holy Souls in Purgatory.

Morning Prayer for the Poor Souls:

Out of the depths I have cried to Thee O Lord! Lord, hear my voice. Let Thine ears be attentive to the voice of my supplication.
If Thou, O Lord, wilt mark iniquities, Lord, who shall stand it?
For with Thee there is mercy: and by reason of Thy law I have waited on Thee, O Lord! My soul hath relied on His word: my soul hath hoped in the Lord. From the morning watch even until night. Let Israel hope in the Lord. For with the Lord there is mercy; and with Him plentiful Redemption. And He will redeem Israel from all his iniquities.
Eternal rest give unto them, O Lord! And let perpetual light shine upon them. May they rest in peace. Amen.

Evening Prayer for the Poor Souls:

V. Lord, hear my prayer.
R. And let my cry come unto Thee.
Bless, O my God! the repose I am about to take, that, renewing my strength, I may be better enabled to serve Thee. Pour down Thy blessings, O Lord! on my parents, relations, friends, and enemies. Protect the Pope, our Bishop, and all the Pastors of Thy holy Church. Assist the poor and the afflicted, and those who are now in their last agony. Look with an eye of pity on the suffering souls in purgatory, particularly

_____
_____
_____

put an end to their torments and lead them forth into everlasting joy.

Eternal rest grant unto them, and let perpetual light shine upon them. Amen.

DATE: _____

Pray today for the souls of all Jewish people who have died.

Morning Prayer for the Poor Souls:

Out of the depths I have cried to Thee O Lord! Lord, hear my voice. Let Thine ears be attentive to the voice of my supplication.
If Thou, O Lord, wilt mark iniquities, Lord, who shall stand it?
For with Thee there is mercy: and by reason of Thy law I have waited on Thee, O Lord! My soul hath relied on His word: my soul hath hoped in the Lord. From the morning watch even until night. Let Israel hope in the Lord. For with the Lord there is mercy; and with Him plentiful Redemption. And He will redeem Israel from all his iniquities.
Eternal rest give unto them, O Lord! And let perpetual light shine upon them. May they rest in peace. Amen.

Evening Prayer for the Poor Souls:

V. Lord, hear my prayer.
R. And let my cry come unto Thee.
Bless, O my God! the repose I am about to take, that, renewing my strength, I may be better enabled to serve Thee. Pour down Thy blessings, O Lord! on my parents, relations, friends, and enemies. Protect the Pope, our Bishop, and all the Pastors of Thy holy Church. Assist the poor and the afflicted, and those who are now in their last agony. Look with an eye of pity on the suffering souls in purgatory, particularly

_____

_____

_____

put an end to their torments and lead them forth into everlasting joy.

Eternal rest grant unto them, and let perpetual light shine upon them. Amen.

DATE: _____

Today, pray for the souls of persecutors of Christians who have died.

Morning Prayer for the Poor Souls:

Out of the depths I have cried to Thee O Lord! Lord, hear my voice. Let Thine ears be attentive to the voice of my supplication.
If Thou, O Lord, wilt mark iniquities, Lord, who shall stand it?
For with Thee there is mercy: and by reason of Thy law I have waited on Thee, O Lord! My soul hath relied on His word: my soul hath hoped in the Lord. From the morning watch even until night. Let Israel hope in the Lord. For with the Lord there is mercy; and with Him plentiful Redemption. And He will redeem Israel from all his iniquities.
Eternal rest give unto them, O Lord! And let perpetual light shine upon them. May they rest in peace. Amen.

Evening Prayer for the Poor Souls:

V. Lord, hear my prayer.
R. And let my cry come unto Thee.
Bless, O my God! the repose I am about to take, that, renewing my strength, I may be better enabled to serve Thee. Pour down Thy blessings, O Lord! on my parents, relations, friends, and enemies. Protect the Pope, our Bishop, and all the Pastors of Thy holy Church. Assist the poor and the afflicted, and those who are now in their last agony. Look with an eye of pity on the suffering souls in purgatory, particularly

_____
_____
_____

put an end to their torments and lead them forth into everlasting joy.

Eternal rest grant unto them, and let perpetual light shine upon them. Amen.

DATE: _____

Light a blessed candle today in remembrance of the Holy Souls.

Morning Prayer for the Poor Souls:

Out of the depths I have cried to Thee O Lord! Lord, hear my voice. Let Thine ears be attentive to the voice of my supplication.
If Thou, O Lord, wilt mark iniquities, Lord, who shall stand it?
For with Thee there is mercy: and by reason of Thy law I have waited on Thee, O Lord! My soul hath relied on His word: my soul hath hoped in the Lord. From the morning watch even until night. Let Israel hope in the Lord. For with the Lord there is mercy; and with Him plentiful Redemption. And He will redeem Israel from all his iniquities.
Eternal rest give unto them, O Lord! And let perpetual light shine upon them. May they rest in peace. Amen.

Evening Prayer for the Poor Souls:

V. Lord, hear my prayer.
R. And let my cry come unto Thee.
Bless, O my God! the repose I am about to take, that, renewing my strength, I may be better enabled to serve Thee. Pour down Thy blessings, O Lord! on my parents, relations, friends, and enemies. Protect the Pope, our Bishop, and all the Pastors of Thy holy Church. Assist the poor and the afflicted, and those who are now in their last agony. Look with an eye of pity on the suffering souls in purgatory, particularly

_____

_____

_____

put an end to their torments and lead them forth into everlasting joy.

Eternal rest grant unto them, and let perpetual light shine upon them. Amen.

DATE: _____

Begin a Novena today for the benefit of the Poor Souls. St. Alphonsus Liguori wrote a powerful one just for the Holy Souls, which may be found online, but any Novena will be appreciated.

Morning Prayer for the Poor Souls:

Out of the depths I have cried to Thee O Lord! Lord, hear my voice. Let Thine ears be attentive to the voice of my supplication.
If Thou, O Lord, wilt mark iniquities, Lord, who shall stand it?
For with Thee there is mercy: and by reason of Thy law I have waited on Thee, O Lord! My soul hath relied on His word: my soul hath hoped in the Lord. From the morning watch even until night. Let Israel hope in the Lord. For with the Lord there is mercy; and with Him plentiful Redemption. And He will redeem Israel from all his iniquities.
Eternal rest give unto them, O Lord! And let perpetual light shine upon them. May they rest in peace. Amen.

Evening Prayer for the Poor Souls:

V. Lord, hear my prayer.
R. And let my cry come unto Thee.
Bless, O my God! the repose I am about to take, that, renewing my strength, I may be better enabled to serve Thee. Pour down Thy blessings, O Lord! on my parents, relations, friends, and enemies. Protect the Pope, our Bishop, and all the Pastors of Thy holy Church. Assist the poor and the afflicted, and those who are now in their last agony. Look with an eye of pity on the suffering souls in purgatory, particularly

_____
_____
_____

put an end to their torments and lead them forth into everlasting joy.

Eternal rest grant unto them, and let perpetual light shine upon them. Amen.

DATE: _____

Give alms to the poor today to benefit the souls in Purgatory. We are told that giving alms is of great benefit to suffering souls.

Morning Prayer for the Poor Souls:

Out of the depths I have cried to Thee O Lord! Lord, hear my voice. Let Thine ears be attentive to the voice of my supplication.
If Thou, O Lord, wilt mark iniquities, Lord, who shall stand it?
For with Thee there is mercy: and by reason of Thy law I have waited on Thee, O Lord! My soul hath relied on His word: my soul hath hoped in the Lord. From the morning watch even until night. Let Israel hope in the Lord. For with the Lord there is mercy; and with Him plentiful Redemption. And He will redeem Israel from all his iniquities.
Eternal rest give unto them, O Lord! And let perpetual light shine upon them. May they rest in peace. Amen.

Evening Prayer for the Poor Souls:

V. Lord, hear my prayer.
R. And let my cry come unto Thee.
Bless, O my God! the repose I am about to take, that, renewing my strength, I may be better enabled to serve Thee. Pour down Thy blessings, O Lord! on my parents, relations, friends, and enemies. Protect the Pope, our Bishop, and all the Pastors of Thy holy Church. Assist the poor and the afflicted, and those who are now in their last agony. Look with an eye of pity on the suffering souls in purgatory, particularly

_____

_____

_____

put an end to their torments and lead them forth into everlasting joy.

Eternal rest grant unto them, and let perpetual light shine upon them. Amen.

DATE: _____

Read aloud today from the Acts of the Apostles to comfort the Holy Souls. The Good News of Jesus' salvation is of great relief to their suffering.

Morning Prayer for the Poor Souls:

Out of the depths I have cried to Thee O Lord! Lord, hear my voice. Let Thine ears be attentive to the voice of my supplication.
If Thou, O Lord, wilt mark iniquities, Lord, who shall stand it?
For with Thee there is mercy: and by reason of Thy law I have waited on Thee, O Lord! My soul hath relied on His word: my soul hath hoped in the Lord. From the morning watch even until night. Let Israel hope in the Lord. For with the Lord there is mercy; and with Him plentiful Redemption. And He will redeem Israel from all his iniquities.
Eternal rest give unto them, O Lord! And let perpetual light shine upon them. May they rest in peace. Amen.

Evening Prayer for the Poor Souls:

V. Lord, hear my prayer.
R. And let my cry come unto Thee.
Bless, O my God! the repose I am about to take, that, renewing my strength, I may be better enabled to serve Thee. Pour down Thy blessings, O Lord! on my parents, relations, friends, and enemies. Protect the Pope, our Bishop, and all the Pastors of Thy holy Church. Assist the poor and the afflicted, and those who are now in their last agony. Look with an eye of pity on the suffering souls in purgatory, particularly

_____
_____

_____

put an end to their torments and lead them forth into everlasting joy.

Eternal rest grant unto them, and let perpetual light shine upon them. Amen.

DATE: _____

Today, ask the saints known as intercessors for the dead to pray with you for their release, including St. Nicholas of Tolentino, St. Gertrude the Great, St. Catherine of Genoa, St. Padre Pio, St. Philip Neri, St. John Macías, St. Faustina Kowalska, St. Joseph and, of course, the Blessed Mother.

Morning Prayer for the Poor Souls:

Out of the depths I have cried to Thee O Lord! Lord, hear my voice. Let Thine ears be attentive to the voice of my supplication.
If Thou, O Lord, wilt mark iniquities, Lord, who shall stand it?
For with Thee there is mercy: and by reason of Thy law I have waited on Thee, O Lord! My soul hath relied on His word: my soul hath hoped in the Lord. From the morning watch even until night. Let Israel hope in the Lord. For with the Lord there is mercy; and with Him plentiful Redemption. And He will redeem Israel from all his iniquities.
Eternal rest give unto them, O Lord! And let perpetual light shine upon them. May they rest in peace. Amen.

Evening Prayer for the Poor Souls:

V. Lord, hear my prayer.
R. And let my cry come unto Thee.
Bless, O my God! the repose I am about to take, that, renewing my strength, I may be better enabled to serve Thee. Pour down Thy blessings, O Lord! on my parents, relations, friends, and enemies. Protect the Pope, our Bishop, and all the Pastors of Thy holy Church. Assist the poor and the afflicted, and those who are now in their last agony. Look with an eye of pity on the suffering souls in purgatory, particularly

_____

_____

_____

put an end to their torments and lead them forth into everlasting joy.

Eternal rest grant unto them, and let perpetual light shine upon them. Amen.

The Month of
_____

DATE: _____

Today, have a Mass said for the soul of a family member or friend who has passed away. This can be through your own parish or through an order or national shrine via their website.

Morning Prayer for the Poor Souls:

Out of the depths I have cried to Thee O Lord! Lord, hear my voice. Let Thine ears be attentive to the voice of my supplication.
If Thou, O Lord, wilt mark iniquities, Lord, who shall stand it?
For with Thee there is mercy: and by reason of Thy law I have waited on Thee, O Lord! My soul hath relied on His word: my soul hath hoped in the Lord. From the morning watch even until night. Let Israel hope in the Lord. For with the Lord there is mercy; and with Him plentiful Redemption. And He will redeem Israel from all his iniquities.
Eternal rest give unto them, O Lord! And let perpetual light shine upon them. May they rest in peace. Amen.

Evening Prayer for the Poor Souls:

V. Lord, hear my prayer.
R. And let my cry come unto Thee.
Bless, O my God! the repose I am about to take, that, renewing my strength, I may be better enabled to serve Thee. Pour down Thy blessings, O Lord! on my parents, relations, friends, and enemies. Protect the Pope, our Bishop, and all the Pastors of Thy holy Church. Assist the poor and the afflicted, and those who are now in their last agony. Look with an eye of pity on the suffering souls in purgatory, particularly

_____
_____
_____

put an end to their torments and lead them forth into everlasting joy.

Eternal rest grant unto them, and let perpetual light shine upon them. Amen.

DATE:

_____

Pray the Rosary today for the release of souls from Purgatory. Mystic saints have told us that the Blessed Mother herself comes to Purgatory to bring souls with her back to Heaven.

Morning Prayer for the Poor Souls:

Out of the depths I have cried to Thee O Lord! Lord, hear my voice. Let Thine ears be attentive to the voice of my supplication.
If Thou, O Lord, wilt mark iniquities, Lord, who shall stand it?
For with Thee there is mercy: and by reason of Thy law I have waited on Thee, O Lord! My soul hath relied on His word: my soul hath hoped in the Lord. From the morning watch even until night. Let Israel hope in the Lord. For with the Lord there is mercy; and with Him plentiful Redemption. And He will redeem Israel from all his iniquities.
Eternal rest give unto them, O Lord! And let perpetual light shine upon them. May they rest in peace. Amen.

Evening Prayer for the Poor Souls:

V. Lord, hear my prayer.
R. And let my cry come unto Thee.
Bless, O my God! the repose I am about to take, that, renewing my strength, I may be better enabled to serve Thee. Pour down Thy blessings, O Lord! on my parents, relations, friends, and enemies. Protect the Pope, our Bishop, and all the Pastors of Thy holy Church. Assist the poor and the afflicted, and those who are now in their last agony. Look with an eye of pity on the suffering souls in purgatory, particularly

_____
_____
_____

put an end to their torments and lead them forth into everlasting joy.

Eternal rest grant unto them, and let perpetual light shine upon them. Amen.

DATE:
_____

Today, ask the Blessed Mother to apply your prayers and works to a poor soul who has no one to pray for them.

Morning Prayer for the Poor Souls:

Out of the depths I have cried to Thee O Lord! Lord, hear my voice. Let Thine ears be attentive to the voice of my supplication.
If Thou, O Lord, wilt mark iniquities, Lord, who shall stand it?
For with Thee there is mercy: and by reason of Thy law I have waited on Thee, O Lord! My soul hath relied on His word: my soul hath hoped in the Lord. From the morning watch even until night. Let Israel hope in the Lord. For with the Lord there is mercy; and with Him plentiful Redemption. And He will redeem Israel from all his iniquities.
Eternal rest give unto them, O Lord! And let perpetual light shine upon them. May they rest in peace. Amen.

Evening Prayer for the Poor Souls:

V. Lord, hear my prayer.
R. And let my cry come unto Thee.
Bless, O my God! the repose I am about to take, that, renewing my strength, I may be better enabled to serve Thee. Pour down Thy blessings, O Lord! on my parents, relations, friends, and enemies. Protect the Pope, our Bishop, and all the Pastors of Thy holy Church. Assist the poor and the afflicted, and those who are now in their last agony. Look with an eye of pity on the suffering souls in purgatory, particularly

_____
_____
_____

put an end to their torments and lead them forth into everlasting joy.

Eternal rest grant unto them, and let perpetual light shine upon them. Amen.

DATE:
_____

We all have a spiritual or physical affliction or burden that we suffer with daily. Today, dedicate your ailment-related suffering to the Poor souls.

Morning Prayer for the Poor Souls:

Out of the depths I have cried to Thee O Lord! Lord, hear my voice. Let Thine ears be attentive to the voice of my supplication.
If Thou, O Lord, wilt mark iniquities, Lord, who shall stand it?
For with Thee there is mercy: and by reason of Thy law I have waited on Thee, O Lord! My soul hath relied on His word: my soul hath hoped in the Lord. From the morning watch even until night. Let Israel hope in the Lord. For with the Lord there is mercy; and with Him plentiful Redemption. And He will redeem Israel from all his iniquities.
Eternal rest give unto them, O Lord! And let perpetual light shine upon them. May they rest in peace. Amen.

Evening Prayer for the Poor Souls:

V. Lord, hear my prayer.
R. And let my cry come unto Thee.
Bless, O my God! the repose I am about to take, that, renewing my strength, I may be better enabled to serve Thee. Pour down Thy blessings, O Lord! on my parents, relations, friends, and enemies. Protect the Pope, our Bishop, and all the Pastors of Thy holy Church. Assist the poor and the afflicted, and those who are now in their last agony. Look with an eye of pity on the suffering souls in purgatory, particularly

_____

_____

_____

put an end to their torments and lead them forth into everlasting joy.

Eternal rest grant unto them, and let perpetual light shine upon them. Amen.

DATE:

_____

Today, visit or call someone elderly or alone and offer your work of mercy for the souls in Purgatory.

Morning Prayer for the Poor Souls:

Out of the depths I have cried to Thee O Lord! Lord, hear my voice. Let Thine ears be attentive to the voice of my supplication.
If Thou, O Lord, wilt mark iniquities, Lord, who shall stand it?
For with Thee there is mercy: and by reason of Thy law I have waited on Thee, O Lord! My soul hath relied on His word: my soul hath hoped in the Lord. From the morning watch even until night. Let Israel hope in the Lord. For with the Lord there is mercy; and with Him plentiful Redemption. And He will redeem Israel from all his iniquities.
Eternal rest give unto them, O Lord! And let perpetual light shine upon them. May they rest in peace. Amen.

Evening Prayer for the Poor Souls:

V. Lord, hear my prayer.
R. And let my cry come unto Thee.
Bless, O my God! the repose I am about to take, that, renewing my strength, I may be better enabled to serve Thee. Pour down Thy blessings, O Lord! on my parents, relations, friends, and enemies. Protect the Pope, our Bishop, and all the Pastors of Thy holy Church. Assist the poor and the afflicted, and those who are now in their last agony. Look with an eye of pity on the suffering souls in purgatory, particularly

_____
_____
_____

put an end to their torments and lead them forth into everlasting joy.

Eternal rest grant unto them, and let perpetual light shine upon them. Amen.

DATE:

_____

During the course of the day today, pray for those you meet and strangers you see on street, asking God to apply your prayers for them to their future time in Purgatory.

Morning Prayer for the Poor Souls:

Out of the depths I have cried to Thee O Lord! Lord, hear my voice. Let Thine ears be attentive to the voice of my supplication.
If Thou, O Lord, wilt mark iniquities, Lord, who shall stand it?
For with Thee there is mercy: and by reason of Thy law I have waited on Thee, O Lord! My soul hath relied on His word: my soul hath hoped in the Lord. From the morning watch even until night. Let Israel hope in the Lord. For with the Lord there is mercy; and with Him plentiful Redemption. And He will redeem Israel from all his iniquities.
Eternal rest give unto them, O Lord! And let perpetual light shine upon them. May they rest in peace. Amen.

Evening Prayer for the Poor Souls:

V. Lord, hear my prayer.
R. And let my cry come unto Thee.
Bless, O my God! the repose I am about to take, that, renewing my strength, I may be better enabled to serve Thee. Pour down Thy blessings, O Lord! on my parents, relations, friends, and enemies. Protect the Pope, our Bishop, and all the Pastors of Thy holy Church. Assist the poor and the afflicted, and those who are now in their last agony. Look with an eye of pity on the suffering souls in purgatory, particularly

_____
_____
_____

put an end to their torments and lead them forth into everlasting joy.

Eternal rest grant unto them, and let perpetual light shine upon them. Amen.

DATE:
_____

Today, ask the Blessed Mother to use your prayers for someone in Purgatory with no one to pray for them.

Morning Prayer for the Poor Souls:

Out of the depths I have cried to Thee O Lord! Lord, hear my voice. Let Thine ears be attentive to the voice of my supplication.
If Thou, O Lord, wilt mark iniquities, Lord, who shall stand it?
For with Thee there is mercy: and by reason of Thy law I have waited on Thee, O Lord! My soul hath relied on His word: my soul hath hoped in the Lord. From the morning watch even until night. Let Israel hope in the Lord. For with the Lord there is mercy; and with Him plentiful Redemption. And He will redeem Israel from all his iniquities.
Eternal rest give unto them, O Lord! And let perpetual light shine upon them. May they rest in peace. Amen.

Evening Prayer for the Poor Souls:

V. Lord, hear my prayer.
R. And let my cry come unto Thee.
Bless, O my God! the repose I am about to take, that, renewing my strength, I may be better enabled to serve Thee. Pour down Thy blessings, O Lord! on my parents, relations, friends, and enemies. Protect the Pope, our Bishop, and all the Pastors of Thy holy Church. Assist the poor and the afflicted, and those who are now in their last agony. Look with an eye of pity on the suffering souls in purgatory, particularly

_____
_____

_____

put an end to their torments and lead them forth into everlasting joy.

Eternal rest grant unto them, and let perpetual light shine upon them. Amen.

DATE:
_____

Today, sprinkle holy water on the carpet of your home or outside your house as a comfort to the Poor Souls.

Morning Prayer for the Poor Souls:

Out of the depths I have cried to Thee O Lord! Lord, hear my voice. Let Thine ears be attentive to the voice of my supplication.
If Thou, O Lord, wilt mark iniquities, Lord, who shall stand it?
For with Thee there is mercy: and by reason of Thy law I have waited on Thee, O Lord! My soul hath relied on His word: my soul hath hoped in the Lord. From the morning watch even until night. Let Israel hope in the Lord. For with the Lord there is mercy; and with Him plentiful Redemption. And He will redeem Israel from all his iniquities.
Eternal rest give unto them, O Lord! And let perpetual light shine upon them. May they rest in peace. Amen.

Evening Prayer for the Poor Souls:

V. Lord, hear my prayer.
R. And let my cry come unto Thee.
Bless, O my God! the repose I am about to take, that, renewing my strength, I may be better enabled to serve Thee. Pour down Thy blessings, O Lord! on my parents, relations, friends, and enemies. Protect the Pope, our Bishop, and all the Pastors of Thy holy Church. Assist the poor and the afflicted, and those who are now in their last agony. Look with an eye of pity on the suffering souls in purgatory, particularly

_____

_____

_____

put an end to their torments and lead them forth into everlasting joy.

Eternal rest grant unto them, and let perpetual light shine upon them. Amen.

DATE:
_____

Today, visit a church if you are able, and pray for the souls who are spending their Purgatorial time there. Catholic mystics have told us that God allows many souls to do so. If you cannot visit a church, think of a local church and pray for any souls who might be there.

Morning Prayer for the Poor Souls:

Out of the depths I have cried to Thee O Lord! Lord, hear my voice. Let Thine ears be attentive to the voice of my supplication.
If Thou, O Lord, wilt mark iniquities, Lord, who shall stand it?
For with Thee there is mercy: and by reason of Thy law I have waited on Thee, O Lord! My soul hath relied on His word: my soul hath hoped in the Lord. From the morning watch even until night. Let Israel hope in the Lord. For with the Lord there is mercy; and with Him plentiful Redemption. And He will redeem Israel from all his iniquities.
Eternal rest give unto them, O Lord! And let perpetual light shine upon them. May they rest in peace. Amen.

Evening Prayer for the Poor Souls:

V. Lord, hear my prayer.
R. And let my cry come unto Thee.
Bless, O my God! the repose I am about to take, that, renewing my strength, I may be better enabled to serve Thee. Pour down Thy blessings, O Lord! on my parents, relations, friends, and enemies. Protect the Pope, our Bishop, and all the Pastors of Thy holy Church. Assist the poor and the afflicted, and those who are now in their last agony. Look with an eye of pity on the suffering souls in purgatory, particularly

_____
_____

put an end to their torments and lead them forth into everlasting joy.

Eternal rest grant unto them, and let perpetual light shine upon them. Amen.

DATE:

_____

Today, visit someone who is sick if you are able, and offer up this work of mercy for the Holy Souls. If you cannot, pray for those in your local hospital or nursing home.

Morning Prayer for the Poor Souls:

Out of the depths I have cried to Thee O Lord! Lord, hear my voice. Let Thine ears be attentive to the voice of my supplication.
If Thou, O Lord, wilt mark iniquities, Lord, who shall stand it?
For with Thee there is mercy: and by reason of Thy law I have waited on Thee, O Lord! My soul hath relied on His word: my soul hath hoped in the Lord. From the morning watch even until night. Let Israel hope in the Lord. For with the Lord there is mercy; and with Him plentiful Redemption. And He will redeem Israel from all his iniquities.
Eternal rest give unto them, O Lord! And let perpetual light shine upon them. May they rest in peace. Amen.

Evening Prayer for the Poor Souls:

V. Lord, hear my prayer.
R. And let my cry come unto Thee.
Bless, O my God! the repose I am about to take, that, renewing my strength, I may be better enabled to serve Thee. Pour down Thy blessings, O Lord! on my parents, relations, friends, and enemies. Protect the Pope, our Bishop, and all the Pastors of Thy holy Church. Assist the poor and the afflicted, and those who are now in their last agony. Look with an eye of pity on the suffering souls in purgatory, particularly

_____
_____

_____

put an end to their torments and lead them forth into everlasting joy.

Eternal rest grant unto them, and let perpetual light shine upon them. Amen.

DATE:
_____

Today pray for the souls of all the atheists who have died.

Morning Prayer for the Poor Souls:

Out of the depths I have cried to Thee O Lord! Lord, hear my voice. Let Thine ears be attentive to the voice of my supplication.
If Thou, O Lord, wilt mark iniquities, Lord, who shall stand it?
For with Thee there is mercy: and by reason of Thy law I have waited on Thee, O Lord! My soul hath relied on His word: my soul hath hoped in the Lord. From the morning watch even until night. Let Israel hope in the Lord. For with the Lord there is mercy; and with Him plentiful Redemption. And He will redeem Israel from all his iniquities.
Eternal rest give unto them, O Lord! And let perpetual light shine upon them. May they rest in peace. Amen.

Evening Prayer for the Poor Souls:

V. Lord, hear my prayer.
R. And let my cry come unto Thee.
Bless, O my God! the repose I am about to take, that, renewing my strength, I may be better enabled to serve Thee. Pour down Thy blessings, O Lord! on my parents, relations, friends, and enemies. Protect the Pope, our Bishop, and all the Pastors of Thy holy Church. Assist the poor and the afflicted, and those who are now in their last agony. Look with an eye of pity on the suffering souls in purgatory, particularly

_____
_____
_____

put an end to their torments and lead them forth into everlasting joy.

Eternal rest grant unto them, and let perpetual light shine upon them. Amen.

DATE: _____

Today, read the obituaries in your local newspaper and pray for the souls who have died in the past several days.

Morning Prayer for the Poor Souls:

Out of the depths I have cried to Thee O Lord! Lord, hear my voice. Let Thine ears be attentive to the voice of my supplication.
If Thou, O Lord, wilt mark iniquities, Lord, who shall stand it?
For with Thee there is mercy: and by reason of Thy law I have waited on Thee, O Lord! My soul hath relied on His word: my soul hath hoped in the Lord. From the morning watch even until night. Let Israel hope in the Lord. For with the Lord there is mercy; and with Him plentiful Redemption. And He will redeem Israel from all his iniquities.
Eternal rest give unto them, O Lord! And let perpetual light shine upon them. May they rest in peace. Amen.

Evening Prayer for the Poor Souls:

V. Lord, hear my prayer.
R. And let my cry come unto Thee.
Bless, O my God! the repose I am about to take, that, renewing my strength, I may be better enabled to serve Thee. Pour down Thy blessings, O Lord! on my parents, relations, friends, and enemies. Protect the Pope, our Bishop, and all the Pastors of Thy holy Church. Assist the poor and the afflicted, and those who are now in their last agony. Look with an eye of pity on the suffering souls in purgatory, particularly

_____

_____

_____

put an end to their torments and lead them forth into everlasting joy.

Eternal rest grant unto them, and let perpetual light shine upon them. Amen.

DATE:

_____

Spend some time in Eucharistic Adoration today for the Poor Souls. If you cannot travel to a church physically, watch live Adoration on EWTN, YouTube or Facebook.

Morning Prayer for the Poor Souls:

Out of the depths I have cried to Thee O Lord! Lord, hear my voice. Let Thine ears be attentive to the voice of my supplication.
If Thou, O Lord, wilt mark iniquities, Lord, who shall stand it?
For with Thee there is mercy: and by reason of Thy law I have waited on Thee, O Lord! My soul hath relied on His word: my soul hath hoped in the Lord. From the morning watch even until night. Let Israel hope in the Lord. For with the Lord there is mercy; and with Him plentiful Redemption. And He will redeem Israel from all his iniquities.
Eternal rest give unto them, O Lord! And let perpetual light shine upon them. May they rest in peace. Amen.

Evening Prayer for the Poor Souls:

V. Lord, hear my prayer.
R. And let my cry come unto Thee.
Bless, O my God! the repose I am about to take, that, renewing my strength, I may be better enabled to serve Thee. Pour down Thy blessings, O Lord! on my parents, relations, friends, and enemies. Protect the Pope, our Bishop, and all the Pastors of Thy holy Church. Assist the poor and the afflicted, and those who are now in their last agony. Look with an eye of pity on the suffering souls in purgatory, particularly

_____

_____

_____

put an end to their torments and lead them forth into everlasting joy.

Eternal rest grant unto them, and let perpetual light shine upon them. Amen.

DATE:

_____

a drive today to a cemetery and pray for the souls of those interred there. If you cannot physically visit a cemetery, think of a cemetery in your city or town and pray for the souls of those buried there.

Morning Prayer for the Poor Souls:

Out of the depths I have cried to Thee O Lord! Lord, hear my voice. Let Thine ears be attentive to the voice of my supplication.
If Thou, O Lord, wilt mark iniquities, Lord, who shall stand it?
For with Thee there is mercy: and by reason of Thy law I have waited on Thee, O Lord! My soul hath relied on His word: my soul hath hoped in the Lord. From the morning watch even until night. Let Israel hope in the Lord. For with the Lord there is mercy; and with Him plentiful Redemption. And He will redeem Israel from all his iniquities.
Eternal rest give unto them, O Lord! And let perpetual light shine upon them. May they rest in peace. Amen.

Evening Prayer for the Poor Souls:

V. Lord, hear my prayer.
R. And let my cry come unto Thee.
Bless, O my God! the repose I am about to take, that, renewing my strength, I may be better enabled to serve Thee. Pour down Thy blessings, O Lord! on my parents, relations, friends, and enemies. Protect the Pope, our Bishop, and all the Pastors of Thy holy Church. Assist the poor and the afflicted, and those who are now in their last agony. Look with an eye of pity on the suffering souls in purgatory, particularly

_____
_____
_____

put an end to their torments and lead them forth into everlasting joy.

Eternal rest grant unto them, and let perpetual light shine upon them. Amen.

DATE:

_____

Today, play some sacred music to comfort the Poor Souls. Mystic saints have told us that these small gestures provide great relief to their suffering.

Morning Prayer for the Poor Souls:

Out of the depths I have cried to Thee O Lord! Lord, hear my voice. Let Thine ears be attentive to the voice of my supplication.
If Thou, O Lord, wilt mark iniquities, Lord, who shall stand it?
For with Thee there is mercy: and by reason of Thy law I have waited on Thee, O Lord! My soul hath relied on His word: my soul hath hoped in the Lord. From the morning watch even until night. Let Israel hope in the Lord. For with the Lord there is mercy; and with Him plentiful Redemption. And He will redeem Israel from all his iniquities.
Eternal rest give unto them, O Lord! And let perpetual light shine upon them. May they rest in peace. Amen.

Evening Prayer for the Poor Souls:

V. Lord, hear my prayer.
R. And let my cry come unto Thee.
Bless, O my God! the repose I am about to take, that, renewing my strength, I may be better enabled to serve Thee. Pour down Thy blessings, O Lord! on my parents, relations, friends, and enemies. Protect the Pope, our Bishop, and all the Pastors of Thy holy Church. Assist the poor and the afflicted, and those who are now in their last agony. Look with an eye of pity on the suffering souls in purgatory, particularly

_____

_____

_____

put an end to their torments and lead them forth into everlasting joy.

Eternal rest grant unto them, and let perpetual light shine upon them. Amen.

DATE:

_____

Today, make reparation to the Sacred Heart of Jesus for the souls in Purgatory who offended His most precious Heart with the following: Adorable Heart of Jesus, glowing with love for us and inflamed with zeal for our salvation. O Heart that understands the misery to which our sins have brought us, infinitely rich in mercy to heal the wounds of our souls, behold me humbly kneeling before You to express the sorrow that fills my heart for the coldness and indifference with which I have so long returned the numberless benefits which You have bestowed upon me.

Morning Prayer for the Poor Souls:

Out of the depths I have cried to Thee O Lord! Lord, hear my voice. Let Thine ears be attentive to the voice of my supplication. If Thou, O Lord, wilt mark iniquities, Lord, who shall stand it? For with Thee there is mercy: and by reason of Thy law I have waited on Thee, O Lord! My soul hath relied on His word: my soul hath hoped in the Lord. From the morning watch even until night. Let Israel hope in the Lord. For with the Lord there is mercy; and with Him plentiful Redemption. And He will redeem Israel from all his iniquities. Eternal rest give unto them, O Lord! And let perpetual light shine upon them. May they rest in peace. Amen.

Evening Prayer for the Poor Souls:

V. Lord, hear my prayer.
R. And let my cry come unto Thee.
Bless, O my God! the repose I am about to take, that, renewing my strength, I may be better enabled to serve Thee. Pour down Thy blessings, O Lord! on my parents, relations, friends, and enemies. Protect the Pope, our Bishop, and all the Pastors of Thy holy Church. Assist the poor and the afflicted, and those who are now in their last agony. Look with an eye of pity on the suffering souls in purgatory, particularly

_____

put an end to their torments and lead them forth into everlasting joy.

Eternal rest grant unto them, and let perpetual light shine upon them. Amen.

DATE:

_____

Start a Mass Collection jar or envelope today for the Holy Souls. Add money to it as you are able, and when you have enough for a donation, have a Mass said for a soul in Purgatory.

Morning Prayer for the Poor Souls:

Out of the depths I have cried to Thee O Lord! Lord, hear my voice. Let Thine ears be attentive to the voice of my supplication.
If Thou, O Lord, wilt mark iniquities, Lord, who shall stand it?
For with Thee there is mercy: and by reason of Thy law I have waited on Thee, O Lord! My soul hath relied on His word: my soul hath hoped in the Lord. From the morning watch even until night. Let Israel hope in the Lord. For with the Lord there is mercy; and with Him plentiful Redemption. And He will redeem Israel from all his iniquities.
Eternal rest give unto them, O Lord! And let perpetual light shine upon them. May they rest in peace. Amen.

Evening Prayer for the Poor Souls:

V. Lord, hear my prayer.
R. And let my cry come unto Thee.
Bless, O my God! the repose I am about to take, that, renewing my strength, I may be better enabled to serve Thee. Pour down Thy blessings, O Lord! on my parents, relations, friends, and enemies. Protect the Pope, our Bishop, and all the Pastors of Thy holy Church. Assist the poor and the afflicted, and those who are now in their last agony. Look with an eye of pity on the suffering souls in purgatory, particularly

_____
_____
_____

put an end to their torments and lead them forth into everlasting joy.

Eternal rest grant unto them, and let perpetual light shine upon them. Amen.

DATE: _____

Go without a meal or snack today if possible, for the benefit of the Holy Souls. If you are in ill health, give up a special treat instead.

Morning Prayer for the Poor Souls:

Out of the depths I have cried to Thee O Lord! Lord, hear my voice. Let Thine ears be attentive to the voice of my supplication.
If Thou, O Lord, wilt mark iniquities, Lord, who shall stand it?
For with Thee there is mercy: and by reason of Thy law I have waited on Thee, O Lord! My soul hath relied on His word: my soul hath hoped in the Lord. From the morning watch even until night. Let Israel hope in the Lord. For with the Lord there is mercy; and with Him plentiful Redemption. And He will redeem Israel from all his iniquities.
Eternal rest give unto them, O Lord! And let perpetual light shine upon them. May they rest in peace. Amen.

Evening Prayer for the Poor Souls:

V. Lord, hear my prayer.
R. And let my cry come unto Thee.
Bless, O my God! the repose I am about to take, that, renewing my strength, I may be better enabled to serve Thee. Pour down Thy blessings, O Lord! on my parents, relations, friends, and enemies. Protect the Pope, our Bishop, and all the Pastors of Thy holy Church. Assist the poor and the afflicted, and those who are now in their last agony. Look with an eye of pity on the suffering souls in purgatory, particularly

_____
_____
_____

put an end to their torments and lead them forth into everlasting joy.

Eternal rest grant unto them, and let perpetual light shine upon them. Amen.

DATE:
_____

Today, say a Divine Mercy chaplet for the Poor Souls.

Morning Prayer for the Poor Souls:

Out of the depths I have cried to Thee O Lord! Lord, hear my voice. Let Thine ears be attentive to the voice of my supplication.
If Thou, O Lord, wilt mark iniquities, Lord, who shall stand it?
For with Thee there is mercy: and by reason of Thy law I have waited on Thee, O Lord! My soul hath relied on His word: my soul hath hoped in the Lord. From the morning watch even until night. Let Israel hope in the Lord. For with the Lord there is mercy; and with Him plentiful Redemption. And He will redeem Israel from all his iniquities.
Eternal rest give unto them, O Lord! And let perpetual light shine upon them. May they rest in peace. Amen.

Evening Prayer for the Poor Souls:

V. Lord, hear my prayer.
R. And let my cry come unto Thee.
Bless, O my God! the repose I am about to take, that, renewing my strength, I may be better enabled to serve Thee. Pour down Thy blessings, O Lord! on my parents, relations, friends, and enemies. Protect the Pope, our Bishop, and all the Pastors of Thy holy Church. Assist the poor and the afflicted, and those who are now in their last agony. Look with an eye of pity on the suffering souls in purgatory, particularly

_____
_____
_____

put an end to their torments and lead them forth into everlasting joy.

Eternal rest grant unto them, and let perpetual light shine upon them. Amen.

DATE: _____

Pray today for the souls of priests and religious in Purgatory.

Morning Prayer for the Poor Souls:

Out of the depths I have cried to Thee O Lord! Lord, hear my voice. Let Thine ears be attentive to the voice of my supplication.
If Thou, O Lord, wilt mark iniquities, Lord, who shall stand it?
For with Thee there is mercy: and by reason of Thy law I have waited on Thee, O Lord! My soul hath relied on His word: my soul hath hoped in the Lord. From the morning watch even until night. Let Israel hope in the Lord. For with the Lord there is mercy; and with Him plentiful Redemption. And He will redeem Israel from all his iniquities.
Eternal rest give unto them, O Lord! And let perpetual light shine upon them. May they rest in peace. Amen.

Evening Prayer for the Poor Souls:

V. Lord, hear my prayer.
R. And let my cry come unto Thee.
Bless, O my God! the repose I am about to take, that, renewing my strength, I may be better enabled to serve Thee. Pour down Thy blessings, O Lord! on my parents, relations, friends, and enemies. Protect the Pope, our Bishop, and all the Pastors of Thy holy Church. Assist the poor and the afflicted, and those who are now in their last agony. Look with an eye of pity on the suffering souls in purgatory, particularly

_____

_____

_____

put an end to their torments and lead them forth into everlasting joy.

Eternal rest grant unto them, and let perpetual light shine upon them. Amen.

DATE: _____

While you are going about your day today, remember your friends and colleagues who have passed away over the years, asking God to release them from Purgatory.

Morning Prayer for the Poor Souls:

Out of the depths I have cried to Thee O Lord! Lord, hear my voice. Let Thine ears be attentive to the voice of my supplication.
If Thou, O Lord, wilt mark iniquities, Lord, who shall stand it?
For with Thee there is mercy: and by reason of Thy law I have waited on Thee, O Lord! My soul hath relied on His word: my soul hath hoped in the Lord. From the morning watch even until night. Let Israel hope in the Lord. For with the Lord there is mercy; and with Him plentiful Redemption. And He will redeem Israel from all his iniquities.
Eternal rest give unto them, O Lord! And let perpetual light shine upon them. May they rest in peace. Amen.

Evening Prayer for the Poor Souls:

V. Lord, hear my prayer.
R. And let my cry come unto Thee.
Bless, O my God! the repose I am about to take, that, renewing my strength, I may be better enabled to serve Thee. Pour down Thy blessings, O Lord! on my parents, relations, friends, and enemies. Protect the Pope, our Bishop, and all the Pastors of Thy holy Church. Assist the poor and the afflicted, and those who are now in their last agony. Look with an eye of pity on the suffering souls in purgatory, particularly

put an end to their torments and lead them forth into everlasting joy.

Eternal rest grant unto them, and let perpetual light shine upon them. Amen.

DATE: _____

Pray today for the dead who heard the Gospel but rejected it. May they be spared Hell and be released from Purgatory to be with Jesus.

Morning Prayer for the Poor Souls:

Out of the depths I have cried to Thee O Lord! Lord, hear my voice. Let Thine ears be attentive to the voice of my supplication.
If Thou, O Lord, wilt mark iniquities, Lord, who shall stand it?
For with Thee there is mercy: and by reason of Thy law I have waited on Thee, O Lord! My soul hath relied on His word: my soul hath hoped in the Lord. From the morning watch even until night. Let Israel hope in the Lord. For with the Lord there is mercy; and with Him plentiful Redemption. And He will redeem Israel from all his iniquities.
Eternal rest give unto them, O Lord! And let perpetual light shine upon them. May they rest in peace. Amen.

Evening Prayer for the Poor Souls:

V. Lord, hear my prayer.
R. And let my cry come unto Thee.
Bless, O my God! the repose I am about to take, that, renewing my strength, I may be better enabled to serve Thee. Pour down Thy blessings, O Lord! on my parents, relations, friends, and enemies. Protect the Pope, our Bishop, and all the Pastors of Thy holy Church. Assist the poor and the afflicted, and those who are now in their last agony. Look with an eye of pity on the suffering souls in purgatory, particularly

_____

_____

_____

put an end to their torments and lead them forth into everlasting joy.

Eternal rest grant unto them, and let perpetual light shine upon them. Amen.

DATE: _____

Today, spend some time reading devotional literature aloud for the comfort of the Poor Souls.

Morning Prayer for the Poor Souls:

Out of the depths I have cried to Thee O Lord! Lord, hear my voice. Let Thine ears be attentive to the voice of my supplication.
If Thou, O Lord, wilt mark iniquities, Lord, who shall stand it?
For with Thee there is mercy: and by reason of Thy law I have waited on Thee, O Lord! My soul hath relied on His word: my soul hath hoped in the Lord. From the morning watch even until night. Let Israel hope in the Lord. For with the Lord there is mercy; and with Him plentiful Redemption. And He will redeem Israel from all his iniquities.
Eternal rest give unto them, O Lord! And let perpetual light shine upon them. May they rest in peace. Amen.

Evening Prayer for the Poor Souls:

V. Lord, hear my prayer.
R. And let my cry come unto Thee.
Bless, O my God! the repose I am about to take, that, renewing my strength, I may be better enabled to serve Thee. Pour down Thy blessings, O Lord! on my parents, relations, friends, and enemies. Protect the Pope, our Bishop, and all the Pastors of Thy holy Church. Assist the poor and the afflicted, and those who are now in their last agony. Look with an eye of pity on the suffering souls in purgatory, particularly

_____

_____

_____

put an end to their torments and lead them forth into everlasting joy.

Eternal rest grant unto them, and let perpetual light shine upon them. Amen.

DATE: _____

Today make the Stations of the Cross for the benefit of the Holy Souls in Purgatory.

Morning Prayer for the Poor Souls:

Out of the depths I have cried to Thee O Lord! Lord, hear my voice. Let Thine ears be attentive to the voice of my supplication.
If Thou, O Lord, wilt mark iniquities, Lord, who shall stand it?
For with Thee there is mercy: and by reason of Thy law I have waited on Thee, O Lord! My soul hath relied on His word: my soul hath hoped in the Lord. From the morning watch even until night. Let Israel hope in the Lord. For with the Lord there is mercy; and with Him plentiful Redemption. And He will redeem Israel from all his iniquities.
Eternal rest give unto them, O Lord! And let perpetual light shine upon them. May they rest in peace. Amen.

Evening Prayer for the Poor Souls:

V. Lord, hear my prayer.
R. And let my cry come unto Thee.
Bless, O my God! the repose I am about to take, that, renewing my strength, I may be better enabled to serve Thee. Pour down Thy blessings, O Lord! on my parents, relations, friends, and enemies. Protect the Pope, our Bishop, and all the Pastors of Thy holy Church. Assist the poor and the afflicted, and those who are now in their last agony. Look with an eye of pity on the suffering souls in purgatory, particularly

_____

_____

_____

put an end to their torments and lead them forth into everlasting joy.

Eternal rest grant unto them, and let perpetual light shine upon them. Amen.

DATE: _____

Pray today for the souls of all Jewish people who have died.

Morning Prayer for the Poor Souls:

Out of the depths I have cried to Thee O Lord! Lord, hear my voice. Let Thine ears be attentive to the voice of my supplication.
If Thou, O Lord, wilt mark iniquities, Lord, who shall stand it?
For with Thee there is mercy: and by reason of Thy law I have waited on Thee, O Lord! My soul hath relied on His word: my soul hath hoped in the Lord. From the morning watch even until night. Let Israel hope in the Lord. For with the Lord there is mercy; and with Him plentiful Redemption. And He will redeem Israel from all his iniquities.
Eternal rest give unto them, O Lord! And let perpetual light shine upon them. May they rest in peace. Amen.

Evening Prayer for the Poor Souls:

V. Lord, hear my prayer.
R. And let my cry come unto Thee.
Bless, O my God! the repose I am about to take, that, renewing my strength, I may be better enabled to serve Thee. Pour down Thy blessings, O Lord! on my parents, relations, friends, and enemies. Protect the Pope, our Bishop, and all the Pastors of Thy holy Church. Assist the poor and the afflicted, and those who are now in their last agony. Look with an eye of pity on the suffering souls in purgatory, particularly

_____
_____
_____

put an end to their torments and lead them forth into everlasting joy.

Eternal rest grant unto them, and let perpetual light shine upon them. Amen.

DATE: _____

Today, pray for the souls of persecutors of Christians who have died.

Morning Prayer for the Poor Souls:

Out of the depths I have cried to Thee O Lord! Lord, hear my voice. Let Thine ears be attentive to the voice of my supplication.
If Thou, O Lord, wilt mark iniquities, Lord, who shall stand it?
For with Thee there is mercy: and by reason of Thy law I have waited on Thee, O Lord! My soul hath relied on His word: my soul hath hoped in the Lord. From the morning watch even until night. Let Israel hope in the Lord. For with the Lord there is mercy; and with Him plentiful Redemption. And He will redeem Israel from all his iniquities.
Eternal rest give unto them, O Lord! And let perpetual light shine upon them. May they rest in peace. Amen.

Evening Prayer for the Poor Souls:

V. Lord, hear my prayer.
R. And let my cry come unto Thee.
Bless, O my God! the repose I am about to take, that, renewing my strength, I may be better enabled to serve Thee. Pour down Thy blessings, O Lord! on my parents, relations, friends, and enemies. Protect the Pope, our Bishop, and all the Pastors of Thy holy Church. Assist the poor and the afflicted, and those who are now in their last agony. Look with an eye of pity on the suffering souls in purgatory, particularly

_____
_____

_____

put an end to their torments and lead them forth into everlasting joy.

Eternal rest grant unto them, and let perpetual light shine upon them. Amen.

DATE: _____

Light a blessed candle today in remembrance of the Holy Souls.

Morning Prayer for the Poor Souls:

Out of the depths I have cried to Thee O Lord! Lord, hear my voice. Let Thine ears be attentive to the voice of my supplication.
If Thou, O Lord, wilt mark iniquities, Lord, who shall stand it?
For with Thee there is mercy: and by reason of Thy law I have waited on Thee, O Lord! My soul hath relied on His word: my soul hath hoped in the Lord. From the morning watch even until night. Let Israel hope in the Lord. For with the Lord there is mercy; and with Him plentiful Redemption. And He will redeem Israel from all his iniquities.
Eternal rest give unto them, O Lord! And let perpetual light shine upon them. May they rest in peace. Amen.

Evening Prayer for the Poor Souls:

V. Lord, hear my prayer.
R. And let my cry come unto Thee.
Bless, O my God! the repose I am about to take, that, renewing my strength, I may be better enabled to serve Thee. Pour down Thy blessings, O Lord! on my parents, relations, friends, and enemies. Protect the Pope, our Bishop, and all the Pastors of Thy holy Church. Assist the poor and the afflicted, and those who are now in their last agony. Look with an eye of pity on the suffering souls in purgatory, particularly

_____

_____

_____

put an end to their torments and lead them forth into everlasting joy.

Eternal rest grant unto them, and let perpetual light shine upon them. Amen.

DATE: _____

Begin a Novena today for the benefit of the Poor Souls. St. Alphonsus Liguori wrote a powerful one just for the Holy Souls, which may be found online, but any Novena will be appreciated.

Morning Prayer for the Poor Souls:

Out of the depths I have cried to Thee O Lord! Lord, hear my voice. Let Thine ears be attentive to the voice of my supplication.
If Thou, O Lord, wilt mark iniquities, Lord, who shall stand it?
For with Thee there is mercy: and by reason of Thy law I have waited on Thee, O Lord! My soul hath relied on His word: my soul hath hoped in the Lord. From the morning watch even until night. Let Israel hope in the Lord. For with the Lord there is mercy; and with Him plentiful Redemption. And He will redeem Israel from all his iniquities.
Eternal rest give unto them, O Lord! And let perpetual light shine upon them. May they rest in peace. Amen.

Evening Prayer for the Poor Souls:

V. Lord, hear my prayer.
R. And let my cry come unto Thee.
Bless, O my God! the repose I am about to take, that, renewing my strength, I may be better enabled to serve Thee. Pour down Thy blessings, O Lord! on my parents, relations, friends, and enemies. Protect the Pope, our Bishop, and all the Pastors of Thy holy Church. Assist the poor and the afflicted, and those who are now in their last agony. Look with an eye of pity on the suffering souls in purgatory, particularly

_____

_____

_____

put an end to their torments and lead them forth into everlasting joy.

Eternal rest grant unto them, and let perpetual light shine upon them. Amen.

DATE: _____

Give alms to the poor today to benefit the souls in Purgatory. We are told that giving alms is of great benefit to suffering souls.

Morning Prayer for the Poor Souls:

Out of the depths I have cried to Thee O Lord! Lord, hear my voice. Let Thine ears be attentive to the voice of my supplication.
If Thou, O Lord, wilt mark iniquities, Lord, who shall stand it?
For with Thee there is mercy: and by reason of Thy law I have waited on Thee, O Lord! My soul hath relied on His word: my soul hath hoped in the Lord. From the morning watch even until night. Let Israel hope in the Lord. For with the Lord there is mercy; and with Him plentiful Redemption. And He will redeem Israel from all his iniquities.
Eternal rest give unto them, O Lord! And let perpetual light shine upon them. May they rest in peace. Amen.

Evening Prayer for the Poor Souls:

V. Lord, hear my prayer.
R. And let my cry come unto Thee.
Bless, O my God! the repose I am about to take, that, renewing my strength, I may be better enabled to serve Thee. Pour down Thy blessings, O Lord! on my parents, relations, friends, and enemies. Protect the Pope, our Bishop, and all the Pastors of Thy holy Church. Assist the poor and the afflicted, and those who are now in their last agony. Look with an eye of pity on the suffering souls in purgatory, particularly

_____
_____

_____

put an end to their torments and lead them forth into everlasting joy.

Eternal rest grant unto them and let perpetual light shine upon them. Amen.

DATE: _____

Read aloud today from the Acts of the Apostles to comfort the Holy Souls. The Good News of Jesus' salvation is of great relief to their suffering.

Morning Prayer for the Poor Souls:

Out of the depths I have cried to Thee O Lord! Lord, hear my voice. Let Thine ears be attentive to the voice of my supplication.
If Thou, O Lord, wilt mark iniquities, Lord, who shall stand it?
For with Thee there is mercy: and by reason of Thy law I have waited on Thee, O Lord! My soul hath relied on His word: my soul hath hoped in the Lord. From the morning watch even until night. Let Israel hope in the Lord. For with the Lord there is mercy; and with Him plentiful Redemption. And He will redeem Israel from all his iniquities.
Eternal rest give unto them, O Lord! And let perpetual light shine upon them. May they rest in peace. Amen.

Evening Prayer for the Poor Souls:

V. Lord, hear my prayer.
R. And let my cry come unto Thee.
Bless, O my God! the repose I am about to take, that, renewing my strength, I may be better enabled to serve Thee. Pour down Thy blessings, O Lord! on my parents, relations, friends, and enemies. Protect the Pope, our Bishop, and all the Pastors of Thy holy Church. Assist the poor and the afflicted, and those who are now in their last agony. Look with an eye of pity on the suffering souls in purgatory, particularly

_____
_____
_____

put an end to their torments and lead them forth into everlasting joy.

Eternal rest grant unto them and let perpetual light shine upon them. Amen.

DATE: _____

Today, ask the saints known as intercessors for the dead to pray with you for their release, including St. Nicholas of Tolentino, St. Gertrude the Great, St. Catherine of Genoa, St. Padre Pio, St. Philip Neri, St. John Macías, St. Faustina Kowalska, St. Joseph and, of course, the Blessed Mother.

Morning Prayer for the Poor Souls:

Out of the depths I have cried to Thee O Lord! Lord, hear my voice. Let Thine ears be attentive to the voice of my supplication.
If Thou, O Lord, wilt mark iniquities, Lord, who shall stand it?
For with Thee there is mercy: and by reason of Thy law I have waited on Thee, O Lord! My soul hath relied on His word: my soul hath hoped in the Lord. From the morning watch even until night. Let Israel hope in the Lord. For with the Lord there is mercy; and with Him plentiful Redemption. And He will redeem Israel from all his iniquities.
Eternal rest give unto them, O Lord! And let perpetual light shine upon them. May they rest in peace. Amen.

Evening Prayer for the Poor Souls:

V. Lord, hear my prayer.
R. And let my cry come unto Thee.
Bless, O my God! the repose I am about to take, that, renewing my strength, I may be better enabled to serve Thee. Pour down Thy blessings, O Lord! on my parents, relations, friends, and enemies. Protect the Pope, our Bishop, and all the Pastors of Thy holy Church. Assist the poor and the afflicted, and those who are now in their last agony. Look with an eye of pity on the suffering souls in purgatory, particularly

_____
_____
_____

put an end to their torments and lead them forth into everlasting joy.

Eternal rest grant unto them and let perpetual light shine upon them. Amen.

DATE: _____

Today, have a Mass said for the soul of a family member or friend who has passed away. This can be through your own parish or through an order or national shrine via their website.

Morning Prayer for the Poor Souls:

Out of the depths I have cried to Thee O Lord! Lord, hear my voice. Let Thine ears be attentive to the voice of my supplication.
If Thou, O Lord, wilt mark iniquities, Lord, who shall stand it?
For with Thee there is mercy: and by reason of Thy law I have waited on Thee, O Lord! My soul hath relied on His word: my soul hath hoped in the Lord. From the morning watch even until night. Let Israel hope in the Lord. For with the Lord there is mercy; and with Him plentiful Redemption. And He will redeem Israel from all his iniquities.
Eternal rest give unto them, O Lord! And let perpetual light shine upon them. May they rest in peace. Amen.

Evening Prayer for the Poor Souls:

V. Lord, hear my prayer.
R. And let my cry come unto Thee.
Bless, O my God! the repose I am about to take, that, renewing my strength, I may be better enabled to serve Thee. Pour down Thy blessings, O Lord! on my parents, relations, friends, and enemies. Protect the Pope, our Bishop, and all the Pastors of Thy holy Church. Assist the poor and the afflicted, and those who are now in their last agony. Look with an eye of pity on the suffering souls in purgatory, particularly

_____
_____
_____

put an end to their torments and lead them forth into everlasting joy.

Eternal rest grant unto them and let perpetual light shine upon them. Amen.

DATE:

_____

Pray the Rosary today for the release of souls from Purgatory. Mystic saints have told us that the Blessed Mother herself comes to Purgatory to bring souls with her back to Heaven.

Morning Prayer for the Poor Souls:

Out of the depths I have cried to Thee O Lord! Lord, hear my voice. Let Thine ears be attentive to the voice of my supplication.
If Thou, O Lord, wilt mark iniquities, Lord, who shall stand it?
For with Thee there is mercy: and by reason of Thy law I have waited on Thee, O Lord! My soul hath relied on His word: my soul hath hoped in the Lord. From the morning watch even until night. Let Israel hope in the Lord. For with the Lord there is mercy; and with Him plentiful Redemption. And He will redeem Israel from all his iniquities.
Eternal rest give unto them, O Lord! And let perpetual light shine upon them. May they rest in peace. Amen.

Evening Prayer for the Poor Souls:

V. Lord, hear my prayer.
R. And let my cry come unto Thee.
Bless, O my God! the repose I am about to take, that, renewing my strength, I may be better enabled to serve Thee. Pour down Thy blessings, O Lord! on my parents, relations, friends, and enemies. Protect the Pope, our Bishop, and all the Pastors of Thy holy Church. Assist the poor and the afflicted, and those who are now in their last agony. Look with an eye of pity on the suffering souls in purgatory, particularly

_____
_____
_____

put an end to their torments and lead them forth into everlasting joy.

Eternal rest grant unto them and let perpetual light shine upon them. Amen.

DATE:

_____

Today, ask the Blessed Mother to apply your prayers and works to a poor soul who has no one to pray for them.

Morning Prayer for the Poor Souls:

Out of the depths I have cried to Thee O Lord! Lord, hear my voice. Let Thine ears be attentive to the voice of my supplication.
If Thou, O Lord, wilt mark iniquities, Lord, who shall stand it?
For with Thee there is mercy: and by reason of Thy law I have waited on Thee, O Lord! My soul hath relied on His word: my soul hath hoped in the Lord. From the morning watch even until night. Let Israel hope in the Lord. For with the Lord there is mercy; and with Him plentiful Redemption. And He will redeem Israel from all his iniquities.
Eternal rest give unto them, O Lord! And let perpetual light shine upon them. May they rest in peace. Amen.

Evening Prayer for the Poor Souls:

V. Lord, hear my prayer.
R. And let my cry come unto Thee.
Bless, O my God! the repose I am about to take, that, renewing my strength, I may be better enabled to serve Thee. Pour down Thy blessings, O Lord! on my parents, relations, friends, and enemies. Protect the Pope, our Bishop, and all the Pastors of Thy holy Church. Assist the poor and the afflicted, and those who are now in their last agony. Look with an eye of pity on the suffering souls in purgatory, particularly

_____
_____
_____

put an end to their torments and lead them forth into everlasting joy.

Eternal rest grant unto them and let perpetual light shine upon them. Amen.

DATE:

_____

We all have a spiritual or physical affliction or burden that we suffer with daily. Today, dedicate your ailment-related suffering to the Poor souls.

Morning Prayer for the Poor Souls:

Out of the depths I have cried to Thee O Lord! Lord, hear my voice. Let Thine ears be attentive to the voice of my supplication.
If Thou, O Lord, wilt mark iniquities, Lord, who shall stand it?
For with Thee there is mercy: and by reason of Thy law I have waited on Thee, O Lord! My soul hath relied on His word: my soul hath hoped in the Lord. From the morning watch even until night. Let Israel hope in the Lord. For with the Lord there is mercy; and with Him plentiful Redemption. And He will redeem Israel from all his iniquities.
Eternal rest give unto them, O Lord! And let perpetual light shine upon them. May they rest in peace. Amen.

Evening Prayer for the Poor Souls:

V. Lord, hear my prayer.
R. And let my cry come unto Thee.
Bless, O my God! the repose I am about to take, that, renewing my strength, I may be better enabled to serve Thee. Pour down Thy blessings, O Lord! on my parents, relations, friends, and enemies. Protect the Pope, our Bishop, and all the Pastors of Thy holy Church. Assist the poor and the afflicted, and those who are now in their last agony. Look with an eye of pity on the suffering souls in purgatory, particularly

_____

_____

_____

put an end to their torments and lead them forth into everlasting joy.

Eternal rest grant unto them and let perpetual light shine upon them. Amen.

DATE:

_____

Today, visit or call someone elderly or alone and offer your work of mercy for the souls in Purgatory.

Morning Prayer for the Poor Souls:

Out of the depths I have cried to Thee O Lord! Lord, hear my voice. Let Thine ears be attentive to the voice of my supplication.
If Thou, O Lord, wilt mark iniquities, Lord, who shall stand it?
For with Thee there is mercy: and by reason of Thy law I have waited on Thee, O Lord! My soul hath relied on His word: my soul hath hoped in the Lord. From the morning watch even until night. Let Israel hope in the Lord. For with the Lord there is mercy; and with Him plentiful Redemption. And He will redeem Israel from all his iniquities.
Eternal rest give unto them, O Lord! And let perpetual light shine upon them. May they rest in peace. Amen.

Evening Prayer for the Poor Souls:

V. Lord, hear my prayer.
R. And let my cry come unto Thee.
Bless, O my God! the repose I am about to take, that, renewing my strength, I may be better enabled to serve Thee. Pour down Thy blessings, O Lord! on my parents, relations, friends, and enemies. Protect the Pope, our Bishop, and all the Pastors of Thy holy Church. Assist the poor and the afflicted, and those who are now in their last agony. Look with an eye of pity on the suffering souls in purgatory, particularly

_____

_____

_____

put an end to their torments and lead them forth into everlasting joy.

Eternal rest grant unto them and let perpetual light shine upon them. Amen.

DATE: _____

During the course of the day today, pray for those you meet and strangers you see on street, asking God to apply your prayers for them to their future time in Purgatory.

Morning Prayer for the Poor Souls:

Out of the depths I have cried to Thee O Lord! Lord, hear my voice. Let Thine ears be attentive to the voice of my supplication.
If Thou, O Lord, wilt mark iniquities, Lord, who shall stand it?
For with Thee there is mercy: and by reason of Thy law I have waited on Thee, O Lord! My soul hath relied on His word: my soul hath hoped in the Lord. From the morning watch even until night. Let Israel hope in the Lord. For with the Lord there is mercy; and with Him plentiful Redemption. And He will redeem Israel from all his iniquities.
Eternal rest give unto them, O Lord! And let perpetual light shine upon them. May they rest in peace. Amen.

Evening Prayer for the Poor Souls:

V. Lord, hear my prayer.
R. And let my cry come unto Thee.
Bless, O my God! the repose I am about to take, that, renewing my strength, I may be better enabled to serve Thee. Pour down Thy blessings, O Lord! on my parents, relations, friends, and enemies. Protect the Pope, our Bishop, and all the Pastors of Thy holy Church. Assist the poor and the afflicted, and those who are now in their last agony. Look with an eye of pity on the suffering souls in purgatory, particularly

_____
_____
_____

put an end to their torments and lead them forth into everlasting joy.

Eternal rest grant unto them and let perpetual light shine upon them. Amen.

DATE:

_____

Today, ask the Blessed Mother to use your prayers for someone in Purgatory with no one to pray for them.

Morning Prayer for the Poor Souls:

Out of the depths I have cried to Thee O Lord! Lord, hear my voice. Let Thine ears be attentive to the voice of my supplication.
If Thou, O Lord, wilt mark iniquities, Lord, who shall stand it?
For with Thee there is mercy: and by reason of Thy law I have waited on Thee, O Lord! My soul hath relied on His word: my soul hath hoped in the Lord. From the morning watch even until night. Let Israel hope in the Lord. For with the Lord there is mercy; and with Him plentiful Redemption. And He will redeem Israel from all his iniquities.
Eternal rest give unto them, O Lord! And let perpetual light shine upon them. May they rest in peace. Amen.

Evening Prayer for the Poor Souls:

V. Lord, hear my prayer.
R. And let my cry come unto Thee.
Bless, O my God! the repose I am about to take, that, renewing my strength, I may be better enabled to serve Thee. Pour down Thy blessings, O Lord! on my parents, relations, friends, and enemies. Protect the Pope, our Bishop, and all the Pastors of Thy holy Church. Assist the poor and the afflicted, and those who are now in their last agony. Look with an eye of pity on the suffering souls in purgatory, particularly

_____
_____
_____

put an end to their torments and lead them forth into everlasting joy.

Eternal rest grant unto them and let perpetual light shine upon them. Amen.

DATE:

_____

Today, sprinkle holy water on the carpet of your home or outside your house as a comfort to the Poor Souls.

Morning Prayer for the Poor Souls:

Out of the depths I have cried to Thee O Lord! Lord, hear my voice. Let Thine ears be attentive to the voice of my supplication.
If Thou, O Lord, wilt mark iniquities, Lord, who shall stand it?
For with Thee there is mercy: and by reason of Thy law I have waited on Thee, O Lord! My soul hath relied on His word: my soul hath hoped in the Lord. From the morning watch even until night. Let Israel hope in the Lord. For with the Lord there is mercy; and with Him plentiful Redemption. And He will redeem Israel from all his iniquities.
Eternal rest give unto them, O Lord! And let perpetual light shine upon them. May they rest in peace. Amen.

Evening Prayer for the Poor Souls:

V. Lord, hear my prayer.
R. And let my cry come unto Thee.
Bless, O my God! the repose I am about to take, that, renewing my strength, I may be better enabled to serve Thee. Pour down Thy blessings, O Lord! on my parents, relations, friends, and enemies. Protect the Pope, our Bishop, and all the Pastors of Thy holy Church. Assist the poor and the afflicted, and those who are now in their last agony. Look with an eye of pity on the suffering souls in purgatory, particularly

_____

_____

_____

put an end to their torments and lead them forth into everlasting joy.

Eternal rest grant unto them and let perpetual light shine upon them. Amen.

DATE:
_____

Today, visit a church if you are able, and pray for the souls who are spending their Purgatorial time there. Catholic mystics have told us that God allows many souls to do so. If you cannot visit a church, think of a local church and pray for any souls who might be there.

Morning Prayer for the Poor Souls:

Out of the depths I have cried to Thee O Lord! Lord, hear my voice. Let Thine ears be attentive to the voice of my supplication.
If Thou, O Lord, wilt mark iniquities, Lord, who shall stand it?
For with Thee there is mercy: and by reason of Thy law I have waited on Thee, O Lord! My soul hath relied on His word: my soul hath hoped in the Lord. From the morning watch even until night. Let Israel hope in the Lord. For with the Lord there is mercy; and with Him plentiful Redemption. And He will redeem Israel from all his iniquities.
Eternal rest give unto them, O Lord! And let perpetual light shine upon them. May they rest in peace. Amen.

Evening Prayer for the Poor Souls:

V. Lord, hear my prayer.
R. And let my cry come unto Thee.
Bless, O my God! the repose I am about to take, that, renewing my strength, I may be better enabled to serve Thee. Pour down Thy blessings, O Lord! on my parents, relations, friends, and enemies. Protect the Pope, our Bishop, and all the Pastors of Thy holy Church. Assist the poor and the afflicted, and those who are now in their last agony. Look with an eye of pity on the suffering souls in purgatory, particularly

_____

_____

put an end to their torments and lead them forth into everlasting joy.

Eternal rest grant unto them and let perpetual light shine upon them. Amen.

DATE:

_____

Today, visit someone who is sick if you are able, and offer up this work of mercy for the Holy Souls. If you cannot, pray for those in your local hospital or nursing home.

Morning Prayer for the Poor Souls:

Out of the depths I have cried to Thee O Lord! Lord, hear my voice. Let Thine ears be attentive to the voice of my supplication.
If Thou, O Lord, wilt mark iniquities, Lord, who shall stand it?
For with Thee there is mercy: and by reason of Thy law I have waited on Thee, O Lord! My soul hath relied on His word: my soul hath hoped in the Lord. From the morning watch even until night. Let Israel hope in the Lord. For with the Lord there is mercy; and with Him plentiful Redemption. And He will redeem Israel from all his iniquities.
Eternal rest give unto them, O Lord! And let perpetual light shine upon them. May they rest in peace. Amen.

Evening Prayer for the Poor Souls:

V. Lord, hear my prayer.
R. And let my cry come unto Thee.
Bless, O my God! the repose I am about to take, that, renewing my strength, I may be better enabled to serve Thee. Pour down Thy blessings, O Lord! on my parents, relations, friends, and enemies. Protect the Pope, our Bishop, and all the Pastors of Thy holy Church. Assist the poor and the afflicted, and those who are now in their last agony. Look with an eye of pity on the suffering souls in purgatory, particularly

_____

_____

_____

put an end to their torments and lead them forth into everlasting joy.

Eternal rest grant unto them and let perpetual light shine upon them. Amen.

DATE:

_____

Today pray for the souls of all the atheists who have died.

Morning Prayer for the Poor Souls:

Out of the depths I have cried to Thee O Lord! Lord, hear my voice. Let Thine ears be attentive to the voice of my supplication.
If Thou, O Lord, wilt mark iniquities, Lord, who shall stand it?
For with Thee there is mercy: and by reason of Thy law I have waited on Thee, O Lord! My soul hath relied on His word: my soul hath hoped in the Lord. From the morning watch even until night. Let Israel hope in the Lord. For with the Lord there is mercy; and with Him plentiful Redemption. And He will redeem Israel from all his iniquities.
Eternal rest give unto them, O Lord! And let perpetual light shine upon them. May they rest in peace. Amen.

Evening Prayer for the Poor Souls:

V. Lord, hear my prayer.
R. And let my cry come unto Thee.
Bless, O my God! the repose I am about to take, that, renewing my strength, I may be better enabled to serve Thee. Pour down Thy blessings, O Lord! on my parents, relations, friends, and enemies. Protect the Pope, our Bishop, and all the Pastors of Thy holy Church. Assist the poor and the afflicted, and those who are now in their last agony. Look with an eye of pity on the suffering souls in purgatory, particularly

_____

_____

_____

put an end to their torments and lead them forth into everlasting joy.

Eternal rest grant unto them and let perpetual light shine upon them. Amen.

DATE: _____

Today, read the obituaries in your local newspaper and pray for the souls who have died in the past several days.

Morning Prayer for the Poor Souls:

Out of the depths I have cried to Thee O Lord! Lord, hear my voice. Let Thine ears be attentive to the voice of my supplication.
If Thou, O Lord, wilt mark iniquities, Lord, who shall stand it?
For with Thee there is mercy: and by reason of Thy law I have waited on Thee, O Lord! My soul hath relied on His word: my soul hath hoped in the Lord. From the morning watch even until night. Let Israel hope in the Lord. For with the Lord there is mercy; and with Him plentiful Redemption. And He will redeem Israel from all his iniquities.
Eternal rest give unto them, O Lord! And let perpetual light shine upon them. May they rest in peace. Amen.

Evening Prayer for the Poor Souls:

V. Lord, hear my prayer.
R. And let my cry come unto Thee.
Bless, O my God! the repose I am about to take, that, renewing my strength, I may be better enabled to serve Thee. Pour down Thy blessings, O Lord! on my parents, relations, friends, and enemies. Protect the Pope, our Bishop, and all the Pastors of Thy holy Church. Assist the poor and the afflicted, and those who are now in their last agony. Look with an eye of pity on the suffering souls in purgatory, particularly

_____

_____

_____

put an end to their torments and lead them forth into everlasting joy.

Eternal rest grant unto them and let perpetual light shine upon them. Amen.

DATE:

_____

Spend some time in Eucharistic Adoration today for the Poor Souls. If you cannot travel to a church physically, watch live Adoration on EWTN, YouTube or Facebook.

***Morning Prayer for the Poor Souls*:**

Out of the depths I have cried to Thee O Lord! Lord, hear my voice. Let Thine ears be attentive to the voice of my supplication.
If Thou, O Lord, wilt mark iniquities, Lord, who shall stand it?
For with Thee there is mercy: and by reason of Thy law I have waited on Thee, O Lord! My soul hath relied on His word: my soul hath hoped in the Lord. From the morning watch even until night. Let Israel hope in the Lord. For with the Lord there is mercy; and with Him plentiful Redemption. And He will redeem Israel from all his iniquities.
Eternal rest give unto them, O Lord! And let perpetual light shine upon them. May they rest in peace. Amen.

Evening Prayer for the Poor Souls:

V. Lord, hear my prayer.
R. And let my cry come unto Thee.
Bless, O my God! the repose I am about to take, that, renewing my strength, I may be better enabled to serve Thee. Pour down Thy blessings, O Lord! on my parents, relations, friends, and enemies. Protect the Pope, our Bishop, and all the Pastors of Thy holy Church. Assist the poor and the afflicted, and those who are now in their last agony. Look with an eye of pity on the suffering souls in purgatory, particularly

_____

_____

_____

put an end to their torments and lead them forth into everlasting joy.

Eternal rest grant unto them and let perpetual light shine upon them. Amen.

DATE:

_____

a drive today to a cemetery and pray for the souls of those interred there. If you cannot physically visit a cemetery, think of a cemetery in your city or town and pray for the souls of those buried there.

Morning Prayer for the Poor Souls:

Out of the depths I have cried to Thee O Lord! Lord, hear my voice. Let Thine ears be attentive to the voice of my supplication.
If Thou, O Lord, wilt mark iniquities, Lord, who shall stand it?
For with Thee there is mercy: and by reason of Thy law I have waited on Thee, O Lord! My soul hath relied on His word: my soul hath hoped in the Lord. From the morning watch even until night. Let Israel hope in the Lord. For with the Lord there is mercy; and with Him plentiful Redemption. And He will redeem Israel from all his iniquities.
Eternal rest give unto them, O Lord! And let perpetual light shine upon them. May they rest in peace. Amen.

Evening Prayer for the Poor Souls:

V. Lord, hear my prayer.
R. And let my cry come unto Thee.
Bless, O my God! the repose I am about to take, that, renewing my strength, I may be better enabled to serve Thee. Pour down Thy blessings, O Lord! on my parents, relations, friends, and enemies. Protect the Pope, our Bishop, and all the Pastors of Thy holy Church. Assist the poor and the afflicted, and those who are now in their last agony. Look with an eye of pity on the suffering souls in purgatory, particularly

_____

_____

_____

put an end to their torments and lead them forth into everlasting joy.

Eternal rest grant unto them and let perpetual light shine upon them. Amen.

DATE:

_____

Today, play some sacred music to comfort the Poor Souls. Mystic saints have told us that these small gestures provide great relief to their suffering.

Morning Prayer for the Poor Souls:

Out of the depths I have cried to Thee O Lord! Lord, hear my voice. Let Thine ears be attentive to the voice of my supplication.
If Thou, O Lord, wilt mark iniquities, Lord, who shall stand it?
For with Thee there is mercy: and by reason of Thy law I have waited on Thee, O Lord! My soul hath relied on His word: my soul hath hoped in the Lord. From the morning watch even until night. Let Israel hope in the Lord. For with the Lord there is mercy; and with Him plentiful Redemption. And He will redeem Israel from all his iniquities.
Eternal rest give unto them, O Lord! And let perpetual light shine upon them. May they rest in peace. Amen.

Evening Prayer for the Poor Souls:

V. Lord, hear my prayer.
R. And let my cry come unto Thee.
Bless, O my God! the repose I am about to take, that, renewing my strength, I may be better enabled to serve Thee. Pour down Thy blessings, O Lord! on my parents, relations, friends, and enemies. Protect the Pope, our Bishop, and all the Pastors of Thy holy Church. Assist the poor and the afflicted, and those who are now in their last agony. Look with an eye of pity on the suffering souls in purgatory, particularly

_____

_____

_____

put an end to their torments and lead them forth into everlasting joy.

Eternal rest grant unto them and let perpetual light shine upon them. Amen.

DATE:

_____

Today, make reparation to the Sacred Heart of Jesus for the souls in Purgatory who offended His most precious Heart with the following: Adorable Heart of Jesus, glowing with love for us and inflamed with zeal for our salvation. O Heart that understands the misery to which our sins have brought us, infinitely rich in mercy to heal the wounds of our souls, behold me humbly kneeling before You to express the sorrow that fills my heart for the coldness and indifference with which I have so long returned the numberless benefits which You have bestowed upon me.

Morning Prayer for the Poor Souls:

Out of the depths I have cried to Thee O Lord! Lord, hear my voice. Let Thine ears be attentive to the voice of my supplication. If Thou, O Lord, wilt mark iniquities, Lord, who shall stand it? For with Thee there is mercy: and by reason of Thy law I have waited on Thee, O Lord! My soul hath relied on His word: my soul hath hoped in the Lord. From the morning watch even until night. Let Israel hope in the Lord. For with the Lord there is mercy; and with Him plentiful Redemption. And He will redeem Israel from all his iniquities. Eternal rest give unto them, O Lord! And let perpetual light shine upon them. May they rest in peace. Amen.

Evening Prayer for the Poor Souls:

V. Lord, hear my prayer.
R. And let my cry come unto Thee.
Bless, O my God! the repose I am about to take, that, renewing my strength, I may be better enabled to serve Thee. Pour down Thy blessings, O Lord! on my parents, relations, friends, and enemies. Protect the Pope, our Bishop, and all the Pastors of Thy holy Church. Assist the poor and the afflicted, and those who are now in their last agony. Look with an eye of pity on the suffering souls in purgatory, particularly

_____

put an end to their torments and lead them forth into everlasting joy.

Eternal rest grant unto them and let perpetual light shine upon them. Amen.

DATE:
_____

Start a Mass Collection jar or envelope today for the Holy Souls. Add money to it as you are able, and when you have enough for a donation, have a Mass said for a soul in Purgatory.

Morning Prayer for the Poor Souls:

Out of the depths I have cried to Thee O Lord! Lord, hear my voice. Let Thine ears be attentive to the voice of my supplication.
If Thou, O Lord, wilt mark iniquities, Lord, who shall stand it?
For with Thee there is mercy: and by reason of Thy law I have waited on Thee, O Lord! My soul hath relied on His word: my soul hath hoped in the Lord. From the morning watch even until night. Let Israel hope in the Lord. For with the Lord there is mercy; and with Him plentiful Redemption. And He will redeem Israel from all his iniquities.
Eternal rest give unto them, O Lord! And let perpetual light shine upon them. May they rest in peace. Amen.

Evening Prayer for the Poor Souls:

V. Lord, hear my prayer.
R. And let my cry come unto Thee.
Bless, O my God! the repose I am about to take, that, renewing my strength, I may be better enabled to serve Thee. Pour down Thy blessings, O Lord! on my parents, relations, friends, and enemies. Protect the Pope, our Bishop, and all the Pastors of Thy holy Church. Assist the poor and the afflicted, and those who are now in their last agony. Look with an eye of pity on the suffering souls in purgatory, particularly

_____
_____
_____

put an end to their torments and lead them forth into everlasting joy.

Eternal rest grant unto them and let perpetual light shine upon them. Amen.

DATE:

_____

Go without a meal or snack today if possible, for the benefit of the Holy Souls. If you are in ill health, give up a special treat instead.

Morning Prayer for the Poor Souls:

Out of the depths I have cried to Thee O Lord! Lord, hear my voice. Let Thine ears be attentive to the voice of my supplication.
If Thou, O Lord, wilt mark iniquities, Lord, who shall stand it?
For with Thee there is mercy: and by reason of Thy law I have waited on Thee, O Lord! My soul hath relied on His word: my soul hath hoped in the Lord. From the morning watch even until night. Let Israel hope in the Lord. For with the Lord there is mercy; and with Him plentiful Redemption. And He will redeem Israel from all his iniquities.
Eternal rest give unto them, O Lord! And let perpetual light shine upon them. May they rest in peace. Amen.

Evening Prayer for the Poor Souls:

V. Lord, hear my prayer.
R. And let my cry come unto Thee.
Bless, O my God! the repose I am about to take, that, renewing my strength, I may be better enabled to serve Thee. Pour down Thy blessings, O Lord! on my parents, relations, friends, and enemies. Protect the Pope, our Bishop, and all the Pastors of Thy holy Church. Assist the poor and the afflicted, and those who are now in their last agony. Look with an eye of pity on the suffering souls in purgatory, particularly

_____

_____

_____

put an end to their torments and lead them forth into everlasting joy.

Eternal rest grant unto them and let perpetual light shine upon them. Amen.

DATE:
_____

Today, say a Divine Mercy chaplet for the Poor Souls.

Morning Prayer for the Poor Souls:

Out of the depths I have cried to Thee O Lord! Lord, hear my voice. Let Thine ears be attentive to the voice of my supplication.
If Thou, O Lord, wilt mark iniquities, Lord, who shall stand it?
For with Thee there is mercy: and by reason of Thy law I have waited on Thee, O Lord! My soul hath relied on His word: my soul hath hoped in the Lord. From the morning watch even until night. Let Israel hope in the Lord. For with the Lord there is mercy; and with Him plentiful Redemption. And He will redeem Israel from all his iniquities.
Eternal rest give unto them, O Lord! And let perpetual light shine upon them. May they rest in peace. Amen.

Evening Prayer for the Poor Souls:

V. Lord, hear my prayer.
R. And let my cry come unto Thee.
Bless, O my God! the repose I am about to take, that, renewing my strength, I may be better enabled to serve Thee. Pour down Thy blessings, O Lord! on my parents, relations, friends, and enemies. Protect the Pope, our Bishop, and all the Pastors of Thy holy Church. Assist the poor and the afflicted, and those who are now in their last agony. Look with an eye of pity on the suffering souls in purgatory, particularly

_____
_____

_____

put an end to their torments and lead them forth into everlasting joy.

Eternal rest grant unto them and let perpetual light shine upon them. Amen.

DATE: _____

Pray today for the souls of priests and religious in Purgatory.

Morning Prayer for the Poor Souls:

Out of the depths I have cried to Thee O Lord! Lord, hear my voice. Let Thine ears be attentive to the voice of my supplication.
If Thou, O Lord, wilt mark iniquities, Lord, who shall stand it?
For with Thee there is mercy: and by reason of Thy law I have waited on Thee, O Lord! My soul hath relied on His word: my soul hath hoped in the Lord. From the morning watch even until night. Let Israel hope in the Lord. For with the Lord there is mercy; and with Him plentiful Redemption. And He will redeem Israel from all his iniquities.
Eternal rest give unto them, O Lord! And let perpetual light shine upon them. May they rest in peace. Amen.

Evening Prayer for the Poor Souls:

V. Lord, hear my prayer.
R. And let my cry come unto Thee.
Bless, O my God! the repose I am about to take, that, renewing my strength, I may be better enabled to serve Thee. Pour down Thy blessings, O Lord! on my parents, relations, friends, and enemies. Protect the Pope, our Bishop, and all the Pastors of Thy holy Church. Assist the poor and the afflicted, and those who are now in their last agony. Look with an eye of pity on the suffering souls in purgatory, particularly

_____

_____

_____

put an end to their torments and lead them forth into everlasting joy.

Eternal rest grant unto them and let perpetual light shine upon them. Amen.

DATE: _____

While you are going about your day today, remember your friends and colleagues who have passed away over the years, asking God to release them from Purgatory.

Morning Prayer for the Poor Souls:

Out of the depths I have cried to Thee O Lord! Lord, hear my voice. Let Thine ears be attentive to the voice of my supplication.
If Thou, O Lord, wilt mark iniquities, Lord, who shall stand it?
For with Thee there is mercy: and by reason of Thy law I have waited on Thee, O Lord! My soul hath relied on His word: my soul hath hoped in the Lord. From the morning watch even until night. Let Israel hope in the Lord. For with the Lord there is mercy; and with Him plentiful Redemption. And He will redeem Israel from all his iniquities.
Eternal rest give unto them, O Lord! And let perpetual light shine upon them. May they rest in peace. Amen.

Evening Prayer for the Poor Souls:

V. Lord, hear my prayer.
R. And let my cry come unto Thee.
Bless, O my God! the repose I am about to take, that, renewing my strength, I may be better enabled to serve Thee. Pour down Thy blessings, O Lord! on my parents, relations, friends, and enemies. Protect the Pope, our Bishop, and all the Pastors of Thy holy Church. Assist the poor and the afflicted, and those who are now in their last agony. Look with an eye of pity on the suffering souls in purgatory, particularly

put an end to their torments and lead them forth into everlasting joy.

Eternal rest grant unto them and let perpetual light shine upon them. Amen.

DATE: _____

Pray today for the dead who heard the Gospel but rejected it. May they be spared Hell and be released from Purgatory to be with Jesus.

Morning Prayer for the Poor Souls:

Out of the depths I have cried to Thee O Lord! Lord, hear my voice. Let Thine ears be attentive to the voice of my supplication.
If Thou, O Lord, wilt mark iniquities, Lord, who shall stand it?
For with Thee there is mercy: and by reason of Thy law I have waited on Thee, O Lord! My soul hath relied on His word: my soul hath hoped in the Lord. From the morning watch even until night. Let Israel hope in the Lord. For with the Lord there is mercy; and with Him plentiful Redemption. And He will redeem Israel from all his iniquities.
Eternal rest give unto them, O Lord! And let perpetual light shine upon them. May they rest in peace. Amen.

Evening Prayer for the Poor Souls:

V. Lord, hear my prayer.
R. And let my cry come unto Thee.
Bless, O my God! the repose I am about to take, that, renewing my strength, I may be better enabled to serve Thee. Pour down Thy blessings, O Lord! on my parents, relations, friends, and enemies. Protect the Pope, our Bishop, and all the Pastors of Thy holy Church. Assist the poor and the afflicted, and those who are now in their last agony. Look with an eye of pity on the suffering souls in purgatory, particularly

_____
_____
_____

put an end to their torments and lead them forth into everlasting joy.

Eternal rest grant unto them and let perpetual light shine upon them. Amen.

DATE: _____

Today, spend some time reading devotional literature aloud for the comfort of the Poor Souls.

Morning Prayer for the Poor Souls:

Out of the depths I have cried to Thee O Lord! Lord, hear my voice. Let Thine ears be attentive to the voice of my supplication.
If Thou, O Lord, wilt mark iniquities, Lord, who shall stand it?
For with Thee there is mercy: and by reason of Thy law I have waited on Thee, O Lord! My soul hath relied on His word: my soul hath hoped in the Lord. From the morning watch even until night. Let Israel hope in the Lord. For with the Lord there is mercy; and with Him plentiful Redemption. And He will redeem Israel from all his iniquities.
Eternal rest give unto them, O Lord! And let perpetual light shine upon them. May they rest in peace. Amen.

Evening Prayer for the Poor Souls:

V. Lord, hear my prayer.
R. And let my cry come unto Thee.
Bless, O my God! the repose I am about to take, that, renewing my strength, I may be better enabled to serve Thee. Pour down Thy blessings, O Lord! on my parents, relations, friends, and enemies. Protect the Pope, our Bishop, and all the Pastors of Thy holy Church. Assist the poor and the afflicted, and those who are now in their last agony. Look with an eye of pity on the suffering souls in purgatory, particularly

_____
_____

_____

put an end to their torments and lead them forth into everlasting joy.

Eternal rest grant unto them and let perpetual light shine upon them. Amen.

DATE: _____

Today make the Stations of the Cross for the benefit of the Holy Souls in Purgatory.

Morning Prayer for the Poor Souls:

Out of the depths I have cried to Thee O Lord! Lord, hear my voice. Let Thine ears be attentive to the voice of my supplication.
If Thou, O Lord, wilt mark iniquities, Lord, who shall stand it?
For with Thee there is mercy: and by reason of Thy law I have waited on Thee, O Lord! My soul hath relied on His word: my soul hath hoped in the Lord. From the morning watch even until night. Let Israel hope in the Lord. For with the Lord there is mercy; and with Him plentiful Redemption. And He will redeem Israel from all his iniquities.
Eternal rest give unto them, O Lord! And let perpetual light shine upon them. May they rest in peace. Amen.

Evening Prayer for the Poor Souls:

V. Lord, hear my prayer.
R. And let my cry come unto Thee.
Bless, O my God! the repose I am about to take, that, renewing my strength, I may be better enabled to serve Thee. Pour down Thy blessings, O Lord! on my parents, relations, friends, and enemies. Protect the Pope, our Bishop, and all the Pastors of Thy holy Church. Assist the poor and the afflicted, and those who are now in their last agony. Look with an eye of pity on the suffering souls in purgatory, particularly

_____

_____

_____

put an end to their torments and lead them forth into everlasting joy.

Eternal rest grant unto them and let perpetual light shine upon them. Amen.

DATE: _____

Pray today for the souls of all Jewish people who have died.

Morning Prayer for the Poor Souls:

Out of the depths I have cried to Thee O Lord! Lord, hear my voice. Let Thine ears be attentive to the voice of my supplication.
If Thou, O Lord, wilt mark iniquities, Lord, who shall stand it?
For with Thee there is mercy: and by reason of Thy law I have waited on Thee, O Lord! My soul hath relied on His word: my soul hath hoped in the Lord. From the morning watch even until night. Let Israel hope in the Lord. For with the Lord there is mercy; and with Him plentiful Redemption. And He will redeem Israel from all his iniquities.
Eternal rest give unto them, O Lord! And let perpetual light shine upon them. May they rest in peace. Amen.

Evening Prayer for the Poor Souls:

V. Lord, hear my prayer.
R. And let my cry come unto Thee.
Bless, O my God! the repose I am about to take, that, renewing my strength, I may be better enabled to serve Thee. Pour down Thy blessings, O Lord! on my parents, relations, friends, and enemies. Protect the Pope, our Bishop, and all the Pastors of Thy holy Church. Assist the poor and the afflicted, and those who are now in their last agony. Look with an eye of pity on the suffering souls in purgatory, particularly

_____

_____

_____

put an end to their torments and lead them forth into everlasting joy.

Eternal rest grant unto them and let perpetual light shine upon them. Amen.

DATE: _____

Today, pray for the souls of persecutors of Christians who have died.

Morning Prayer for the Poor Souls:

Out of the depths I have cried to Thee O Lord! Lord, hear my voice. Let Thine ears be attentive to the voice of my supplication.
If Thou, O Lord, wilt mark iniquities, Lord, who shall stand it?
For with Thee there is mercy: and by reason of Thy law I have waited on Thee, O Lord! My soul hath relied on His word: my soul hath hoped in the Lord. From the morning watch even until night. Let Israel hope in the Lord. For with the Lord there is mercy; and with Him plentiful Redemption. And He will redeem Israel from all his iniquities.
Eternal rest give unto them, O Lord! And let perpetual light shine upon them. May they rest in peace. Amen.

Evening Prayer for the Poor Souls:

V. Lord, hear my prayer.
R. And let my cry come unto Thee.
Bless, O my God! the repose I am about to take, that, renewing my strength, I may be better enabled to serve Thee. Pour down Thy blessings, O Lord! on my parents, relations, friends, and enemies. Protect the Pope, our Bishop, and all the Pastors of Thy holy Church. Assist the poor and the afflicted, and those who are now in their last agony. Look with an eye of pity on the suffering souls in purgatory, particularly

_____
_____
_____

put an end to their torments and lead them forth into everlasting joy.

Eternal rest grant unto them and let perpetual light shine upon them. Amen.

DATE: _____

Light a blessed candle today in remembrance of the Holy Souls.

Morning Prayer for the Poor Souls:

Out of the depths I have cried to Thee O Lord! Lord, hear my voice. Let Thine ears be attentive to the voice of my supplication.
If Thou, O Lord, wilt mark iniquities, Lord, who shall stand it?
For with Thee there is mercy: and by reason of Thy law I have waited on Thee, O Lord! My soul hath relied on His word: my soul hath hoped in the Lord. From the morning watch even until night. Let Israel hope in the Lord. For with the Lord there is mercy; and with Him plentiful Redemption. And He will redeem Israel from all his iniquities.
Eternal rest give unto them, O Lord! And let perpetual light shine upon them. May they rest in peace. Amen.

Evening Prayer for the Poor Souls:

V. Lord, hear my prayer.
R. And let my cry come unto Thee.
Bless, O my God! the repose I am about to take, that, renewing my strength, I may be better enabled to serve Thee. Pour down Thy blessings, O Lord! on my parents, relations, friends, and enemies. Protect the Pope, our Bishop, and all the Pastors of Thy holy Church. Assist the poor and the afflicted, and those who are now in their last agony. Look with an eye of pity on the suffering souls in purgatory, particularly

_____

_____

_____

put an end to their torments and lead them forth into everlasting joy.

Eternal rest grant unto them and let perpetual light shine upon them. Amen.

DATE: _____

Begin a Novena today for the benefit of the Poor Souls. St. Alphonsus Liguori wrote a powerful one just for the Holy Souls, which may be found online, but any Novena will be appreciated.

Morning Prayer for the Poor Souls:

Out of the depths I have cried to Thee O Lord! Lord, hear my voice. Let Thine ears be attentive to the voice of my supplication.
If Thou, O Lord, wilt mark iniquities, Lord, who shall stand it?
For with Thee there is mercy: and by reason of Thy law I have waited on Thee, O Lord! My soul hath relied on His word: my soul hath hoped in the Lord. From the morning watch even until night. Let Israel hope in the Lord. For with the Lord there is mercy; and with Him plentiful Redemption. And He will redeem Israel from all his iniquities.
Eternal rest give unto them, O Lord! And let perpetual light shine upon them. May they rest in peace. Amen.

Evening Prayer for the Poor Souls:

V. Lord, hear my prayer.
R. And let my cry come unto Thee.
Bless, O my God! the repose I am about to take, that, renewing my strength, I may be better enabled to serve Thee. Pour down Thy blessings, O Lord! on my parents, relations, friends, and enemies. Protect the Pope, our Bishop, and all the Pastors of Thy holy Church. Assist the poor and the afflicted, and those who are now in their last agony. Look with an eye of pity on the suffering souls in purgatory, particularly

_____
_____

_____

put an end to their torments and lead them forth into everlasting joy.

Eternal rest grant unto them, and let perpetual light shine upon them. Amen.

DATE: _____

Give alms to the poor today to benefit the souls in Purgatory. We are told that giving alms is of great benefit to suffering souls.

Morning Prayer for the Poor Souls:

Out of the depths I have cried to Thee O Lord! Lord, hear my voice. Let Thine ears be attentive to the voice of my supplication.
If Thou, O Lord, wilt mark iniquities, Lord, who shall stand it?
For with Thee there is mercy: and by reason of Thy law I have waited on Thee, O Lord! My soul hath relied on His word: my soul hath hoped in the Lord. From the morning watch even until night. Let Israel hope in the Lord. For with the Lord there is mercy; and with Him plentiful Redemption. And He will redeem Israel from all his iniquities.
Eternal rest give unto them, O Lord! And let perpetual light shine upon them. May they rest in peace. Amen.

Evening Prayer for the Poor Souls:

V. Lord, hear my prayer.
R. And let my cry come unto Thee.
Bless, O my God! the repose I am about to take, that, renewing my strength, I may be better enabled to serve Thee. Pour down Thy blessings, O Lord! on my parents, relations, friends, and enemies. Protect the Pope, our Bishop, and all the Pastors of Thy holy Church. Assist the poor and the afflicted, and those who are now in their last agony. Look with an eye of pity on the suffering souls in purgatory, particularly

_____

_____

_____

put an end to their torments and lead them forth into everlasting joy.

Eternal rest grant unto them, and let perpetual light shine upon them. Amen.

DATE: _____

Read aloud today from the Acts of the Apostles to comfort the Holy Souls. The Good News of Jesus' salvation is of great relief to their suffering.

Morning Prayer for the Poor Souls:

Out of the depths I have cried to Thee O Lord! Lord, hear my voice. Let Thine ears be attentive to the voice of my supplication.
If Thou, O Lord, wilt mark iniquities, Lord, who shall stand it?
For with Thee there is mercy: and by reason of Thy law I have waited on Thee, O Lord! My soul hath relied on His word: my soul hath hoped in the Lord. From the morning watch even until night. Let Israel hope in the Lord. For with the Lord there is mercy; and with Him plentiful Redemption. And He will redeem Israel from all his iniquities.
Eternal rest give unto them, O Lord! And let perpetual light shine upon them. May they rest in peace. Amen.

Evening Prayer for the Poor Souls:

V. Lord, hear my prayer.
R. And let my cry come unto Thee.
Bless, O my God! the repose I am about to take, that, renewing my strength, I may be better enabled to serve Thee. Pour down Thy blessings, O Lord! on my parents, relations, friends, and enemies. Protect the Pope, our Bishop, and all the Pastors of Thy holy Church. Assist the poor and the afflicted, and those who are now in their last agony. Look with an eye of pity on the suffering souls in purgatory, particularly

_____
_____

_____

put an end to their torments and lead them forth into everlasting joy.

Eternal rest grant unto them and let perpetual light shine upon them. Amen.

DATE: _____

Today, ask the saints known as intercessors for the dead to pray with you for their release, including St. Nicholas of Tolentino, St. Gertrude the Great, St. Catherine of Genoa, St. Padre Pio, St. Philip Neri, St. John Macías, St. Faustina Kowalska, St. Joseph and, of course, the Blessed Mother.

Morning Prayer for the Poor Souls:

Out of the depths I have cried to Thee O Lord! Lord, hear my voice. Let Thine ears be attentive to the voice of my supplication.
If Thou, O Lord, wilt mark iniquities, Lord, who shall stand it?
For with Thee there is mercy: and by reason of Thy law I have waited on Thee, O Lord! My soul hath relied on His word: my soul hath hoped in the Lord. From the morning watch even until night. Let Israel hope in the Lord. For with the Lord there is mercy; and with Him plentiful Redemption. And He will redeem Israel from all his iniquities.
Eternal rest give unto them, O Lord! And let perpetual light shine upon them. May they rest in peace. Amen.

Evening Prayer for the Poor Souls:

V. Lord, hear my prayer.
R. And let my cry come unto Thee.
Bless, O my God! the repose I am about to take, that, renewing my strength, I may be better enabled to serve Thee. Pour down Thy blessings, O Lord! on my parents, relations, friends, and enemies. Protect the Pope, our Bishop, and all the Pastors of Thy holy Church. Assist the poor and the afflicted, and those who are now in their last agony. Look with an eye of pity on the suffering souls in purgatory, particularly

_____
_____
_____

put an end to their torments and lead them forth into everlasting joy.

Eternal rest grant unto them and let perpetual light shine upon them. Amen.

DATE: _____

Today, have a Mass said for the soul of a family member or friend who has passed away. This can be through your own parish or through an order or national shrine via their website.

Morning Prayer for the Poor Souls:

Out of the depths I have cried to Thee O Lord! Lord, hear my voice. Let Thine ears be attentive to the voice of my supplication.
If Thou, O Lord, wilt mark iniquities, Lord, who shall stand it?
For with Thee there is mercy: and by reason of Thy law I have waited on Thee, O Lord! My soul hath relied on His word: my soul hath hoped in the Lord. From the morning watch even until night. Let Israel hope in the Lord. For with the Lord there is mercy; and with Him plentiful Redemption. And He will redeem Israel from all his iniquities.
Eternal rest give unto them, O Lord! And let perpetual light shine upon them. May they rest in peace. Amen.

Evening Prayer for the Poor Souls:

V. Lord, hear my prayer.
R. And let my cry come unto Thee.
Bless, O my God! the repose I am about to take, that, renewing my strength, I may be better enabled to serve Thee. Pour down Thy blessings, O Lord! on my parents, relations, friends, and enemies. Protect the Pope, our Bishop, and all the Pastors of Thy holy Church. Assist the poor and the afflicted, and those who are now in their last agony. Look with an eye of pity on the suffering souls in purgatory, particularly

_____
_____
_____

put an end to their torments and lead them forth into everlasting joy.

Eternal rest grant unto them, and let perpetual light shine upon them. Amen.

DATE:
_____

Pray the Rosary today for the release of souls from Purgatory. Mystic saints have told us that the Blessed Mother herself comes to Purgatory to bring souls with her back to Heaven.

Morning Prayer for the Poor Souls:

Out of the depths I have cried to Thee O Lord! Lord, hear my voice. Let Thine ears be attentive to the voice of my supplication.
If Thou, O Lord, wilt mark iniquities, Lord, who shall stand it?
For with Thee there is mercy: and by reason of Thy law I have waited on Thee, O Lord! My soul hath relied on His word: my soul hath hoped in the Lord. From the morning watch even until night. Let Israel hope in the Lord. For with the Lord there is mercy; and with Him plentiful Redemption. And He will redeem Israel from all his iniquities.
Eternal rest give unto them, O Lord! And let perpetual light shine upon them. May they rest in peace. Amen.

Evening Prayer for the Poor Souls:

V. Lord, hear my prayer.
R. And let my cry come unto Thee.
Bless, O my God! the repose I am about to take, that, renewing my strength, I may be better enabled to serve Thee. Pour down Thy blessings, O Lord! on my parents, relations, friends, and enemies. Protect the Pope, our Bishop, and all the Pastors of Thy holy Church. Assist the poor and the afflicted, and those who are now in their last agony. Look with an eye of pity on the suffering souls in purgatory, particularly

_____
_____
_____

put an end to their torments and lead them forth into everlasting joy.

Eternal rest grant unto them, and let perpetual light shine upon them. Amen.

DATE:

_____

Today, ask the Blessed Mother to apply your prayers and works to a poor soul who has no one to pray for them.

Morning Prayer for the Poor Souls:

Out of the depths I have cried to Thee O Lord! Lord, hear my voice. Let Thine ears be attentive to the voice of my supplication.
If Thou, O Lord, wilt mark iniquities, Lord, who shall stand it?
For with Thee there is mercy: and by reason of Thy law I have waited on Thee, O Lord! My soul hath relied on His word: my soul hath hoped in the Lord. From the morning watch even until night. Let Israel hope in the Lord. For with the Lord there is mercy; and with Him plentiful Redemption. And He will redeem Israel from all his iniquities.
Eternal rest give unto them, O Lord! And let perpetual light shine upon them. May they rest in peace. Amen.

Evening Prayer for the Poor Souls:

V. Lord, hear my prayer.
R. And let my cry come unto Thee.
Bless, O my God! the repose I am about to take, that, renewing my strength, I may be better enabled to serve Thee. Pour down Thy blessings, O Lord! on my parents, relations, friends, and enemies. Protect the Pope, our Bishop, and all the Pastors of Thy holy Church. Assist the poor and the afflicted, and those who are now in their last agony. Look with an eye of pity on the suffering souls in purgatory, particularly

_____
_____

_____

put an end to their torments and lead them forth into everlasting joy.

Eternal rest grant unto them, and let perpetual light shine upon them. Amen.

DATE:

_____

We all have a spiritual or physical affliction or burden that we suffer with daily. Today, dedicate your ailment-related suffering to the Poor souls.

Morning Prayer for the Poor Souls:

Out of the depths I have cried to Thee O Lord! Lord, hear my voice. Let Thine ears be attentive to the voice of my supplication.
If Thou, O Lord, wilt mark iniquities, Lord, who shall stand it?
For with Thee there is mercy: and by reason of Thy law I have waited on Thee, O Lord! My soul hath relied on His word: my soul hath hoped in the Lord. From the morning watch even until night. Let Israel hope in the Lord. For with the Lord there is mercy; and with Him plentiful Redemption. And He will redeem Israel from all his iniquities.
Eternal rest give unto them, O Lord! And let perpetual light shine upon them. May they rest in peace. Amen.

Evening Prayer for the Poor Souls:

V. Lord, hear my prayer.
R. And let my cry come unto Thee.
Bless, O my God! the repose I am about to take, that, renewing my strength, I may be better enabled to serve Thee. Pour down Thy blessings, O Lord! on my parents, relations, friends, and enemies. Protect the Pope, our Bishop, and all the Pastors of Thy holy Church. Assist the poor and the afflicted, and those who are now in their last agony. Look with an eye of pity on the suffering souls in purgatory, particularly

_____

_____

_____

put an end to their torments and lead them forth into everlasting joy.

Eternal rest grant unto them, and let perpetual light shine upon them. Amen.

DATE:

_____

Today, visit or call someone elderly or alone and offer your work of mercy for the souls in Purgatory.

Morning Prayer for the Poor Souls:

Out of the depths I have cried to Thee O Lord! Lord, hear my voice. Let Thine ears be attentive to the voice of my supplication.
If Thou, O Lord, wilt mark iniquities, Lord, who shall stand it?
For with Thee there is mercy: and by reason of Thy law I have waited on Thee, O Lord! My soul hath relied on His word: my soul hath hoped in the Lord. From the morning watch even until night. Let Israel hope in the Lord. For with the Lord there is mercy; and with Him plentiful Redemption. And He will redeem Israel from all his iniquities.
Eternal rest give unto them, O Lord! And let perpetual light shine upon them. May they rest in peace. Amen.

Evening Prayer for the Poor Souls:

V. Lord, hear my prayer.
R. And let my cry come unto Thee.
Bless, O my God! the repose I am about to take, that, renewing my strength, I may be better enabled to serve Thee. Pour down Thy blessings, O Lord! on my parents, relations, friends, and enemies. Protect the Pope, our Bishop, and all the Pastors of Thy holy Church. Assist the poor and the afflicted, and those who are now in their last agony. Look with an eye of pity on the suffering souls in purgatory, particularly

_____
_____
_____

put an end to their torments and lead them forth into everlasting joy.

Eternal rest grant unto them, and let perpetual light shine upon them. Amen.

DATE:
_____

During the course of the day today, pray for those you meet and strangers you see on street, asking God to apply your prayers for them to their future time in Purgatory.

Morning Prayer for the Poor Souls:

Out of the depths I have cried to Thee O Lord! Lord, hear my voice. Let Thine ears be attentive to the voice of my supplication.
If Thou, O Lord, wilt mark iniquities, Lord, who shall stand it?
For with Thee there is mercy: and by reason of Thy law I have waited on Thee, O Lord! My soul hath relied on His word: my soul hath hoped in the Lord. From the morning watch even until night. Let Israel hope in the Lord.
For with the Lord there is mercy; and with Him plentiful Redemption. And He will redeem Israel from all his iniquities.
Eternal rest give unto them, O Lord! And let perpetual light shine upon them. May they rest in peace. Amen.

Evening Prayer for the Poor Souls:

V. Lord, hear my prayer.
R. And let my cry come unto Thee.
Bless, O my God! the repose I am about to take, that, renewing my strength, I may be better enabled to serve Thee. Pour down Thy blessings, O Lord! on my parents, relations, friends, and enemies. Protect the Pope, our Bishop, and all the Pastors of Thy holy Church. Assist the poor and the afflicted, and those who are now in their last agony. Look with an eye of pity on the suffering souls in purgatory, particularly

_____
_____

_____

put an end to their torments and lead them forth into everlasting joy.

Eternal rest grant unto them, and let perpetual light shine upon them. Amen.

DATE: _____

Today, ask the Blessed Mother to use your prayers for someone in Purgatory with no one to pray for them.

Morning Prayer for the Poor Souls:

Out of the depths I have cried to Thee O Lord! Lord, hear my voice. Let Thine ears be attentive to the voice of my supplication.
If Thou, O Lord, wilt mark iniquities, Lord, who shall stand it?
For with Thee there is mercy: and by reason of Thy law I have waited on Thee, O Lord! My soul hath relied on His word: my soul hath hoped in the Lord. From the morning watch even until night. Let Israel hope in the Lord. For with the Lord there is mercy; and with Him plentiful Redemption. And He will redeem Israel from all his iniquities.
Eternal rest give unto them, O Lord! And let perpetual light shine upon them. May they rest in peace. Amen.

Evening Prayer for the Poor Souls:

V. Lord, hear my prayer.
R. And let my cry come unto Thee.
Bless, O my God! the repose I am about to take, that, renewing my strength, I may be better enabled to serve Thee. Pour down Thy blessings, O Lord! on my parents, relations, friends, and enemies. Protect the Pope, our Bishop, and all the Pastors of Thy holy Church. Assist the poor and the afflicted, and those who are now in their last agony. Look with an eye of pity on the suffering souls in purgatory, particularly

_____

_____

_____

put an end to their torments and lead them forth into everlasting joy.

Eternal rest grant unto them, and let perpetual light shine upon them. Amen.

DATE:
_____

Today, sprinkle holy water on the carpet of your home or outside your house as a comfort to the Poor Souls.

Morning Prayer for the Poor Souls:

Out of the depths I have cried to Thee O Lord! Lord, hear my voice. Let Thine ears be attentive to the voice of my supplication.
If Thou, O Lord, wilt mark iniquities, Lord, who shall stand it?
For with Thee there is mercy: and by reason of Thy law I have waited on Thee, O Lord! My soul hath relied on His word: my soul hath hoped in the Lord. From the morning watch even until night. Let Israel hope in the Lord. For with the Lord there is mercy; and with Him plentiful Redemption. And He will redeem Israel from all his iniquities.
Eternal rest give unto them, O Lord! And let perpetual light shine upon them. May they rest in peace. Amen.

Evening Prayer for the Poor Souls:

V. Lord, hear my prayer.
R. And let my cry come unto Thee.
Bless, O my God! the repose I am about to take, that, renewing my strength, I may be better enabled to serve Thee. Pour down Thy blessings, O Lord! on my parents, relations, friends, and enemies. Protect the Pope, our Bishop, and all the Pastors of Thy holy Church. Assist the poor and the afflicted, and those who are now in their last agony. Look with an eye of pity on the suffering souls in purgatory, particularly

_____
_____
_____

put an end to their torments and lead them forth into everlasting joy.

Eternal rest grant unto them, and let perpetual light shine upon them. Amen.

DATE:

_____

Today, visit a church if you are able, and pray for the souls who are spending their Purgatorial time there. Catholic mystics have told us that God allows many souls to do so. If you cannot visit a church, think of a local church and pray for any souls who might be there.

Morning Prayer for the Poor Souls:

Out of the depths I have cried to Thee O Lord! Lord, hear my voice. Let Thine ears be attentive to the voice of my supplication.
If Thou, O Lord, wilt mark iniquities, Lord, who shall stand it?
For with Thee there is mercy: and by reason of Thy law I have waited on Thee, O Lord! My soul hath relied on His word: my soul hath hoped in the Lord. From the morning watch even until night. Let Israel hope in the Lord. For with the Lord there is mercy; and with Him plentiful Redemption. And He will redeem Israel from all his iniquities.
Eternal rest give unto them, O Lord! And let perpetual light shine upon them. May they rest in peace. Amen.

Evening Prayer for the Poor Souls:

V. Lord, hear my prayer.
R. And let my cry come unto Thee.
Bless, O my God! the repose I am about to take, that, renewing my strength, I may be better enabled to serve Thee. Pour down Thy blessings, O Lord! on my parents, relations, friends, and enemies. Protect the Pope, our Bishop, and all the Pastors of Thy holy Church. Assist the poor and the afflicted, and those who are now in their last agony. Look with an eye of pity on the suffering souls in purgatory, particularly

_____

_____

put an end to their torments and lead them forth into everlasting joy.

Eternal rest grant unto them, and let perpetual light shine upon them. Amen.

DATE:
_____

Today, visit someone who is sick if you are able, and offer up this work of mercy for the Holy Souls. If you cannot, pray for those in your local hospital or nursing home.

Morning Prayer for the Poor Souls:

Out of the depths I have cried to Thee O Lord! Lord, hear my voice. Let Thine ears be attentive to the voice of my supplication.
If Thou, O Lord, wilt mark iniquities, Lord, who shall stand it?
For with Thee there is mercy: and by reason of Thy law I have waited on Thee, O Lord! My soul hath relied on His word: my soul hath hoped in the Lord. From the morning watch even until night. Let Israel hope in the Lord. For with the Lord there is mercy; and with Him plentiful Redemption. And He will redeem Israel from all his iniquities.
Eternal rest give unto them, O Lord! And let perpetual light shine upon them. May they rest in peace. Amen.

Evening Prayer for the Poor Souls:

V. Lord, hear my prayer.
R. And let my cry come unto Thee.
Bless, O my God! the repose I am about to take, that, renewing my strength, I may be better enabled to serve Thee. Pour down Thy blessings, O Lord! on my parents, relations, friends, and enemies. Protect the Pope, our Bishop, and all the Pastors of Thy holy Church. Assist the poor and the afflicted, and those who are now in their last agony. Look with an eye of pity on the suffering souls in purgatory, particularly

_____
_____
_____

put an end to their torments and lead them forth into everlasting joy.

Eternal rest grant unto them, and let perpetual light shine upon them. Amen.

DATE:

_____

Today pray for the souls of all the atheists who have died.

Morning Prayer for the Poor Souls:

Out of the depths I have cried to Thee O Lord! Lord, hear my voice. Let Thine ears be attentive to the voice of my supplication.
If Thou, O Lord, wilt mark iniquities, Lord, who shall stand it?
For with Thee there is mercy: and by reason of Thy law I have waited on Thee, O Lord! My soul hath relied on His word: my soul hath hoped in the Lord. From the morning watch even until night. Let Israel hope in the Lord. For with the Lord there is mercy; and with Him plentiful Redemption. And He will redeem Israel from all his iniquities.
Eternal rest give unto them, O Lord! And let perpetual light shine upon them. May they rest in peace. Amen.

Evening Prayer for the Poor Souls:

V. Lord, hear my prayer.
R. And let my cry come unto Thee.
Bless, O my God! the repose I am about to take, that, renewing my strength, I may be better enabled to serve Thee. Pour down Thy blessings, O Lord! on my parents, relations, friends, and enemies. Protect the Pope, our Bishop, and all the Pastors of Thy holy Church. Assist the poor and the afflicted, and those who are now in their last agony. Look with an eye of pity on the suffering souls in purgatory, particularly

_____

_____

_____

put an end to their torments and lead them forth into everlasting joy.

Eternal rest grant unto them, and let perpetual light shine upon them. Amen.

DATE:
_____

Today, read the obituaries in your local newspaper and pray for the souls who have died in the past several days.

Morning Prayer for the Poor Souls:

Out of the depths I have cried to Thee O Lord! Lord, hear my voice. Let Thine ears be attentive to the voice of my supplication.
If Thou, O Lord, wilt mark iniquities, Lord, who shall stand it?
For with Thee there is mercy: and by reason of Thy law I have waited on Thee, O Lord! My soul hath relied on His word: my soul hath hoped in the Lord. From the morning watch even until night. Let Israel hope in the Lord. For with the Lord there is mercy; and with Him plentiful Redemption. And He will redeem Israel from all his iniquities.
Eternal rest give unto them, O Lord! And let perpetual light shine upon them. May they rest in peace. Amen.

Evening Prayer for the Poor Souls:

V. Lord, hear my prayer.
R. And let my cry come unto Thee.
Bless, O my God! the repose I am about to take, that, renewing my strength, I may be better enabled to serve Thee. Pour down Thy blessings, O Lord! on my parents, relations, friends, and enemies. Protect the Pope, our Bishop, and all the Pastors of Thy holy Church. Assist the poor and the afflicted, and those who are now in their last agony. Look with an eye of pity on the suffering souls in purgatory, particularly

_____
_____
_____

put an end to their torments and lead them forth into everlasting joy.

Eternal rest grant unto them, and let perpetual light shine upon them. Amen.

DATE:
_____

Spend some time in Eucharistic Adoration today for the Poor Souls. If you cannot travel to a church physically, watch live Adoration on EWTN, YouTube or Facebook.

Morning Prayer for the Poor Souls:

Out of the depths I have cried to Thee O Lord! Lord, hear my voice. Let Thine ears be attentive to the voice of my supplication.
If Thou, O Lord, wilt mark iniquities, Lord, who shall stand it?
For with Thee there is mercy: and by reason of Thy law I have waited on Thee, O Lord! My soul hath relied on His word: my soul hath hoped in the Lord. From the morning watch even until night. Let Israel hope in the Lord. For with the Lord there is mercy; and with Him plentiful Redemption. And He will redeem Israel from all his iniquities.
Eternal rest give unto them, O Lord! And let perpetual light shine upon them. May they rest in peace. Amen.

Evening Prayer for the Poor Souls:

V. Lord, hear my prayer.
R. And let my cry come unto Thee.
Bless, O my God! the repose I am about to take, that, renewing my strength, I may be better enabled to serve Thee. Pour down Thy blessings, O Lord! on my parents, relations, friends, and enemies. Protect the Pope, our Bishop, and all the Pastors of Thy holy Church. Assist the poor and the afflicted, and those who are now in their last agony. Look with an eye of pity on the suffering souls in purgatory, particularly

_____
_____
_____

put an end to their torments and lead them forth into everlasting joy.

Eternal rest grant unto them, and let perpetual light shine upon them. Amen.

DATE:

_____

a drive today to a cemetery and pray for the souls of those interred there. If you cannot physically visit a cemetery, think of a cemetery in your city or town and pray for the souls of those buried there.

Morning Prayer for the Poor Souls:

Out of the depths I have cried to Thee O Lord! Lord, hear my voice. Let Thine ears be attentive to the voice of my supplication.
If Thou, O Lord, wilt mark iniquities, Lord, who shall stand it?
For with Thee there is mercy: and by reason of Thy law I have waited on Thee, O Lord! My soul hath relied on His word: my soul hath hoped in the Lord. From the morning watch even until night. Let Israel hope in the Lord. For with the Lord there is mercy; and with Him plentiful Redemption. And He will redeem Israel from all his iniquities.
Eternal rest give unto them, O Lord! And let perpetual light shine upon them. May they rest in peace. Amen.

Evening Prayer for the Poor Souls:

V. Lord, hear my prayer.
R. And let my cry come unto Thee.
Bless, O my God! the repose I am about to take, that, renewing my strength, I may be better enabled to serve Thee. Pour down Thy blessings, O Lord! on my parents, relations, friends, and enemies. Protect the Pope, our Bishop, and all the Pastors of Thy holy Church. Assist the poor and the afflicted, and those who are now in their last agony. Look with an eye of pity on the suffering souls in purgatory, particularly

_____

_____

put an end to their torments and lead them forth into everlasting joy.

Eternal rest grant unto them, and let perpetual light shine upon them. Amen.

DATE:

_____

Today, play some sacred music to comfort the Poor Souls. Mystic saints have told us that these small gestures provide great relief to their suffering.

Morning Prayer for the Poor Souls:

Out of the depths I have cried to Thee O Lord! Lord, hear my voice. Let Thine ears be attentive to the voice of my supplication.
If Thou, O Lord, wilt mark iniquities, Lord, who shall stand it?
For with Thee there is mercy: and by reason of Thy law I have waited on Thee, O Lord! My soul hath relied on His word: my soul hath hoped in the Lord. From the morning watch even until night. Let Israel hope in the Lord. For with the Lord there is mercy; and with Him plentiful Redemption. And He will redeem Israel from all his iniquities.
Eternal rest give unto them, O Lord! And let perpetual light shine upon them. May they rest in peace. Amen.

Evening Prayer for the Poor Souls:

V. Lord, hear my prayer.
R. And let my cry come unto Thee.
Bless, O my God! the repose I am about to take, that, renewing my strength, I may be better enabled to serve Thee. Pour down Thy blessings, O Lord! on my parents, relations, friends, and enemies. Protect the Pope, our Bishop, and all the Pastors of Thy holy Church. Assist the poor and the afflicted, and those who are now in their last agony. Look with an eye of pity on the suffering souls in purgatory, particularly

_____
_____

_____

put an end to their torments and lead them forth into everlasting joy.

Eternal rest grant unto them, and let perpetual light shine upon them. Amen.

DATE:

_____

Today, make reparation to the Sacred Heart of Jesus for the souls in Purgatory who offended His most precious Heart with the following: Adorable Heart of Jesus, glowing with love for us and inflamed with zeal for our salvation. O Heart that understands the misery to which our sins have brought us, infinitely rich in mercy to heal the wounds of our souls, behold me humbly kneeling before You to express the sorrow that fills my heart for the coldness and indifference with which I have so long returned the numberless benefits which You have bestowed upon me.

Morning Prayer for the Poor Souls:

Out of the depths I have cried to Thee O Lord! Lord, hear my voice. Let Thine ears be attentive to the voice of my supplication. If Thou, O Lord, wilt mark iniquities, Lord, who shall stand it? For with Thee there is mercy: and by reason of Thy law I have waited on Thee, O Lord! My soul hath relied on His word: my soul hath hoped in the Lord. From the morning watch even until night. Let Israel hope in the Lord. For with the Lord there is mercy; and with Him plentiful Redemption. And He will redeem Israel from all his iniquities. Eternal rest give unto them, O Lord! And let perpetual light shine upon them. May they rest in peace. Amen.

Evening Prayer for the Poor Souls:

V. Lord, hear my prayer.
R. And let my cry come unto Thee.
Bless, O my God! the repose I am about to take, that, renewing my strength, I may be better enabled to serve Thee. Pour down Thy blessings, O Lord! on my parents, relations, friends, and enemies. Protect the Pope, our Bishop, and all the Pastors of Thy holy Church. Assist the poor and the afflicted, and those who are now in their last agony. Look with an eye of pity on the suffering souls in purgatory, particularly

_____

put an end to their torments and lead them forth into everlasting joy.

Eternal rest grant unto them, and let perpetual light shine upon them. Amen.

DATE:
_____

Start a Mass Collection jar or envelope today for the Holy Souls. Add money to it as you are able, and when you have enough for a donation, have a Mass said for a soul in Purgatory.

Morning Prayer for the Poor Souls:

Out of the depths I have cried to Thee O Lord! Lord, hear my voice. Let Thine ears be attentive to the voice of my supplication.
If Thou, O Lord, wilt mark iniquities, Lord, who shall stand it?
For with Thee there is mercy: and by reason of Thy law I have waited on Thee, O Lord! My soul hath relied on His word: my soul hath hoped in the Lord. From the morning watch even until night. Let Israel hope in the Lord. For with the Lord there is mercy; and with Him plentiful Redemption. And He will redeem Israel from all his iniquities.
Eternal rest give unto them, O Lord! And let perpetual light shine upon them. May they rest in peace. Amen.

Evening Prayer for the Poor Souls:

V. Lord, hear my prayer.
R. And let my cry come unto Thee.
Bless, O my God! the repose I am about to take, that, renewing my strength, I may be better enabled to serve Thee. Pour down Thy blessings, O Lord! on my parents, relations, friends, and enemies. Protect the Pope, our Bishop, and all the Pastors of Thy holy Church. Assist the poor and the afflicted, and those who are now in their last agony. Look with an eye of pity on the suffering souls in purgatory, particularly

_____
_____
_____

put an end to their torments and lead them forth into everlasting joy.

Eternal rest grant unto them, and let perpetual light shine upon them. Amen.

DATE:
_____

Go without a meal or snack today if possible, for the benefit of the Holy Souls. If you are in ill health, give up a special treat instead.

Morning Prayer for the Poor Souls:

Out of the depths I have cried to Thee O Lord! Lord, hear my voice. Let Thine ears be attentive to the voice of my supplication.
If Thou, O Lord, wilt mark iniquities, Lord, who shall stand it?
For with Thee there is mercy: and by reason of Thy law I have waited on Thee, O Lord! My soul hath relied on His word: my soul hath hoped in the Lord. From the morning watch even until night. Let Israel hope in the Lord. For with the Lord there is mercy; and with Him plentiful Redemption. And He will redeem Israel from all his iniquities.
Eternal rest give unto them, O Lord! And let perpetual light shine upon them. May they rest in peace. Amen.

Evening Prayer for the Poor Souls:

V. Lord, hear my prayer.
R. And let my cry come unto Thee.
Bless, O my God! the repose I am about to take, that, renewing my strength, I may be better enabled to serve Thee. Pour down Thy blessings, O Lord! on my parents, relations, friends, and enemies. Protect the Pope, our Bishop, and all the Pastors of Thy holy Church. Assist the poor and the afflicted, and those who are now in their last agony. Look with an eye of pity on the suffering souls in purgatory, particularly

_____
_____
_____

put an end to their torments and lead them forth into everlasting joy.

Eternal rest grant unto them, and let perpetual light shine upon them. Amen.

DATE:
_____

Today, say a Divine Mercy chaplet for the Poor Souls.

Morning Prayer for the Poor Souls:

Out of the depths I have cried to Thee O Lord! Lord, hear my voice. Let Thine ears be attentive to the voice of my supplication.
If Thou, O Lord, wilt mark iniquities, Lord, who shall stand it?
For with Thee there is mercy: and by reason of Thy law I have waited on Thee, O Lord! My soul hath relied on His word: my soul hath hoped in the Lord. From the morning watch even until night. Let Israel hope in the Lord. For with the Lord there is mercy; and with Him plentiful Redemption. And He will redeem Israel from all his iniquities.
Eternal rest give unto them, O Lord! And let perpetual light shine upon them. May they rest in peace. Amen.

Evening Prayer for the Poor Souls:

V. Lord, hear my prayer.
R. And let my cry come unto Thee.
Bless, O my God! the repose I am about to take, that, renewing my strength, I may be better enabled to serve Thee. Pour down Thy blessings, O Lord! on my parents, relations, friends, and enemies. Protect the Pope, our Bishop, and all the Pastors of Thy holy Church. Assist the poor and the afflicted, and those who are now in their last agony. Look with an eye of pity on the suffering souls in purgatory, particularly

_____

_____

_____

put an end to their torments and lead them forth into everlasting joy.

Eternal rest grant unto them, and let perpetual light shine upon them. Amen.

DATE: _____

Pray today for the souls of priests and religious in Purgatory.

Morning Prayer for the Poor Souls:

Out of the depths I have cried to Thee O Lord! Lord, hear my voice. Let Thine ears be attentive to the voice of my supplication.
If Thou, O Lord, wilt mark iniquities, Lord, who shall stand it?
For with Thee there is mercy: and by reason of Thy law I have waited on Thee, O Lord! My soul hath relied on His word: my soul hath hoped in the Lord. From the morning watch even until night. Let Israel hope in the Lord. For with the Lord there is mercy; and with Him plentiful Redemption. And He will redeem Israel from all his iniquities.
Eternal rest give unto them, O Lord! And let perpetual light shine upon them. May they rest in peace. Amen.

Evening Prayer for the Poor Souls:

V. Lord, hear my prayer.
R. And let my cry come unto Thee.
Bless, O my God! the repose I am about to take, that, renewing my strength, I may be better enabled to serve Thee. Pour down Thy blessings, O Lord! on my parents, relations, friends, and enemies. Protect the Pope, our Bishop, and all the Pastors of Thy holy Church. Assist the poor and the afflicted, and those who are now in their last agony. Look with an eye of pity on the suffering souls in purgatory, particularly

_____
_____
_____

put an end to their torments and lead them forth into everlasting joy.

Eternal rest grant unto them, and let perpetual light shine upon them. Amen.

DATE: _____

While you are going about your day today, remember your friends and colleagues who have passed away over the years, asking God to release them from Purgatory.

Morning Prayer for the Poor Souls:

Out of the depths I have cried to Thee O Lord! Lord, hear my voice. Let Thine ears be attentive to the voice of my supplication.
If Thou, O Lord, wilt mark iniquities, Lord, who shall stand it?
For with Thee there is mercy: and by reason of Thy law I have waited on Thee, O Lord! My soul hath relied on His word: my soul hath hoped in the Lord. From the morning watch even until night. Let Israel hope in the Lord. For with the Lord there is mercy; and with Him plentiful Redemption. And He will redeem Israel from all his iniquities.
Eternal rest give unto them, O Lord! And let perpetual light shine upon them. May they rest in peace. Amen.

Evening Prayer for the Poor Souls:

V. Lord, hear my prayer.
R. And let my cry come unto Thee.
Bless, O my God! the repose I am about to take, that, renewing my strength, I may be better enabled to serve Thee. Pour down Thy blessings, O Lord! on my parents, relations, friends, and enemies. Protect the Pope, our Bishop, and all the Pastors of Thy holy Church. Assist the poor and the afflicted, and those who are now in their last agony. Look with an eye of pity on the suffering souls in purgatory, particularly

put an end to their torments and lead them forth into everlasting joy.

Eternal rest grant unto them, and let perpetual light shine upon them. Amen.

DATE: _____

Pray today for the dead who heard the Gospel but rejected it. May they be spared Hell and be released from Purgatory to be with Jesus.

Morning Prayer for the Poor Souls:

Out of the depths I have cried to Thee O Lord! Lord, hear my voice. Let Thine ears be attentive to the voice of my supplication.
If Thou, O Lord, wilt mark iniquities, Lord, who shall stand it?
For with Thee there is mercy: and by reason of Thy law I have waited on Thee, O Lord! My soul hath relied on His word: my soul hath hoped in the Lord. From the morning watch even until night. Let Israel hope in the Lord. For with the Lord there is mercy; and with Him plentiful Redemption. And He will redeem Israel from all his iniquities.
Eternal rest give unto them, O Lord! And let perpetual light shine upon them. May they rest in peace. Amen.

Evening Prayer for the Poor Souls:

V. Lord, hear my prayer.
R. And let my cry come unto Thee.
Bless, O my God! the repose I am about to take, that, renewing my strength, I may be better enabled to serve Thee. Pour down Thy blessings, O Lord! on my parents, relations, friends, and enemies. Protect the Pope, our Bishop, and all the Pastors of Thy holy Church. Assist the poor and the afflicted, and those who are now in their last agony. Look with an eye of pity on the suffering souls in purgatory, particularly

_____

_____

_____

put an end to their torments and lead them forth into everlasting joy.

Eternal rest grant unto them, and let perpetual light shine upon them. Amen.

DATE: _____

Today, spend some time reading devotional literature aloud for the comfort of the Poor Souls.

Morning Prayer for the Poor Souls:

Out of the depths I have cried to Thee O Lord! Lord, hear my voice. Let Thine ears be attentive to the voice of my supplication.
If Thou, O Lord, wilt mark iniquities, Lord, who shall stand it?
For with Thee there is mercy: and by reason of Thy law I have waited on Thee, O Lord! My soul hath relied on His word: my soul hath hoped in the Lord. From the morning watch even until night. Let Israel hope in the Lord. For with the Lord there is mercy; and with Him plentiful Redemption. And He will redeem Israel from all his iniquities.
Eternal rest give unto them, O Lord! And let perpetual light shine upon them. May they rest in peace. Amen.

Evening Prayer for the Poor Souls:

V. Lord, hear my prayer.
R. And let my cry come unto Thee.
Bless, O my God! the repose I am about to take, that, renewing my strength, I may be better enabled to serve Thee. Pour down Thy blessings, O Lord! on my parents, relations, friends, and enemies. Protect the Pope, our Bishop, and all the Pastors of Thy holy Church. Assist the poor and the afflicted, and those who are now in their last agony. Look with an eye of pity on the suffering souls in purgatory, particularly

_____

_____

_____

put an end to their torments and lead them forth into everlasting joy.

Eternal rest grant unto them, and let perpetual light shine upon them. Amen.

DATE: _____

Today make the Stations of the Cross for the benefit of the Holy Souls in Purgatory.

Morning Prayer for the Poor Souls:

Out of the depths I have cried to Thee O Lord! Lord, hear my voice. Let Thine ears be attentive to the voice of my supplication.
If Thou, O Lord, wilt mark iniquities, Lord, who shall stand it?
For with Thee there is mercy: and by reason of Thy law I have waited on Thee, O Lord! My soul hath relied on His word: my soul hath hoped in the Lord. From the morning watch even until night. Let Israel hope in the Lord. For with the Lord there is mercy; and with Him plentiful Redemption. And He will redeem Israel from all his iniquities.
Eternal rest give unto them, O Lord! And let perpetual light shine upon them. May they rest in peace. Amen.

Evening Prayer for the Poor Souls:

V. Lord, hear my prayer.
R. And let my cry come unto Thee.
Bless, O my God! the repose I am about to take, that, renewing my strength, I may be better enabled to serve Thee. Pour down Thy blessings, O Lord! on my parents, relations, friends, and enemies. Protect the Pope, our Bishop, and all the Pastors of Thy holy Church. Assist the poor and the afflicted, and those who are now in their last agony. Look with an eye of pity on the suffering souls in purgatory, particularly

_____

_____

_____

put an end to their torments and lead them forth into everlasting joy.

Eternal rest grant unto them, and let perpetual light shine upon them. Amen.

DATE: _____

Pray today for the souls of all Jewish people who have died.

Morning Prayer for the Poor Souls:

Out of the depths I have cried to Thee O Lord! Lord, hear my voice. Let Thine ears be attentive to the voice of my supplication.
If Thou, O Lord, wilt mark iniquities, Lord, who shall stand it?
For with Thee there is mercy: and by reason of Thy law I have waited on Thee, O Lord! My soul hath relied on His word: my soul hath hoped in the Lord. From the morning watch even until night. Let Israel hope in the Lord. For with the Lord there is mercy; and with Him plentiful Redemption. And He will redeem Israel from all his iniquities.
Eternal rest give unto them, O Lord! And let perpetual light shine upon them. May they rest in peace. Amen.

Evening Prayer for the Poor Souls:

V. Lord, hear my prayer.
R. And let my cry come unto Thee.
Bless, O my God! the repose I am about to take, that, renewing my strength, I may be better enabled to serve Thee. Pour down Thy blessings, O Lord! on my parents, relations, friends, and enemies. Protect the Pope, our Bishop, and all the Pastors of Thy holy Church. Assist the poor and the afflicted, and those who are now in their last agony. Look with an eye of pity on the suffering souls in purgatory, particularly

_____
_____

_____

put an end to their torments and lead them forth into everlasting joy.

Eternal rest grant unto them, and let perpetual light shine upon them. Amen.

DATE: _____

Today, pray for the souls of persecutors of Christians who have died.

Morning Prayer for the Poor Souls:

Out of the depths I have cried to Thee O Lord! Lord, hear my voice. Let Thine ears be attentive to the voice of my supplication.
If Thou, O Lord, wilt mark iniquities, Lord, who shall stand it?
For with Thee there is mercy: and by reason of Thy law I have waited on Thee, O Lord! My soul hath relied on His word: my soul hath hoped in the Lord. From the morning watch even until night. Let Israel hope in the Lord. For with the Lord there is mercy; and with Him plentiful Redemption. And He will redeem Israel from all his iniquities.
Eternal rest give unto them, O Lord! And let perpetual light shine upon them. May they rest in peace. Amen.

Evening Prayer for the Poor Souls:

V. Lord, hear my prayer.
R. And let my cry come unto Thee.
Bless, O my God! the repose I am about to take, that, renewing my strength, I may be better enabled to serve Thee. Pour down Thy blessings, O Lord! on my parents, relations, friends, and enemies. Protect the Pope, our Bishop, and all the Pastors of Thy holy Church. Assist the poor and the afflicted, and those who are now in their last agony. Look with an eye of pity on the suffering souls in purgatory, particularly

_____

_____

_____

put an end to their torments and lead them forth into everlasting joy.

Eternal rest grant unto them, and let perpetual light shine upon them. Amen.

DATE: _____

Light a blessed candle today in remembrance of the Holy Souls.

Morning Prayer for the Poor Souls:

Out of the depths I have cried to Thee O Lord! Lord, hear my voice. Let Thine ears be attentive to the voice of my supplication.
If Thou, O Lord, wilt mark iniquities, Lord, who shall stand it?
For with Thee there is mercy: and by reason of Thy law I have waited on Thee, O Lord! My soul hath relied on His word: my soul hath hoped in the Lord. From the morning watch even until night. Let Israel hope in the Lord. For with the Lord there is mercy; and with Him plentiful Redemption. And He will redeem Israel from all his iniquities.
Eternal rest give unto them, O Lord! And let perpetual light shine upon them. May they rest in peace. Amen.

Evening Prayer for the Poor Souls:

V. Lord, hear my prayer.
R. And let my cry come unto Thee.
Bless, O my God! the repose I am about to take, that, renewing my strength, I may be better enabled to serve Thee. Pour down Thy blessings, O Lord! on my parents, relations, friends, and enemies. Protect the Pope, our Bishop, and all the Pastors of Thy holy Church. Assist the poor and the afflicted, and those who are now in their last agony. Look with an eye of pity on the suffering souls in purgatory, particularly

_____

_____

_____

put an end to their torments and lead them forth into everlasting joy.

Eternal rest grant unto them, and let perpetual light shine upon them. Amen.

DATE: _____

Begin a Novena today for the benefit of the Poor Souls. St. Alphonsus Liguori wrote a powerful one just for the Holy Souls, which may be found online, but any Novena will be appreciated.

Morning Prayer for the Poor Souls:

Out of the depths I have cried to Thee O Lord! Lord, hear my voice. Let Thine ears be attentive to the voice of my supplication.
If Thou, O Lord, wilt mark iniquities, Lord, who shall stand it?
For with Thee there is mercy: and by reason of Thy law I have waited on Thee, O Lord! My soul hath relied on His word: my soul hath hoped in the Lord. From the morning watch even until night. Let Israel hope in the Lord. For with the Lord there is mercy; and with Him plentiful Redemption. And He will redeem Israel from all his iniquities.
Eternal rest give unto them, O Lord! And let perpetual light shine upon them. May they rest in peace. Amen.

Evening Prayer for the Poor Souls:

V. Lord, hear my prayer.
R. And let my cry come unto Thee.
Bless, O my God! the repose I am about to take, that, renewing my strength, I may be better enabled to serve Thee. Pour down Thy blessings, O Lord! on my parents, relations, friends, and enemies. Protect the Pope, our Bishop, and all the Pastors of Thy holy Church. Assist the poor and the afflicted, and those who are now in their last agony. Look with an eye of pity on the suffering souls in purgatory, particularly

_____
_____

_____

put an end to their torments and lead them forth into everlasting joy.

Eternal rest grant unto them, and let perpetual light shine upon them. Amen.

DATE: _____

Give alms to the poor today to benefit the souls in Purgatory. We are told that giving alms is of great benefit to suffering souls.

Morning Prayer for the Poor Souls:

Out of the depths I have cried to Thee O Lord! Lord, hear my voice. Let Thine ears be attentive to the voice of my supplication.
If Thou, O Lord, wilt mark iniquities, Lord, who shall stand it?
For with Thee there is mercy: and by reason of Thy law I have waited on Thee, O Lord! My soul hath relied on His word: my soul hath hoped in the Lord. From the morning watch even until night. Let Israel hope in the Lord. For with the Lord there is mercy; and with Him plentiful Redemption. And He will redeem Israel from all his iniquities.
Eternal rest give unto them, O Lord! And let perpetual light shine upon them. May they rest in peace. Amen.

Evening Prayer for the Poor Souls:

V. Lord, hear my prayer.
R. And let my cry come unto Thee.
Bless, O my God! the repose I am about to take, that, renewing my strength, I may be better enabled to serve Thee. Pour down Thy blessings, O Lord! on my parents, relations, friends, and enemies. Protect the Pope, our Bishop, and all the Pastors of Thy holy Church. Assist the poor and the afflicted, and those who are now in their last agony. Look with an eye of pity on the suffering souls in purgatory, particularly

_____

_____

_____

put an end to their torments and lead them forth into everlasting joy.

Eternal rest grant unto them, and let perpetual light shine upon them. Amen.

DATE: _____

Read aloud today from the Acts of the Apostles to comfort the Holy Souls. The Good News of Jesus' salvation is of great relief to their suffering.

Morning Prayer for the Poor Souls:

Out of the depths I have cried to Thee O Lord! Lord, hear my voice. Let Thine ears be attentive to the voice of my supplication.
If Thou, O Lord, wilt mark iniquities, Lord, who shall stand it?
For with Thee there is mercy: and by reason of Thy law I have waited on Thee, O Lord! My soul hath relied on His word: my soul hath hoped in the Lord. From the morning watch even until night. Let Israel hope in the Lord. For with the Lord there is mercy; and with Him plentiful Redemption. And He will redeem Israel from all his iniquities.
Eternal rest give unto them, O Lord! And let perpetual light shine upon them. May they rest in peace. Amen.

Evening Prayer for the Poor Souls:

V. Lord, hear my prayer.
R. And let my cry come unto Thee.
Bless, O my God! the repose I am about to take, that, renewing my strength, I may be better enabled to serve Thee. Pour down Thy blessings, O Lord! on my parents, relations, friends, and enemies. Protect the Pope, our Bishop, and all the Pastors of Thy holy Church. Assist the poor and the afflicted, and those who are now in their last agony. Look with an eye of pity on the suffering souls in purgatory, particularly

_____

_____

_____

put an end to their torments and lead them forth into everlasting joy.

Eternal rest grant unto them, and let perpetual light shine upon them. Amen.

DATE: _____

Today, ask the saints known as intercessors for the dead to pray with you for their release, including St. Nicholas of Tolentino, St. Gertrude the Great, St. Catherine of Genoa, St. Padre Pio, St. Philip Neri, St. John Macías, St. Faustina Kowalska, St. Joseph and, of course, the Blessed Mother.

Morning Prayer for the Poor Souls:

Out of the depths I have cried to Thee O Lord! Lord, hear my voice. Let Thine ears be attentive to the voice of my supplication.
If Thou, O Lord, wilt mark iniquities, Lord, who shall stand it?
For with Thee there is mercy: and by reason of Thy law I have waited on Thee, O Lord! My soul hath relied on His word: my soul hath hoped in the Lord. From the morning watch even until night. Let Israel hope in the Lord. For with the Lord there is mercy; and with Him plentiful Redemption. And He will redeem Israel from all his iniquities.
Eternal rest give unto them, O Lord! And let perpetual light shine upon them. May they rest in peace. Amen.

Evening Prayer for the Poor Souls:

V. Lord, hear my prayer.
R. And let my cry come unto Thee.
Bless, O my God! the repose I am about to take, that, renewing my strength, I may be better enabled to serve Thee. Pour down Thy blessings, O Lord! on my parents, relations, friends, and enemies. Protect the Pope, our Bishop, and all the Pastors of Thy holy Church. Assist the poor and the afflicted, and those who are now in their last agony. Look with an eye of pity on the suffering souls in purgatory, particularly

_____

_____

_____

put an end to their torments and lead them forth into everlasting joy.

Eternal rest grant unto them, and let perpetual light shine upon them. Amen.

DATE: _____

Today, have a Mass said for the soul of a family member or friend who has passed away. This can be through your own parish or through an order or national shrine via their website.

Morning Prayer for the Poor Souls:

Out of the depths I have cried to Thee O Lord! Lord, hear my voice. Let Thine ears be attentive to the voice of my supplication.
If Thou, O Lord, wilt mark iniquities, Lord, who shall stand it?
For with Thee there is mercy: and by reason of Thy law I have waited on Thee, O Lord! My soul hath relied on His word: my soul hath hoped in the Lord. From the morning watch even until night. Let Israel hope in the Lord. For with the Lord there is mercy; and with Him plentiful Redemption. And He will redeem Israel from all his iniquities.
Eternal rest give unto them, O Lord! And let perpetual light shine upon them. May they rest in peace. Amen.

Evening Prayer for the Poor Souls:

V. Lord, hear my prayer.
R. And let my cry come unto Thee.
Bless, O my God! the repose I am about to take, that, renewing my strength, I may be better enabled to serve Thee. Pour down Thy blessings, O Lord! on my parents, relations, friends, and enemies. Protect the Pope, our Bishop, and all the Pastors of Thy holy Church. Assist the poor and the afflicted, and those who are now in their last agony. Look with an eye of pity on the suffering souls in purgatory, particularly

_____
_____

_____

put an end to their torments and lead them forth into everlasting joy.

Eternal rest grant unto them, and let perpetual light shine upon them. Amen.

DATE:

_____

Pray the Rosary today for the release of souls from Purgatory. Mystic saints have told us that the Blessed Mother herself comes to Purgatory to bring souls with her back to Heaven.

Morning Prayer for the Poor Souls:

Out of the depths I have cried to Thee O Lord! Lord, hear my voice. Let Thine ears be attentive to the voice of my supplication.
If Thou, O Lord, wilt mark iniquities, Lord, who shall stand it?
For with Thee there is mercy: and by reason of Thy law I have waited on Thee, O Lord! My soul hath relied on His word: my soul hath hoped in the Lord. From the morning watch even until night. Let Israel hope in the Lord. For with the Lord there is mercy; and with Him plentiful Redemption. And He will redeem Israel from all his iniquities.
Eternal rest give unto them, O Lord! And let perpetual light shine upon them. May they rest in peace. Amen.

Evening Prayer for the Poor Souls:

V. Lord, hear my prayer.
R. And let my cry come unto Thee.
Bless, O my God! the repose I am about to take, that, renewing my strength, I may be better enabled to serve Thee. Pour down Thy blessings, O Lord! on my parents, relations, friends, and enemies. Protect the Pope, our Bishop, and all the Pastors of Thy holy Church. Assist the poor and the afflicted, and those who are now in their last agony. Look with an eye of pity on the suffering souls in purgatory, particularly

_____
_____
_____

put an end to their torments and lead them forth into everlasting joy.

Eternal rest grant unto them, and let perpetual light shine upon them. Amen.

DATE:

_____

Today, ask the Blessed Mother to apply your prayers and works to a poor soul who has no one to pray for them.

Morning Prayer for the Poor Souls:

Out of the depths I have cried to Thee O Lord! Lord, hear my voice. Let Thine ears be attentive to the voice of my supplication.
If Thou, O Lord, wilt mark iniquities, Lord, who shall stand it?
For with Thee there is mercy: and by reason of Thy law I have waited on Thee, O Lord! My soul hath relied on His word: my soul hath hoped in the Lord. From the morning watch even until night. Let Israel hope in the Lord. For with the Lord there is mercy; and with Him plentiful Redemption. And He will redeem Israel from all his iniquities.
Eternal rest give unto them, O Lord! And let perpetual light shine upon them. May they rest in peace. Amen.

Evening Prayer for the Poor Souls:

V. Lord, hear my prayer.
R. And let my cry come unto Thee.
Bless, O my God! the repose I am about to take, that, renewing my strength, I may be better enabled to serve Thee. Pour down Thy blessings, O Lord! on my parents, relations, friends, and enemies. Protect the Pope, our Bishop, and all the Pastors of Thy holy Church. Assist the poor and the afflicted, and those who are now in their last agony. Look with an eye of pity on the suffering souls in purgatory, particularly

_____
_____
_____

put an end to their torments and lead them forth into everlasting joy.

Eternal rest grant unto them, and let perpetual light shine upon them. Amen.

DATE:

_____

We all have a spiritual or physical affliction or burden that we suffer with daily. Today, dedicate your ailment-related suffering to the Poor souls.

Morning Prayer for the Poor Souls:

Out of the depths I have cried to Thee O Lord! Lord, hear my voice. Let Thine ears be attentive to the voice of my supplication.
If Thou, O Lord, wilt mark iniquities, Lord, who shall stand it?
For with Thee there is mercy: and by reason of Thy law I have waited on Thee, O Lord! My soul hath relied on His word: my soul hath hoped in the Lord. From the morning watch even until night. Let Israel hope in the Lord. For with the Lord there is mercy; and with Him plentiful Redemption. And He will redeem Israel from all his iniquities.
Eternal rest give unto them, O Lord! And let perpetual light shine upon them. May they rest in peace. Amen.

Evening Prayer for the Poor Souls:

V. Lord, hear my prayer.
R. And let my cry come unto Thee.
Bless, O my God! the repose I am about to take, that, renewing my strength, I may be better enabled to serve Thee. Pour down Thy blessings, O Lord! on my parents, relations, friends, and enemies. Protect the Pope, our Bishop, and all the Pastors of Thy holy Church. Assist the poor and the afflicted, and those who are now in their last agony. Look with an eye of pity on the suffering souls in purgatory, particularly

_____

_____

_____

put an end to their torments and lead them forth into everlasting joy.

Eternal rest grant unto them, and let perpetual light shine upon them. Amen.

DATE:
_____

Today, visit or call someone elderly or alone and offer your work of mercy for the souls in Purgatory.

Morning Prayer for the Poor Souls:

Out of the depths I have cried to Thee O Lord! Lord, hear my voice. Let Thine ears be attentive to the voice of my supplication.
If Thou, O Lord, wilt mark iniquities, Lord, who shall stand it?
For with Thee there is mercy: and by reason of Thy law I have waited on Thee, O Lord! My soul hath relied on His word: my soul hath hoped in the Lord. From the morning watch even until night. Let Israel hope in the Lord. For with the Lord there is mercy; and with Him plentiful Redemption. And He will redeem Israel from all his iniquities.
Eternal rest give unto them, O Lord! And let perpetual light shine upon them. May they rest in peace. Amen.

Evening Prayer for the Poor Souls:

V. Lord, hear my prayer.
R. And let my cry come unto Thee.
Bless, O my God! the repose I am about to take, that, renewing my strength, I may be better enabled to serve Thee. Pour down Thy blessings, O Lord! on my parents, relations, friends, and enemies. Protect the Pope, our Bishop, and all the Pastors of Thy holy Church. Assist the poor and the afflicted, and those who are now in their last agony. Look with an eye of pity on the suffering souls in purgatory, particularly

_____

_____

_____

put an end to their torments and lead them forth into everlasting joy.

Eternal rest grant unto them, and let perpetual light shine upon them. Amen.

DATE:
_____

During the course of the day today, pray for those you meet and strangers you see on street, asking God to apply your prayers for them to their future time in Purgatory.

Morning Prayer for the Poor Souls:

Out of the depths I have cried to Thee O Lord! Lord, hear my voice. Let Thine ears be attentive to the voice of my supplication.
If Thou, O Lord, wilt mark iniquities, Lord, who shall stand it?
For with Thee there is mercy: and by reason of Thy law I have waited on Thee, O Lord! My soul hath relied on His word: my soul hath hoped in the Lord. From the morning watch even until night. Let Israel hope in the Lord. For with the Lord there is mercy; and with Him plentiful Redemption. And He will redeem Israel from all his iniquities.
Eternal rest give unto them, O Lord! And let perpetual light shine upon them. May they rest in peace. Amen.

Evening Prayer for the Poor Souls:

V. Lord, hear my prayer.
R. And let my cry come unto Thee.
Bless, O my God! the repose I am about to take, that, renewing my strength, I may be better enabled to serve Thee. Pour down Thy blessings, O Lord! on my parents, relations, friends, and enemies. Protect the Pope, our Bishop, and all the Pastors of Thy holy Church. Assist the poor and the afflicted, and those who are now in their last agony. Look with an eye of pity on the suffering souls in purgatory, particularly

_____
_____
_____

put an end to their torments and lead them forth into everlasting joy.

Eternal rest grant unto them, and let perpetual light shine upon them. Amen.

DATE:

_____

Today, ask the Blessed Mother to use your prayers for someone in Purgatory with no one to pray for them.

Morning Prayer for the Poor Souls:

Out of the depths I have cried to Thee O Lord! Lord, hear my voice. Let Thine ears be attentive to the voice of my supplication.
If Thou, O Lord, wilt mark iniquities, Lord, who shall stand it?
For with Thee there is mercy: and by reason of Thy law I have waited on Thee, O Lord! My soul hath relied on His word: my soul hath hoped in the Lord. From the morning watch even until night. Let Israel hope in the Lord. For with the Lord there is mercy; and with Him plentiful Redemption. And He will redeem Israel from all his iniquities.
Eternal rest give unto them, O Lord! And let perpetual light shine upon them. May they rest in peace. Amen.

Evening Prayer for the Poor Souls:

V. Lord, hear my prayer.
R. And let my cry come unto Thee.
Bless, O my God! the repose I am about to take, that, renewing my strength, I may be better enabled to serve Thee. Pour down Thy blessings, O Lord! on my parents, relations, friends, and enemies. Protect the Pope, our Bishop, and all the Pastors of Thy holy Church. Assist the poor and the afflicted, and those who are now in their last agony. Look with an eye of pity on the suffering souls in purgatory, particularly

_____

_____

_____

put an end to their torments and lead them forth into everlasting joy.

Eternal rest grant unto them, and let perpetual light shine upon them. Amen.

DATE:
_____

Today, sprinkle holy water on the carpet of your home or outside your house as a comfort to the Poor Souls.

Morning Prayer for the Poor Souls:

Out of the depths I have cried to Thee O Lord! Lord, hear my voice. Let Thine ears be attentive to the voice of my supplication.
If Thou, O Lord, wilt mark iniquities, Lord, who shall stand it?
For with Thee there is mercy: and by reason of Thy law I have waited on Thee, O Lord! My soul hath relied on His word: my soul hath hoped in the Lord. From the morning watch even until night. Let Israel hope in the Lord. For with the Lord there is mercy; and with Him plentiful Redemption. And He will redeem Israel from all his iniquities.
Eternal rest give unto them, O Lord! And let perpetual light shine upon them. May they rest in peace. Amen.

Evening Prayer for the Poor Souls:

V. Lord, hear my prayer.
R. And let my cry come unto Thee.
Bless, O my God! the repose I am about to take, that, renewing my strength, I may be better enabled to serve Thee. Pour down Thy blessings, O Lord! on my parents, relations, friends, and enemies. Protect the Pope, our Bishop, and all the Pastors of Thy holy Church. Assist the poor and the afflicted, and those who are now in their last agony. Look with an eye of pity on the suffering souls in purgatory, particularly

_____
_____
_____

put an end to their torments and lead them forth into everlasting joy.

Eternal rest grant unto them, and let perpetual light shine upon them. Amen.

DATE:
_____

Today, visit a church if you are able, and pray for the souls who are spending their Purgatorial time there. Catholic mystics have told us that God allows many souls to do so. If you cannot visit a church, think of a local church and pray for any souls who might be there.

Morning Prayer for the Poor Souls:

Out of the depths I have cried to Thee O Lord! Lord, hear my voice. Let Thine ears be attentive to the voice of my supplication.
If Thou, O Lord, wilt mark iniquities, Lord, who shall stand it?
For with Thee there is mercy: and by reason of Thy law I have waited on Thee, O Lord! My soul hath relied on His word: my soul hath hoped in the Lord. From the morning watch even until night. Let Israel hope in the Lord. For with the Lord there is mercy; and with Him plentiful Redemption. And He will redeem Israel from all his iniquities.
Eternal rest give unto them, O Lord! And let perpetual light shine upon them. May they rest in peace. Amen.

Evening Prayer for the Poor Souls:

V. Lord, hear my prayer.
R. And let my cry come unto Thee.
Bless, O my God! the repose I am about to take, that, renewing my strength, I may be better enabled to serve Thee. Pour down Thy blessings, O Lord! on my parents, relations, friends, and enemies. Protect the Pope, our Bishop, and all the Pastors of Thy holy Church. Assist the poor and the afflicted, and those who are now in their last agony. Look with an eye of pity on the suffering souls in purgatory, particularly

_____
_____

put an end to their torments and lead them forth into everlasting joy.

Eternal rest grant unto them, and let perpetual light shine upon them. Amen.

DATE:

_____

Today, visit someone who is sick if you are able, and offer up this work of mercy for the Holy Souls. If you cannot, pray for those in your local hospital or nursing home.

Morning Prayer for the Poor Souls:

Out of the depths I have cried to Thee O Lord! Lord, hear my voice. Let Thine ears be attentive to the voice of my supplication.
If Thou, O Lord, wilt mark iniquities, Lord, who shall stand it?
For with Thee there is mercy: and by reason of Thy law I have waited on Thee, O Lord! My soul hath relied on His word: my soul hath hoped in the Lord. From the morning watch even until night. Let Israel hope in the Lord. For with the Lord there is mercy; and with Him plentiful Redemption. And He will redeem Israel from all his iniquities.
Eternal rest give unto them, O Lord! And let perpetual light shine upon them. May they rest in peace. Amen.

Evening Prayer for the Poor Souls:

V. Lord, hear my prayer.
R. And let my cry come unto Thee.
Bless, O my God! the repose I am about to take, that, renewing my strength, I may be better enabled to serve Thee. Pour down Thy blessings, O Lord! on my parents, relations, friends, and enemies. Protect the Pope, our Bishop, and all the Pastors of Thy holy Church. Assist the poor and the afflicted, and those who are now in their last agony. Look with an eye of pity on the suffering souls in purgatory, particularly

_____

_____

_____

put an end to their torments and lead them forth into everlasting joy.

Eternal rest grant unto them, and let perpetual light shine upon them. Amen.

DATE:

_____

Today pray for the souls of all the atheists who have died.

Morning Prayer for the Poor Souls:

Out of the depths I have cried to Thee O Lord! Lord, hear my voice. Let Thine ears be attentive to the voice of my supplication.
If Thou, O Lord, wilt mark iniquities, Lord, who shall stand it?
For with Thee there is mercy: and by reason of Thy law I have waited on Thee, O Lord! My soul hath relied on His word: my soul hath hoped in the Lord. From the morning watch even until night. Let Israel hope in the Lord. For with the Lord there is mercy; and with Him plentiful Redemption. And He will redeem Israel from all his iniquities.
Eternal rest give unto them, O Lord! And let perpetual light shine upon them. May they rest in peace. Amen.

Evening Prayer for the Poor Souls:

V. Lord, hear my prayer.
R. And let my cry come unto Thee.
Bless, O my God! the repose I am about to take, that, renewing my strength, I may be better enabled to serve Thee. Pour down Thy blessings, O Lord! on my parents, relations, friends, and enemies. Protect the Pope, our Bishop, and all the Pastors of Thy holy Church. Assist the poor and the afflicted, and those who are now in their last agony. Look with an eye of pity on the suffering souls in purgatory, particularly

_____

_____

_____

put an end to their torments and lead them forth into everlasting joy.

Eternal rest grant unto them, and let perpetual light shine upon them. Amen.

DATE:

_____

Today, read the obituaries in your local newspaper and pray for the souls who have died in the past several days.

Morning Prayer for the Poor Souls:

Out of the depths I have cried to Thee O Lord! Lord, hear my voice. Let Thine ears be attentive to the voice of my supplication.
If Thou, O Lord, wilt mark iniquities, Lord, who shall stand it?
For with Thee there is mercy: and by reason of Thy law I have waited on Thee, O Lord! My soul hath relied on His word: my soul hath hoped in the Lord. From the morning watch even until night. Let Israel hope in the Lord. For with the Lord there is mercy; and with Him plentiful Redemption. And He will redeem Israel from all his iniquities.
Eternal rest give unto them, O Lord! And let perpetual light shine upon them. May they rest in peace. Amen.

Evening Prayer for the Poor Souls:

V. Lord, hear my prayer.
R. And let my cry come unto Thee.
Bless, O my God! the repose I am about to take, that, renewing my strength, I may be better enabled to serve Thee. Pour down Thy blessings, O Lord! on my parents, relations, friends, and enemies. Protect the Pope, our Bishop, and all the Pastors of Thy holy Church. Assist the poor and the afflicted, and those who are now in their last agony. Look with an eye of pity on the suffering souls in purgatory, particularly

_____

_____

_____

put an end to their torments and lead them forth into everlasting joy.

Eternal rest grant unto them, and let perpetual light shine upon them. Amen.

DATE:
_____

Spend some time in Eucharistic Adoration today for the Poor Souls. If you cannot travel to a church physically, watch live Adoration on EWTN, YouTube or Facebook.

Morning Prayer for the Poor Souls:

Out of the depths I have cried to Thee O Lord! Lord, hear my voice. Let Thine ears be attentive to the voice of my supplication.
If Thou, O Lord, wilt mark iniquities, Lord, who shall stand it?
For with Thee there is mercy: and by reason of Thy law I have waited on Thee, O Lord! My soul hath relied on His word: my soul hath hoped in the Lord. From the morning watch even until night. Let Israel hope in the Lord. For with the Lord there is mercy; and with Him plentiful Redemption. And He will redeem Israel from all his iniquities.
Eternal rest give unto them, O Lord! And let perpetual light shine upon them. May they rest in peace. Amen.

Evening Prayer for the Poor Souls:

V. Lord, hear my prayer.
R. And let my cry come unto Thee.
Bless, O my God! the repose I am about to take, that, renewing my strength, I may be better enabled to serve Thee. Pour down Thy blessings, O Lord! on my parents, relations, friends, and enemies. Protect the Pope, our Bishop, and all the Pastors of Thy holy Church. Assist the poor and the afflicted, and those who are now in their last agony. Look with an eye of pity on the suffering souls in purgatory, particularly

_____
_____

_____

put an end to their torments and lead them forth into everlasting joy.

Eternal rest grant unto them, and let perpetual light shine upon them. Amen.

DATE:

_____

a drive today to a cemetery and pray for the souls of those interred there. If you cannot physically visit a cemetery, think of a cemetery in your city or town and pray for the souls of those buried there.

Morning Prayer for the Poor Souls:

Out of the depths I have cried to Thee O Lord! Lord, hear my voice. Let Thine ears be attentive to the voice of my supplication.
If Thou, O Lord, wilt mark iniquities, Lord, who shall stand it?
For with Thee there is mercy: and by reason of Thy law I have waited on Thee, O Lord! My soul hath relied on His word: my soul hath hoped in the Lord. From the morning watch even until night. Let Israel hope in the Lord. For with the Lord there is mercy; and with Him plentiful Redemption. And He will redeem Israel from all his iniquities.
Eternal rest give unto them, O Lord! And let perpetual light shine upon them. May they rest in peace. Amen.

Evening Prayer for the Poor Souls:

V. Lord, hear my prayer.
R. And let my cry come unto Thee.
Bless, O my God! the repose I am about to take, that, renewing my strength, I may be better enabled to serve Thee. Pour down Thy blessings, O Lord! on my parents, relations, friends, and enemies. Protect the Pope, our Bishop, and all the Pastors of Thy holy Church. Assist the poor and the afflicted, and those who are now in their last agony. Look with an eye of pity on the suffering souls in purgatory, particularly

_____
_____
_____

put an end to their torments and lead them forth into everlasting joy.

Eternal rest grant unto them, and let perpetual light shine upon them. Amen.

DATE:

_____

Today, play some sacred music to comfort the Poor Souls. Mystic saints have told us that these small gestures provide great relief to their suffering.

Morning Prayer for the Poor Souls:

Out of the depths I have cried to Thee O Lord! Lord, hear my voice. Let Thine ears be attentive to the voice of my supplication.
If Thou, O Lord, wilt mark iniquities, Lord, who shall stand it?
For with Thee there is mercy: and by reason of Thy law I have waited on Thee, O Lord! My soul hath relied on His word: my soul hath hoped in the Lord. From the morning watch even until night. Let Israel hope in the Lord. For with the Lord there is mercy; and with Him plentiful Redemption. And He will redeem Israel from all his iniquities.
Eternal rest give unto them, O Lord! And let perpetual light shine upon them. May they rest in peace. Amen.

Evening Prayer for the Poor Souls:

V. Lord, hear my prayer.
R. And let my cry come unto Thee.
Bless, O my God! the repose I am about to take, that, renewing my strength, I may be better enabled to serve Thee. Pour down Thy blessings, O Lord! on my parents, relations, friends, and enemies. Protect the Pope, our Bishop, and all the Pastors of Thy holy Church. Assist the poor and the afflicted, and those who are now in their last agony. Look with an eye of pity on the suffering souls in purgatory, particularly

_____
_____
_____

put an end to their torments and lead them forth into everlasting joy.

Eternal rest grant unto them, and let perpetual light shine upon them. Amen.

DATE:

Today, make reparation to the Sacred Heart of Jesus for the souls in Purgatory who offended His most precious Heart with the following: Adorable Heart of Jesus, glowing with love for us and inflamed with zeal for our salvation. O Heart that understands the misery to which our sins have brought us, infinitely rich in mercy to heal the wounds of our souls, behold me humbly kneeling before You to express the sorrow that fills my heart for the coldness and indifference with which I have so long returned the numberless benefits which You have bestowed upon me.

Morning Prayer for the Poor Souls:

Out of the depths I have cried to Thee O Lord! Lord, hear my voice. Let Thine ears be attentive to the voice of my supplication. If Thou, O Lord, wilt mark iniquities, Lord, who shall stand it? For with Thee there is mercy: and by reason of Thy law I have waited on Thee, O Lord! My soul hath relied on His word: my soul hath hoped in the Lord. From the morning watch even until night. Let Israel hope in the Lord. For with the Lord there is mercy; and with Him plentiful Redemption. And He will redeem Israel from all his iniquities. Eternal rest give unto them, O Lord! And let perpetual light shine upon them. May they rest in peace. Amen.

Evening Prayer for the Poor Souls:

V. Lord, hear my prayer.
R. And let my cry come unto Thee.
Bless, O my God! the repose I am about to take, that, renewing my strength, I may be better enabled to serve Thee. Pour down Thy blessings, O Lord! on my parents, relations, friends, and enemies. Protect the Pope, our Bishop, and all the Pastors of Thy holy Church. Assist the poor and the afflicted, and those who are now in their last agony. Look with an eye of pity on the suffering souls in purgatory, particularly

---

put an end to their torments and lead them forth into everlasting joy.

Eternal rest grant unto them, and let perpetual light shine upon them. Amen.

DATE:

_____

Start a Mass Collection jar or envelope today for the Holy Souls. Add money to it as you are able, and when you have enough for a donation, have a Mass said for a soul in Purgatory.

Morning Prayer for the Poor Souls:

Out of the depths I have cried to Thee O Lord! Lord, hear my voice. Let Thine ears be attentive to the voice of my supplication.
If Thou, O Lord, wilt mark iniquities, Lord, who shall stand it?
For with Thee there is mercy: and by reason of Thy law I have waited on Thee, O Lord! My soul hath relied on His word: my soul hath hoped in the Lord. From the morning watch even until night. Let Israel hope in the Lord. For with the Lord there is mercy; and with Him plentiful Redemption. And He will redeem Israel from all his iniquities.
Eternal rest give unto them, O Lord! And let perpetual light shine upon them. May they rest in peace. Amen.

Evening Prayer for the Poor Souls:

V. Lord, hear my prayer.
R. And let my cry come unto Thee.
Bless, O my God! the repose I am about to take, that, renewing my strength, I may be better enabled to serve Thee. Pour down Thy blessings, O Lord! on my parents, relations, friends, and enemies. Protect the Pope, our Bishop, and all the Pastors of Thy holy Church. Assist the poor and the afflicted, and those who are now in their last agony. Look with an eye of pity on the suffering souls in purgatory, particularly

_____

_____

_____

put an end to their torments and lead them forth into everlasting joy.

Eternal rest grant unto them, and let perpetual light shine upon them. Amen.

DATE:
_____

Go without a meal or snack today if possible, for the benefit of the Holy Souls. If you are in ill health, give up a special treat instead.

Morning Prayer for the Poor Souls:

Out of the depths I have cried to Thee O Lord! Lord, hear my voice. Let Thine ears be attentive to the voice of my supplication.
If Thou, O Lord, wilt mark iniquities, Lord, who shall stand it?
For with Thee there is mercy: and by reason of Thy law I have waited on Thee, O Lord! My soul hath relied on His word: my soul hath hoped in the Lord. From the morning watch even until night. Let Israel hope in the Lord. For with the Lord there is mercy; and with Him plentiful Redemption. And He will redeem Israel from all his iniquities.
Eternal rest give unto them, O Lord! And let perpetual light shine upon them. May they rest in peace. Amen.

Evening Prayer for the Poor Souls:

V. Lord, hear my prayer.
R. And let my cry come unto Thee.
Bless, O my God! the repose I am about to take, that, renewing my strength, I may be better enabled to serve Thee. Pour down Thy blessings, O Lord! on my parents, relations, friends, and enemies. Protect the Pope, our Bishop, and all the Pastors of Thy holy Church. Assist the poor and the afflicted, and those who are now in their last agony. Look with an eye of pity on the suffering souls in purgatory, particularly

_____

_____

_____

put an end to their torments and lead them forth into everlasting joy.

Eternal rest grant unto them, and let perpetual light shine upon them. Amen.

DATE:
_____

Today, say a Divine Mercy chaplet for the Poor Souls.

Morning Prayer for the Poor Souls:

Out of the depths I have cried to Thee O Lord! Lord, hear my voice. Let Thine ears be attentive to the voice of my supplication.
If Thou, O Lord, wilt mark iniquities, Lord, who shall stand it?
For with Thee there is mercy: and by reason of Thy law I have waited on Thee, O Lord! My soul hath relied on His word: my soul hath hoped in the Lord. From the morning watch even until night. Let Israel hope in the Lord. For with the Lord there is mercy; and with Him plentiful Redemption. And He will redeem Israel from all his iniquities.
Eternal rest give unto them, O Lord! And let perpetual light shine upon them. May they rest in peace. Amen.

Evening Prayer for the Poor Souls:

V. Lord, hear my prayer.
R. And let my cry come unto Thee.
Bless, O my God! the repose I am about to take, that, renewing my strength, I may be better enabled to serve Thee. Pour down Thy blessings, O Lord! on my parents, relations, friends, and enemies. Protect the Pope, our Bishop, and all the Pastors of Thy holy Church. Assist the poor and the afflicted, and those who are now in their last agony. Look with an eye of pity on the suffering souls in purgatory, particularly

_____
_____

_____

put an end to their torments and lead them forth into everlasting joy.

Eternal rest grant unto them, and let perpetual light shine upon them. Amen.

DATE: _____

Pray today for the souls of priests and religious in Purgatory.

Morning Prayer for the Poor Souls:

Out of the depths I have cried to Thee O Lord! Lord, hear my voice. Let Thine ears be attentive to the voice of my supplication.
If Thou, O Lord, wilt mark iniquities, Lord, who shall stand it?
For with Thee there is mercy: and by reason of Thy law I have waited on Thee, O Lord! My soul hath relied on His word: my soul hath hoped in the Lord. From the morning watch even until night. Let Israel hope in the Lord. For with the Lord there is mercy; and with Him plentiful Redemption. And He will redeem Israel from all his iniquities.
Eternal rest give unto them, O Lord! And let perpetual light shine upon them. May they rest in peace. Amen.

Evening Prayer for the Poor Souls:

V. Lord, hear my prayer.
R. And let my cry come unto Thee.
Bless, O my God! the repose I am about to take, that, renewing my strength, I may be better enabled to serve Thee. Pour down Thy blessings, O Lord! on my parents, relations, friends, and enemies. Protect the Pope, our Bishop, and all the Pastors of Thy holy Church. Assist the poor and the afflicted, and those who are now in their last agony. Look with an eye of pity on the suffering souls in purgatory, particularly

_____

_____

_____

put an end to their torments and lead them forth into everlasting joy.

Eternal rest grant unto them, and let perpetual light shine upon them. Amen.

DATE: _____

While you are going about your day today, remember your friends and colleagues who have passed away over the years, asking God to release them from Purgatory.

Morning Prayer for the Poor Souls:

Out of the depths I have cried to Thee O Lord! Lord, hear my voice. Let Thine ears be attentive to the voice of my supplication.
If Thou, O Lord, wilt mark iniquities, Lord, who shall stand it?
For with Thee there is mercy: and by reason of Thy law I have waited on Thee, O Lord! My soul hath relied on His word: my soul hath hoped in the Lord. From the morning watch even until night. Let Israel hope in the Lord. For with the Lord there is mercy; and with Him plentiful Redemption. And He will redeem Israel from all his iniquities.
Eternal rest give unto them, O Lord! And let perpetual light shine upon them. May they rest in peace. Amen.

Evening Prayer for the Poor Souls:

V. Lord, hear my prayer.
R. And let my cry come unto Thee.
Bless, O my God! the repose I am about to take, that, renewing my strength, I may be better enabled to serve Thee. Pour down Thy blessings, O Lord! on my parents, relations, friends, and enemies. Protect the Pope, our Bishop, and all the Pastors of Thy holy Church. Assist the poor and the afflicted, and those who are now in their last agony. Look with an eye of pity on the suffering souls in purgatory, particularly

put an end to their torments and lead them forth into everlasting joy.

Eternal rest grant unto them, and let perpetual light shine upon them. Amen.

DATE: _____

Pray today for the dead who heard the Gospel but rejected it. May they be spared Hell and be released from Purgatory to be with Jesus.

Morning Prayer for the Poor Souls:

Out of the depths I have cried to Thee O Lord! Lord, hear my voice. Let Thine ears be attentive to the voice of my supplication.
If Thou, O Lord, wilt mark iniquities, Lord, who shall stand it?
For with Thee there is mercy: and by reason of Thy law I have waited on Thee, O Lord! My soul hath relied on His word: my soul hath hoped in the Lord. From the morning watch even until night. Let Israel hope in the Lord. For with the Lord there is mercy; and with Him plentiful Redemption. And He will redeem Israel from all his iniquities.
Eternal rest give unto them, O Lord! And let perpetual light shine upon them. May they rest in peace. Amen.

Evening Prayer for the Poor Souls:

V. Lord, hear my prayer.
R. And let my cry come unto Thee.
Bless, O my God! the repose I am about to take, that, renewing my strength, I may be better enabled to serve Thee. Pour down Thy blessings, O Lord! on my parents, relations, friends, and enemies. Protect the Pope, our Bishop, and all the Pastors of Thy holy Church. Assist the poor and the afflicted, and those who are now in their last agony. Look with an eye of pity on the suffering souls in purgatory, particularly

_____

_____

_____

put an end to their torments and lead them forth into everlasting joy.

Eternal rest grant unto them, and let perpetual light shine upon them. Amen.

DATE: _____

Today, spend some time reading devotional literature aloud for the comfort of the Poor Souls.

Morning Prayer for the Poor Souls:

Out of the depths I have cried to Thee O Lord! Lord, hear my voice. Let Thine ears be attentive to the voice of my supplication.
If Thou, O Lord, wilt mark iniquities, Lord, who shall stand it?
For with Thee there is mercy: and by reason of Thy law I have waited on Thee, O Lord! My soul hath relied on His word: my soul hath hoped in the Lord. From the morning watch even until night. Let Israel hope in the Lord. For with the Lord there is mercy; and with Him plentiful Redemption. And He will redeem Israel from all his iniquities.
Eternal rest give unto them, O Lord! And let perpetual light shine upon them. May they rest in peace. Amen.

Evening Prayer for the Poor Souls:

V. Lord, hear my prayer.
R. And let my cry come unto Thee.
Bless, O my God! the repose I am about to take, that, renewing my strength, I may be better enabled to serve Thee. Pour down Thy blessings, O Lord! on my parents, relations, friends, and enemies. Protect the Pope, our Bishop, and all the Pastors of Thy holy Church. Assist the poor and the afflicted, and those who are now in their last agony. Look with an eye of pity on the suffering souls in purgatory, particularly

_____

_____

_____

put an end to their torments and lead them forth into everlasting joy.

Eternal rest grant unto them, and let perpetual light shine upon them. Amen.

DATE: _____

Today make the Stations of the Cross for the benefit of the Holy Souls in Purgatory.

Morning Prayer for the Poor Souls:

Out of the depths I have cried to Thee O Lord! Lord, hear my voice. Let Thine ears be attentive to the voice of my supplication.
If Thou, O Lord, wilt mark iniquities, Lord, who shall stand it?
For with Thee there is mercy: and by reason of Thy law I have waited on Thee, O Lord! My soul hath relied on His word: my soul hath hoped in the Lord. From the morning watch even until night. Let Israel hope in the Lord. For with the Lord there is mercy; and with Him plentiful Redemption. And He will redeem Israel from all his iniquities.
Eternal rest give unto them, O Lord! And let perpetual light shine upon them. May they rest in peace. Amen.

Evening Prayer for the Poor Souls:

V. Lord, hear my prayer.
R. And let my cry come unto Thee.
Bless, O my God! the repose I am about to take, that, renewing my strength, I may be better enabled to serve Thee. Pour down Thy blessings, O Lord! on my parents, relations, friends, and enemies. Protect the Pope, our Bishop, and all the Pastors of Thy holy Church. Assist the poor and the afflicted, and those who are now in their last agony. Look with an eye of pity on the suffering souls in purgatory, particularly

_____

_____

_____

put an end to their torments and lead them forth into everlasting joy.

Eternal rest grant unto them, and let perpetual light shine upon them. Amen.

DATE: _____

Pray today for the souls of all Jewish people who have died.

Morning Prayer for the Poor Souls:

Out of the depths I have cried to Thee O Lord! Lord, hear my voice. Let Thine ears be attentive to the voice of my supplication.
If Thou, O Lord, wilt mark iniquities, Lord, who shall stand it?
For with Thee there is mercy: and by reason of Thy law I have waited on Thee, O Lord! My soul hath relied on His word: my soul hath hoped in the Lord. From the morning watch even until night. Let Israel hope in the Lord. For with the Lord there is mercy; and with Him plentiful Redemption. And He will redeem Israel from all his iniquities.
Eternal rest give unto them, O Lord! And let perpetual light shine upon them. May they rest in peace. Amen.

Evening Prayer for the Poor Souls:

V. Lord, hear my prayer.
R. And let my cry come unto Thee.
Bless, O my God! the repose I am about to take, that, renewing my strength, I may be better enabled to serve Thee. Pour down Thy blessings, O Lord! on my parents, relations, friends, and enemies. Protect the Pope, our Bishop, and all the Pastors of Thy holy Church. Assist the poor and the afflicted, and those who are now in their last agony. Look with an eye of pity on the suffering souls in purgatory, particularly

_____
_____

_____

put an end to their torments and lead them forth into everlasting joy.

Eternal rest grant unto them, and let perpetual light shine upon them. Amen.

DATE: _____

Today, pray for the souls of persecutors of Christians who have died.

Morning Prayer for the Poor Souls:

Out of the depths I have cried to Thee O Lord! Lord, hear my voice. Let Thine ears be attentive to the voice of my supplication.
If Thou, O Lord, wilt mark iniquities, Lord, who shall stand it?
For with Thee there is mercy: and by reason of Thy law I have waited on Thee, O Lord! My soul hath relied on His word: my soul hath hoped in the Lord. From the morning watch even until night. Let Israel hope in the Lord. For with the Lord there is mercy; and with Him plentiful Redemption. And He will redeem Israel from all his iniquities.
Eternal rest give unto them, O Lord! And let perpetual light shine upon them. May they rest in peace. Amen.

Evening Prayer for the Poor Souls:

V. Lord, hear my prayer.
R. And let my cry come unto Thee.
Bless, O my God! the repose I am about to take, that, renewing my strength, I may be better enabled to serve Thee. Pour down Thy blessings, O Lord! on my parents, relations, friends, and enemies. Protect the Pope, our Bishop, and all the Pastors of Thy holy Church. Assist the poor and the afflicted, and those who are now in their last agony. Look with an eye of pity on the suffering souls in purgatory, particularly

_____
_____

_____

put an end to their torments and lead them forth into everlasting joy.

Eternal rest grant unto them, and let perpetual light shine upon them. Amen.

DATE: _____

Light a blessed candle today in remembrance of the Holy Souls.

Morning Prayer for the Poor Souls:

Out of the depths I have cried to Thee O Lord! Lord, hear my voice. Let Thine ears be attentive to the voice of my supplication.
If Thou, O Lord, wilt mark iniquities, Lord, who shall stand it?
For with Thee there is mercy: and by reason of Thy law I have waited on Thee, O Lord! My soul hath relied on His word: my soul hath hoped in the Lord. From the morning watch even until night. Let Israel hope in the Lord. For with the Lord there is mercy; and with Him plentiful Redemption. And He will redeem Israel from all his iniquities.
Eternal rest give unto them, O Lord! And let perpetual light shine upon them. May they rest in peace. Amen.

Evening Prayer for the Poor Souls:

V. Lord, hear my prayer.
R. And let my cry come unto Thee.
Bless, O my God! the repose I am about to take, that, renewing my strength, I may be better enabled to serve Thee. Pour down Thy blessings, O Lord! on my parents, relations, friends, and enemies. Protect the Pope, our Bishop, and all the Pastors of Thy holy Church. Assist the poor and the afflicted, and those who are now in their last agony. Look with an eye of pity on the suffering souls in purgatory, particularly

_____
_____
_____

put an end to their torments and lead them forth into everlasting joy.

Eternal rest grant unto them, and let perpetual light shine upon them. Amen.

DATE: _____

Begin a Novena today for the benefit of the Poor Souls. St. Alphonsus Liguori wrote a powerful one just for the Holy Souls, which may be found online, but any Novena will be appreciated.

Morning Prayer for the Poor Souls:

Out of the depths I have cried to Thee O Lord! Lord, hear my voice. Let Thine ears be attentive to the voice of my supplication.
If Thou, O Lord, wilt mark iniquities, Lord, who shall stand it?
For with Thee there is mercy: and by reason of Thy law I have waited on Thee, O Lord! My soul hath relied on His word: my soul hath hoped in the Lord. From the morning watch even until night. Let Israel hope in the Lord. For with the Lord there is mercy; and with Him plentiful Redemption. And He will redeem Israel from all his iniquities.
Eternal rest give unto them, O Lord! And let perpetual light shine upon them. May they rest in peace. Amen.

Evening Prayer for the Poor Souls:

V. Lord, hear my prayer.
R. And let my cry come unto Thee.
Bless, O my God! the repose I am about to take, that, renewing my strength, I may be better enabled to serve Thee. Pour down Thy blessings, O Lord! on my parents, relations, friends, and enemies. Protect the Pope, our Bishop, and all the Pastors of Thy holy Church. Assist the poor and the afflicted, and those who are now in their last agony. Look with an eye of pity on the suffering souls in purgatory, particularly

_____

_____

_____

put an end to their torments and lead them forth into everlasting joy.

Eternal rest grant unto them, and let perpetual light shine upon them. Amen.

DATE: _____

Give alms to the poor today to benefit the souls in Purgatory. We are told that giving alms is of great benefit to suffering souls.

Morning Prayer for the Poor Souls:

Out of the depths I have cried to Thee O Lord! Lord, hear my voice. Let Thine ears be attentive to the voice of my supplication.
If Thou, O Lord, wilt mark iniquities, Lord, who shall stand it?
For with Thee there is mercy: and by reason of Thy law I have waited on Thee, O Lord! My soul hath relied on His word: my soul hath hoped in the Lord. From the morning watch even until night. Let Israel hope in the Lord. For with the Lord there is mercy; and with Him plentiful Redemption. And He will redeem Israel from all his iniquities.
Eternal rest give unto them, O Lord! And let perpetual light shine upon them. May they rest in peace. Amen.

Evening Prayer for the Poor Souls:

V. Lord, hear my prayer.
R. And let my cry come unto Thee.
Bless, O my God! the repose I am about to take, that, renewing my strength, I may be better enabled to serve Thee. Pour down Thy blessings, O Lord! on my parents, relations, friends, and enemies. Protect the Pope, our Bishop, and all the Pastors of Thy holy Church. Assist the poor and the afflicted, and those who are now in their last agony. Look with an eye of pity on the suffering souls in purgatory, particularly

_____
_____
_____

put an end to their torments and lead them forth into everlasting joy.

Eternal rest grant unto them, and let perpetual light shine upon them. Amen.

DATE: _____

Read aloud today from the Acts of the Apostles to comfort the Holy Souls. The Good News of Jesus' salvation is of great relief to their suffering.

Morning Prayer for the Poor Souls:

Out of the depths I have cried to Thee O Lord! Lord, hear my voice. Let Thine ears be attentive to the voice of my supplication.
If Thou, O Lord, wilt mark iniquities, Lord, who shall stand it?
For with Thee there is mercy: and by reason of Thy law I have waited on Thee, O Lord! My soul hath relied on His word: my soul hath hoped in the Lord. From the morning watch even until night. Let Israel hope in the Lord. For with the Lord there is mercy; and with Him plentiful Redemption. And He will redeem Israel from all his iniquities.
Eternal rest give unto them, O Lord! And let perpetual light shine upon them. May they rest in peace. Amen.

Evening Prayer for the Poor Souls:

V. Lord, hear my prayer.
R. And let my cry come unto Thee.
Bless, O my God! the repose I am about to take, that, renewing my strength, I may be better enabled to serve Thee. Pour down Thy blessings, O Lord! on my parents, relations, friends, and enemies. Protect the Pope, our Bishop, and all the Pastors of Thy holy Church. Assist the poor and the afflicted, and those who are now in their last agony. Look with an eye of pity on the suffering souls in purgatory, particularly

_____

_____

_____

put an end to their torments and lead them forth into everlasting joy.

Eternal rest grant unto them, and let perpetual light shine upon them. Amen.

DATE: _____

Today, ask the saints known as intercessors for the dead to pray with you for their release, including St. Nicholas of Tolentino, St. Gertrude the Great, St. Catherine of Genoa, St. Padre Pio, St. Philip Neri, St. John Macías, St. Faustina Kowalska, St. Joseph and, of course, the Blessed Mother.

Morning Prayer for the Poor Souls:

Out of the depths I have cried to Thee O Lord! Lord, hear my voice. Let Thine ears be attentive to the voice of my supplication.
If Thou, O Lord, wilt mark iniquities, Lord, who shall stand it?
For with Thee there is mercy: and by reason of Thy law I have waited on Thee, O Lord! My soul hath relied on His word: my soul hath hoped in the Lord. From the morning watch even until night. Let Israel hope in the Lord. For with the Lord there is mercy; and with Him plentiful Redemption. And He will redeem Israel from all his iniquities.
Eternal rest give unto them, O Lord! And let perpetual light shine upon them. May they rest in peace. Amen.

Evening Prayer for the Poor Souls:

V. Lord, hear my prayer.
R. And let my cry come unto Thee.
Bless, O my God! the repose I am about to take, that, renewing my strength, I may be better enabled to serve Thee. Pour down Thy blessings, O Lord! on my parents, relations, friends, and enemies. Protect the Pope, our Bishop, and all the Pastors of Thy holy Church. Assist the poor and the afflicted, and those who are now in their last agony. Look with an eye of pity on the suffering souls in purgatory, particularly

_____

_____

_____

put an end to their torments and lead them forth into everlasting joy.

Eternal rest grant unto them, and let perpetual light shine upon them. Amen.

The Month of
_____

DATE: _____

Today, have a Mass said for the soul of a family member or friend who has passed away. This can be through your own parish or through an order or national shrine via their website.

Morning Prayer for the Poor Souls:

Out of the depths I have cried to Thee O Lord! Lord, hear my voice. Let Thine ears be attentive to the voice of my supplication.
If Thou, O Lord, wilt mark iniquities, Lord, who shall stand it?
For with Thee there is mercy: and by reason of Thy law I have waited on Thee, O Lord! My soul hath relied on His word: my soul hath hoped in the Lord. From the morning watch even until night. Let Israel hope in the Lord. For with the Lord there is mercy; and with Him plentiful Redemption. And He will redeem Israel from all his iniquities.
Eternal rest give unto them, O Lord! And let perpetual light shine upon them. May they rest in peace. Amen.

Evening Prayer for the Poor Souls:

V. Lord, hear my prayer.
R. And let my cry come unto Thee.
Bless, O my God! the repose I am about to take, that, renewing my strength, I may be better enabled to serve Thee. Pour down Thy blessings, O Lord! on my parents, relations, friends, and enemies. Protect the Pope, our Bishop, and all the Pastors of Thy holy Church. Assist the poor and the afflicted, and those who are now in their last agony. Look with an eye of pity on the suffering souls in purgatory, particularly

_____

_____

_____

put an end to their torments and lead them forth into everlasting joy.

Eternal rest grant unto them, and let perpetual light shine upon them. Amen.

DATE:
_____

Pray the Rosary today for the release of souls from Purgatory. Mystic saints have told us that the Blessed Mother herself comes to Purgatory to bring souls with her back to Heaven.

Morning Prayer for the Poor Souls:

Out of the depths I have cried to Thee O Lord! Lord, hear my voice. Let Thine ears be attentive to the voice of my supplication.
If Thou, O Lord, wilt mark iniquities, Lord, who shall stand it?
For with Thee there is mercy: and by reason of Thy law I have waited on Thee, O Lord! My soul hath relied on His word: my soul hath hoped in the Lord. From the morning watch even until night. Let Israel hope in the Lord. For with the Lord there is mercy; and with Him plentiful Redemption. And He will redeem Israel from all his iniquities.
Eternal rest give unto them, O Lord! And let perpetual light shine upon them. May they rest in peace. Amen.

Evening Prayer for the Poor Souls:

V. Lord, hear my prayer.
R. And let my cry come unto Thee.
Bless, O my God! the repose I am about to take, that, renewing my strength, I may be better enabled to serve Thee. Pour down Thy blessings, O Lord! on my parents, relations, friends, and enemies. Protect the Pope, our Bishop, and all the Pastors of Thy holy Church. Assist the poor and the afflicted, and those who are now in their last agony. Look with an eye of pity on the suffering souls in purgatory, particularly

_____
_____
_____

put an end to their torments and lead them forth into everlasting joy.

Eternal rest grant unto them, and let perpetual light shine upon them. Amen.

DATE:

_____

Today, ask the Blessed Mother to apply your prayers and works to a poor soul who has no one to pray for them.

Morning Prayer for the Poor Souls:

Out of the depths I have cried to Thee O Lord! Lord, hear my voice. Let Thine ears be attentive to the voice of my supplication.
If Thou, O Lord, wilt mark iniquities, Lord, who shall stand it?
For with Thee there is mercy: and by reason of Thy law I have waited on Thee, O Lord! My soul hath relied on His word: my soul hath hoped in the Lord. From the morning watch even until night. Let Israel hope in the Lord. For with the Lord there is mercy; and with Him plentiful Redemption. And He will redeem Israel from all his iniquities.
Eternal rest give unto them, O Lord! And let perpetual light shine upon them. May they rest in peace. Amen.

Evening Prayer for the Poor Souls:

V. Lord, hear my prayer.
R. And let my cry come unto Thee.
Bless, O my God! the repose I am about to take, that, renewing my strength, I may be better enabled to serve Thee. Pour down Thy blessings, O Lord! on my parents, relations, friends, and enemies. Protect the Pope, our Bishop, and all the Pastors of Thy holy Church. Assist the poor and the afflicted, and those who are now in their last agony. Look with an eye of pity on the suffering souls in purgatory, particularly

_____
_____

_____

put an end to their torments and lead them forth into everlasting joy.

Eternal rest grant unto them, and let perpetual light shine upon them. Amen.

DATE:
_____

We all have a spiritual or physical affliction or burden that we suffer with daily. Today, dedicate your ailment-related suffering to the Poor souls.

Morning Prayer for the Poor Souls:

Out of the depths I have cried to Thee O Lord! Lord, hear my voice. Let Thine ears be attentive to the voice of my supplication.
If Thou, O Lord, wilt mark iniquities, Lord, who shall stand it?
For with Thee there is mercy: and by reason of Thy law I have waited on Thee, O Lord! My soul hath relied on His word: my soul hath hoped in the Lord. From the morning watch even until night. Let Israel hope in the Lord. For with the Lord there is mercy; and with Him plentiful Redemption. And He will redeem Israel from all his iniquities.
Eternal rest give unto them, O Lord! And let perpetual light shine upon them. May they rest in peace. Amen.

Evening Prayer for the Poor Souls:

V. Lord, hear my prayer.
R. And let my cry come unto Thee.
Bless, O my God! the repose I am about to take, that, renewing my strength, I may be better enabled to serve Thee. Pour down Thy blessings, O Lord! on my parents, relations, friends, and enemies. Protect the Pope, our Bishop, and all the Pastors of Thy holy Church. Assist the poor and the afflicted, and those who are now in their last agony. Look with an eye of pity on the suffering souls in purgatory, particularly

_____

_____

_____

put an end to their torments and lead them forth into everlasting joy.

Eternal rest grant unto them, and let perpetual light shine upon them. Amen.

DATE:

_____

Today, visit or call someone elderly or alone and offer your work of mercy for the souls in Purgatory.

Morning Prayer for the Poor Souls:

Out of the depths I have cried to Thee O Lord! Lord, hear my voice. Let Thine ears be attentive to the voice of my supplication.
If Thou, O Lord, wilt mark iniquities, Lord, who shall stand it?
For with Thee there is mercy: and by reason of Thy law I have waited on Thee, O Lord! My soul hath relied on His word: my soul hath hoped in the Lord. From the morning watch even until night. Let Israel hope in the Lord. For with the Lord there is mercy; and with Him plentiful Redemption. And He will redeem Israel from all his iniquities.
Eternal rest give unto them, O Lord! And let perpetual light shine upon them. May they rest in peace. Amen.

Evening Prayer for the Poor Souls:

V. Lord, hear my prayer.
R. And let my cry come unto Thee.
Bless, O my God! the repose I am about to take, that, renewing my strength, I may be better enabled to serve Thee. Pour down Thy blessings, O Lord! on my parents, relations, friends, and enemies. Protect the Pope, our Bishop, and all the Pastors of Thy holy Church. Assist the poor and the afflicted, and those who are now in their last agony. Look with an eye of pity on the suffering souls in purgatory, particularly

_____

_____

_____

put an end to their torments and lead them forth into everlasting joy.

Eternal rest grant unto them, and let perpetual light shine upon them. Amen.

DATE:

_____

During the course of the day today, pray for those you meet and strangers you see on street, asking God to apply your prayers for them to their future time in Purgatory.

Morning Prayer for the Poor Souls:

Out of the depths I have cried to Thee O Lord! Lord, hear my voice. Let Thine ears be attentive to the voice of my supplication.
If Thou, O Lord, wilt mark iniquities, Lord, who shall stand it?
For with Thee there is mercy: and by reason of Thy law I have waited on Thee, O Lord! My soul hath relied on His word: my soul hath hoped in the Lord. From the morning watch even until night. Let Israel hope in the Lord. For with the Lord there is mercy; and with Him plentiful Redemption. And He will redeem Israel from all his iniquities.
Eternal rest give unto them, O Lord! And let perpetual light shine upon them. May they rest in peace. Amen.

Evening Prayer for the Poor Souls:

V. Lord, hear my prayer.
R. And let my cry come unto Thee.
Bless, O my God! the repose I am about to take, that, renewing my strength, I may be better enabled to serve Thee. Pour down Thy blessings, O Lord! on my parents, relations, friends, and enemies. Protect the Pope, our Bishop, and all the Pastors of Thy holy Church. Assist the poor and the afflicted, and those who are now in their last agony. Look with an eye of pity on the suffering souls in purgatory, particularly

_____
_____
_____

put an end to their torments and lead them forth into everlasting joy.

Eternal rest grant unto them, and let perpetual light shine upon them. Amen.

DATE:

_____

Today, ask the Blessed Mother to use your prayers for someone in Purgatory with no one to pray for them.

Morning Prayer for the Poor Souls:

Out of the depths I have cried to Thee O Lord! Lord, hear my voice. Let Thine ears be attentive to the voice of my supplication.
If Thou, O Lord, wilt mark iniquities, Lord, who shall stand it?
For with Thee there is mercy: and by reason of Thy law I have waited on Thee, O Lord! My soul hath relied on His word: my soul hath hoped in the Lord. From the morning watch even until night. Let Israel hope in the Lord. For with the Lord there is mercy; and with Him plentiful Redemption. And He will redeem Israel from all his iniquities.
Eternal rest give unto them, O Lord! And let perpetual light shine upon them. May they rest in peace. Amen.

Evening Prayer for the Poor Souls:

V. Lord, hear my prayer.
R. And let my cry come unto Thee.
Bless, O my God! the repose I am about to take, that, renewing my strength, I may be better enabled to serve Thee. Pour down Thy blessings, O Lord! on my parents, relations, friends, and enemies. Protect the Pope, our Bishop, and all the Pastors of Thy holy Church. Assist the poor and the afflicted, and those who are now in their last agony. Look with an eye of pity on the suffering souls in purgatory, particularly

_____

_____

_____

put an end to their torments and lead them forth into everlasting joy.

Eternal rest grant unto them, and let perpetual light shine upon them. Amen.

DATE:

_____

Today, sprinkle holy water on the carpet of your home or outside your house as a comfort to the Poor Souls.

Morning Prayer for the Poor Souls:

Out of the depths I have cried to Thee O Lord! Lord, hear my voice. Let Thine ears be attentive to the voice of my supplication.
If Thou, O Lord, wilt mark iniquities, Lord, who shall stand it?
For with Thee there is mercy: and by reason of Thy law I have waited on Thee, O Lord! My soul hath relied on His word: my soul hath hoped in the Lord. From the morning watch even until night. Let Israel hope in the Lord. For with the Lord there is mercy; and with Him plentiful Redemption. And He will redeem Israel from all his iniquities.
Eternal rest give unto them, O Lord! And let perpetual light shine upon them. May they rest in peace. Amen.

Evening Prayer for the Poor Souls:

V. Lord, hear my prayer.
R. And let my cry come unto Thee.
Bless, O my God! the repose I am about to take, that, renewing my strength, I may be better enabled to serve Thee. Pour down Thy blessings, O Lord! on my parents, relations, friends, and enemies. Protect the Pope, our Bishop, and all the Pastors of Thy holy Church. Assist the poor and the afflicted, and those who are now in their last agony. Look with an eye of pity on the suffering souls in purgatory, particularly

_____

_____

_____

put an end to their torments and lead them forth into everlasting joy.

Eternal rest grant unto them, and let perpetual light shine upon them. Amen.

DATE:

_____

Today, visit a church if you are able, and pray for the souls who are spending their Purgatorial time there. Catholic mystics have told us that God allows many souls to do so. If you cannot visit a church, think of a local church and pray for any souls who might be there.

Morning Prayer for the Poor Souls:

Out of the depths I have cried to Thee O Lord! Lord, hear my voice. Let Thine ears be attentive to the voice of my supplication.
If Thou, O Lord, wilt mark iniquities, Lord, who shall stand it?
For with Thee there is mercy: and by reason of Thy law I have waited on Thee, O Lord! My soul hath relied on His word: my soul hath hoped in the Lord. From the morning watch even until night. Let Israel hope in the Lord. For with the Lord there is mercy; and with Him plentiful Redemption. And He will redeem Israel from all his iniquities.
Eternal rest give unto them, O Lord! And let perpetual light shine upon them. May they rest in peace. Amen.

Evening Prayer for the Poor Souls:

V. Lord, hear my prayer.
R. And let my cry come unto Thee.
Bless, O my God! the repose I am about to take, that, renewing my strength, I may be better enabled to serve Thee. Pour down Thy blessings, O Lord! on my parents, relations, friends, and enemies. Protect the Pope, our Bishop, and all the Pastors of Thy holy Church. Assist the poor and the afflicted, and those who are now in their last agony. Look with an eye of pity on the suffering souls in purgatory, particularly

_____

_____

put an end to their torments and lead them forth into everlasting joy.

Eternal rest grant unto them, and let perpetual light shine upon them. Amen.

DATE:
_____

Today, visit someone who is sick if you are able, and offer up this work of mercy for the Holy Souls. If you cannot, pray for those in your local hospital or nursing home.

Morning Prayer for the Poor Souls:

Out of the depths I have cried to Thee O Lord! Lord, hear my voice. Let Thine ears be attentive to the voice of my supplication.
If Thou, O Lord, wilt mark iniquities, Lord, who shall stand it?
For with Thee there is mercy: and by reason of Thy law I have waited on Thee, O Lord! My soul hath relied on His word: my soul hath hoped in the Lord. From the morning watch even until night. Let Israel hope in the Lord. For with the Lord there is mercy; and with Him plentiful Redemption. And He will redeem Israel from all his iniquities.
Eternal rest give unto them, O Lord! And let perpetual light shine upon them. May they rest in peace. Amen.

Evening Prayer for the Poor Souls:

V. Lord, hear my prayer.
R. And let my cry come unto Thee.
Bless, O my God! the repose I am about to take, that, renewing my strength, I may be better enabled to serve Thee. Pour down Thy blessings, O Lord! on my parents, relations, friends, and enemies. Protect the Pope, our Bishop, and all the Pastors of Thy holy Church. Assist the poor and the afflicted, and those who are now in their last agony. Look with an eye of pity on the suffering souls in purgatory, particularly

_____
_____

_____

put an end to their torments and lead them forth into everlasting joy.

Eternal rest grant unto them, and let perpetual light shine upon them. Amen.

DATE:

_____

Today pray for the souls of all the atheists who have died.

Morning Prayer for the Poor Souls:

Out of the depths I have cried to Thee O Lord! Lord, hear my voice. Let Thine ears be attentive to the voice of my supplication.
If Thou, O Lord, wilt mark iniquities, Lord, who shall stand it?
For with Thee there is mercy: and by reason of Thy law I have waited on Thee, O Lord! My soul hath relied on His word: my soul hath hoped in the Lord. From the morning watch even until night. Let Israel hope in the Lord. For with the Lord there is mercy; and with Him plentiful Redemption. And He will redeem Israel from all his iniquities.
Eternal rest give unto them, O Lord! And let perpetual light shine upon them. May they rest in peace. Amen.

Evening Prayer for the Poor Souls:

V. Lord, hear my prayer.
R. And let my cry come unto Thee.
Bless, O my God! the repose I am about to take, that, renewing my strength, I may be better enabled to serve Thee. Pour down Thy blessings, O Lord! on my parents, relations, friends, and enemies. Protect the Pope, our Bishop, and all the Pastors of Thy holy Church. Assist the poor and the afflicted, and those who are now in their last agony. Look with an eye of pity on the suffering souls in purgatory, particularly

_____

_____

_____

put an end to their torments and lead them forth into everlasting joy.

Eternal rest grant unto them, and let perpetual light shine upon them. Amen.

DATE:
_____

Today, read the obituaries in your local newspaper and pray for the souls who have died in the past several days.

Morning Prayer for the Poor Souls:

Out of the depths I have cried to Thee O Lord! Lord, hear my voice. Let Thine ears be attentive to the voice of my supplication.
If Thou, O Lord, wilt mark iniquities, Lord, who shall stand it?
For with Thee there is mercy: and by reason of Thy law I have waited on Thee, O Lord! My soul hath relied on His word: my soul hath hoped in the Lord. From the morning watch even until night. Let Israel hope in the Lord. For with the Lord there is mercy; and with Him plentiful Redemption. And He will redeem Israel from all his iniquities.
Eternal rest give unto them, O Lord! And let perpetual light shine upon them. May they rest in peace. Amen.

Evening Prayer for the Poor Souls:

V. Lord, hear my prayer.
R. And let my cry come unto Thee.
Bless, O my God! the repose I am about to take, that, renewing my strength, I may be better enabled to serve Thee. Pour down Thy blessings, O Lord! on my parents, relations, friends, and enemies. Protect the Pope, our Bishop, and all the Pastors of Thy holy Church. Assist the poor and the afflicted, and those who are now in their last agony. Look with an eye of pity on the suffering souls in purgatory, particularly

_____
_____

_____

put an end to their torments and lead them forth into everlasting joy.

Eternal rest grant unto them, and let perpetual light shine upon them. Amen.

DATE:
_____

Spend some time in Eucharistic Adoration today for the Poor Souls. If you cannot travel to a church physically, watch live Adoration on EWTN, YouTube or Facebook.

Morning Prayer for the Poor Souls:

Out of the depths I have cried to Thee O Lord! Lord, hear my voice. Let Thine ears be attentive to the voice of my supplication.
If Thou, O Lord, wilt mark iniquities, Lord, who shall stand it?
For with Thee there is mercy: and by reason of Thy law I have waited on Thee, O Lord! My soul hath relied on His word: my soul hath hoped in the Lord. From the morning watch even until night. Let Israel hope in the Lord. For with the Lord there is mercy; and with Him plentiful Redemption. And He will redeem Israel from all his iniquities.
Eternal rest give unto them, O Lord! And let perpetual light shine upon them. May they rest in peace. Amen.

Evening Prayer for the Poor Souls:

V. Lord, hear my prayer.
R. And let my cry come unto Thee.
Bless, O my God! the repose I am about to take, that, renewing my strength, I may be better enabled to serve Thee. Pour down Thy blessings, O Lord! on my parents, relations, friends, and enemies. Protect the Pope, our Bishop, and all the Pastors of Thy holy Church. Assist the poor and the afflicted, and those who are now in their last agony. Look with an eye of pity on the suffering souls in purgatory, particularly

_____

_____

_____

put an end to their torments and lead them forth into everlasting joy.

Eternal rest grant unto them, and let perpetual light shine upon them. Amen.

DATE:
_____

a drive today to a cemetery and pray for the souls of those interred there. If you cannot physically visit a cemetery, think of a cemetery in your city or town and pray for the souls of those buried there.

Morning Prayer for the Poor Souls:

Out of the depths I have cried to Thee O Lord! Lord, hear my voice. Let Thine ears be attentive to the voice of my supplication.
If Thou, O Lord, wilt mark iniquities, Lord, who shall stand it?
For with Thee there is mercy: and by reason of Thy law I have waited on Thee, O Lord! My soul hath relied on His word: my soul hath hoped in the Lord. From the morning watch even until night. Let Israel hope in the Lord. For with the Lord there is mercy; and with Him plentiful Redemption. And He will redeem Israel from all his iniquities.
Eternal rest give unto them, O Lord! And let perpetual light shine upon them. May they rest in peace. Amen.

Evening Prayer for the Poor Souls:

V. Lord, hear my prayer.
R. And let my cry come unto Thee.
Bless, O my God! the repose I am about to take, that, renewing my strength, I may be better enabled to serve Thee. Pour down Thy blessings, O Lord! on my parents, relations, friends, and enemies. Protect the Pope, our Bishop, and all the Pastors of Thy holy Church. Assist the poor and the afflicted, and those who are now in their last agony. Look with an eye of pity on the suffering souls in purgatory, particularly

_____
_____
_____

put an end to their torments and lead them forth into everlasting joy.

Eternal rest grant unto them, and let perpetual light shine upon them. Amen.

DATE:

_____

Today, play some sacred music to comfort the Poor Souls. Mystic saints have told us that these small gestures provide great relief to their suffering.

Morning Prayer for the Poor Souls:

Out of the depths I have cried to Thee O Lord! Lord, hear my voice. Let Thine ears be attentive to the voice of my supplication.
If Thou, O Lord, wilt mark iniquities, Lord, who shall stand it?
For with Thee there is mercy: and by reason of Thy law I have waited on Thee, O Lord! My soul hath relied on His word: my soul hath hoped in the Lord. From the morning watch even until night. Let Israel hope in the Lord. For with the Lord there is mercy; and with Him plentiful Redemption. And He will redeem Israel from all his iniquities.
Eternal rest give unto them, O Lord! And let perpetual light shine upon them. May they rest in peace. Amen.

Evening Prayer for the Poor Souls:

V. Lord, hear my prayer.
R. And let my cry come unto Thee.
Bless, O my God! the repose I am about to take, that, renewing my strength, I may be better enabled to serve Thee. Pour down Thy blessings, O Lord! on my parents, relations, friends, and enemies. Protect the Pope, our Bishop, and all the Pastors of Thy holy Church. Assist the poor and the afflicted, and those who are now in their last agony. Look with an eye of pity on the suffering souls in purgatory, particularly

_____
_____
_____

put an end to their torments and lead them forth into everlasting joy.

Eternal rest grant unto them, and let perpetual light shine upon them. Amen.

DATE:
_____

Today, make reparation to the Sacred Heart of Jesus for the souls in Purgatory who offended His most precious Heart with the following: Adorable Heart of Jesus, glowing with love for us and inflamed with zeal for our salvation. O Heart that understands the misery to which our sins have brought us, infinitely rich in mercy to heal the wounds of our souls, behold me humbly kneeling before You to express the sorrow that fills my heart for the coldness and indifference with which I have so long returned the numberless benefits which You have bestowed upon me.

Morning Prayer for the Poor Souls:

Out of the depths I have cried to Thee O Lord! Lord, hear my voice. Let Thine ears be attentive to the voice of my supplication. If Thou, O Lord, wilt mark iniquities, Lord, who shall stand it? For with Thee there is mercy: and by reason of Thy law I have waited on Thee, O Lord! My soul hath relied on His word: my soul hath hoped in the Lord. From the morning watch even until night. Let Israel hope in the Lord. For with the Lord there is mercy; and with Him plentiful Redemption. And He will redeem Israel from all his iniquities. Eternal rest give unto them, O Lord! And let perpetual light shine upon them. May they rest in peace. Amen.

Evening Prayer for the Poor Souls:

V. Lord, hear my prayer.
R. And let my cry come unto Thee.
Bless, O my God! the repose I am about to take, that, renewing my strength, I may be better enabled to serve Thee. Pour down Thy blessings, O Lord! on my parents, relations, friends, and enemies. Protect the Pope, our Bishop, and all the Pastors of Thy holy Church. Assist the poor and the afflicted, and those who are now in their last agony. Look with an eye of pity on the suffering souls in purgatory, particularly

_____

put an end to their torments and lead them forth into everlasting joy.

Eternal rest grant unto them, and let perpetual light shine upon them. Amen.

DATE:

_____

Start a Mass Collection jar or envelope today for the Holy Souls. Add money to it as you are able, and when you have enough for a donation, have a Mass said for a soul in Purgatory.

Morning Prayer for the Poor Souls:

Out of the depths I have cried to Thee O Lord! Lord, hear my voice. Let Thine ears be attentive to the voice of my supplication.
If Thou, O Lord, wilt mark iniquities, Lord, who shall stand it?
For with Thee there is mercy: and by reason of Thy law I have waited on Thee, O Lord! My soul hath relied on His word: my soul hath hoped in the Lord. From the morning watch even until night. Let Israel hope in the Lord. For with the Lord there is mercy; and with Him plentiful Redemption. And He will redeem Israel from all his iniquities.
Eternal rest give unto them, O Lord! And let perpetual light shine upon them. May they rest in peace. Amen.

Evening Prayer for the Poor Souls:

V. Lord, hear my prayer.
R. And let my cry come unto Thee.
Bless, O my God! the repose I am about to take, that, renewing my strength, I may be better enabled to serve Thee. Pour down Thy blessings, O Lord! on my parents, relations, friends, and enemies. Protect the Pope, our Bishop, and all the Pastors of Thy holy Church. Assist the poor and the afflicted, and those who are now in their last agony. Look with an eye of pity on the suffering souls in purgatory, particularly

_____
_____
_____

put an end to their torments and lead them forth into everlasting joy.

Eternal rest grant unto them, and let perpetual light shine upon them. Amen.

DATE:
_____

Go without a meal or snack today if possible, for the benefit of the Holy Souls. If you are in ill health, give up a special treat instead.

Morning Prayer for the Poor Souls:

Out of the depths I have cried to Thee O Lord! Lord, hear my voice. Let Thine ears be attentive to the voice of my supplication.
If Thou, O Lord, wilt mark iniquities, Lord, who shall stand it?
For with Thee there is mercy: and by reason of Thy law I have waited on Thee, O Lord! My soul hath relied on His word: my soul hath hoped in the Lord. From the morning watch even until night. Let Israel hope in the Lord. For with the Lord there is mercy; and with Him plentiful Redemption. And He will redeem Israel from all his iniquities.
Eternal rest give unto them, O Lord! And let perpetual light shine upon them. May they rest in peace. Amen.

Evening Prayer for the Poor Souls:

V. Lord, hear my prayer.
R. And let my cry come unto Thee.
Bless, O my God! the repose I am about to take, that, renewing my strength, I may be better enabled to serve Thee. Pour down Thy blessings, O Lord! on my parents, relations, friends, and enemies. Protect the Pope, our Bishop, and all the Pastors of Thy holy Church. Assist the poor and the afflicted, and those who are now in their last agony. Look with an eye of pity on the suffering souls in purgatory, particularly

_____
_____
_____

put an end to their torments and lead them forth into everlasting joy.

Eternal rest grant unto them, and let perpetual light shine upon them. Amen.

DATE:
_____

Today, say a Divine Mercy chaplet for the Poor Souls.

Morning Prayer for the Poor Souls:

Out of the depths I have cried to Thee O Lord! Lord, hear my voice. Let Thine ears be attentive to the voice of my supplication.
If Thou, O Lord, wilt mark iniquities, Lord, who shall stand it?
For with Thee there is mercy: and by reason of Thy law I have waited on Thee, O Lord! My soul hath relied on His word: my soul hath hoped in the Lord. From the morning watch even until night. Let Israel hope in the Lord. For with the Lord there is mercy; and with Him plentiful Redemption. And He will redeem Israel from all his iniquities.
Eternal rest give unto them, O Lord! And let perpetual light shine upon them. May they rest in peace. Amen.

Evening Prayer for the Poor Souls:

V. Lord, hear my prayer.
R. And let my cry come unto Thee.
Bless, O my God! the repose I am about to take, that, renewing my strength, I may be better enabled to serve Thee. Pour down Thy blessings, O Lord! on my parents, relations, friends, and enemies. Protect the Pope, our Bishop, and all the Pastors of Thy holy Church. Assist the poor and the afflicted, and those who are now in their last agony. Look with an eye of pity on the suffering souls in purgatory, particularly

_____
_____
_____

put an end to their torments and lead them forth into everlasting joy.

Eternal rest grant unto them, and let perpetual light shine upon them. Amen.

DATE: _____

Pray today for the souls of priests and religious in Purgatory.

Morning Prayer for the Poor Souls:

Out of the depths I have cried to Thee O Lord! Lord, hear my voice. Let Thine ears be attentive to the voice of my supplication.
If Thou, O Lord, wilt mark iniquities, Lord, who shall stand it?
For with Thee there is mercy: and by reason of Thy law I have waited on Thee, O Lord! My soul hath relied on His word: my soul hath hoped in the Lord. From the morning watch even until night. Let Israel hope in the Lord. For with the Lord there is mercy; and with Him plentiful Redemption. And He will redeem Israel from all his iniquities.
Eternal rest give unto them, O Lord! And let perpetual light shine upon them. May they rest in peace. Amen.

Evening Prayer for the Poor Souls:

V. Lord, hear my prayer.
R. And let my cry come unto Thee.
Bless, O my God! the repose I am about to take, that, renewing my strength, I may be better enabled to serve Thee. Pour down Thy blessings, O Lord! on my parents, relations, friends, and enemies. Protect the Pope, our Bishop, and all the Pastors of Thy holy Church. Assist the poor and the afflicted, and those who are now in their last agony. Look with an eye of pity on the suffering souls in purgatory, particularly

_____
_____

_____

put an end to their torments and lead them forth into everlasting joy.

Eternal rest grant unto them, and let perpetual light shine upon them. Amen.

DATE: _____

While you are going about your day today, remember your friends and colleagues who have passed away over the years, asking God to release them from Purgatory.

Morning Prayer for the Poor Souls:

Out of the depths I have cried to Thee O Lord! Lord, hear my voice. Let Thine ears be attentive to the voice of my supplication.
If Thou, O Lord, wilt mark iniquities, Lord, who shall stand it?
For with Thee there is mercy: and by reason of Thy law I have waited on Thee, O Lord! My soul hath relied on His word: my soul hath hoped in the Lord. From the morning watch even until night. Let Israel hope in the Lord. For with the Lord there is mercy; and with Him plentiful Redemption. And He will redeem Israel from all his iniquities.
Eternal rest give unto them, O Lord! And let perpetual light shine upon them. May they rest in peace. Amen.

Evening Prayer for the Poor Souls:

V. Lord, hear my prayer.
R. And let my cry come unto Thee.
Bless, O my God! the repose I am about to take, that, renewing my strength, I may be better enabled to serve Thee. Pour down Thy blessings, O Lord! on my parents, relations, friends, and enemies. Protect the Pope, our Bishop, and all the Pastors of Thy holy Church. Assist the poor and the afflicted, and those who are now in their last agony. Look with an eye of pity on the suffering souls in purgatory, particularly

put an end to their torments and lead them forth into everlasting joy.

Eternal rest grant unto them and let perpetual light shine upon them. Amen.

DATE: _____

Pray today for the dead who heard the Gospel but rejected it. May they be spared Hell and be released from Purgatory to be with Jesus.

Morning Prayer for the Poor Souls:

Out of the depths I have cried to Thee O Lord! Lord, hear my voice. Let Thine ears be attentive to the voice of my supplication.
If Thou, O Lord, wilt mark iniquities, Lord, who shall stand it?
For with Thee there is mercy: and by reason of Thy law I have waited on Thee, O Lord! My soul hath relied on His word: my soul hath hoped in the Lord. From the morning watch even until night. Let Israel hope in the Lord. For with the Lord there is mercy; and with Him plentiful Redemption. And He will redeem Israel from all his iniquities.
Eternal rest give unto them, O Lord! And let perpetual light shine upon them. May they rest in peace. Amen.

Evening Prayer for the Poor Souls:

V. Lord, hear my prayer.
R. And let my cry come unto Thee.
Bless, O my God! the repose I am about to take, that, renewing my strength, I may be better enabled to serve Thee. Pour down Thy blessings, O Lord! on my parents, relations, friends, and enemies. Protect the Pope, our Bishop, and all the Pastors of Thy holy Church. Assist the poor and the afflicted, and those who are now in their last agony. Look with an eye of pity on the suffering souls in purgatory, particularly

_____

_____

_____

put an end to their torments and lead them forth into everlasting joy.

Eternal rest grant unto them and let perpetual light shine upon them. Amen.

DATE: _____

Today, spend some time reading devotional literature aloud for the comfort of the Poor Souls.

Morning Prayer for the Poor Souls:

Out of the depths I have cried to Thee O Lord! Lord, hear my voice. Let Thine ears be attentive to the voice of my supplication.
If Thou, O Lord, wilt mark iniquities, Lord, who shall stand it?
For with Thee there is mercy: and by reason of Thy law I have waited on Thee, O Lord! My soul hath relied on His word: my soul hath hoped in the Lord. From the morning watch even until night. Let Israel hope in the Lord. For with the Lord there is mercy; and with Him plentiful Redemption. And He will redeem Israel from all his iniquities.
Eternal rest give unto them, O Lord! And let perpetual light shine upon them. May they rest in peace. Amen.

Evening Prayer for the Poor Souls:

V. Lord, hear my prayer.
R. And let my cry come unto Thee.
Bless, O my God! the repose I am about to take, that, renewing my strength, I may be better enabled to serve Thee. Pour down Thy blessings, O Lord! on my parents, relations, friends, and enemies. Protect the Pope, our Bishop, and all the Pastors of Thy holy Church. Assist the poor and the afflicted, and those who are now in their last agony. Look with an eye of pity on the suffering souls in purgatory, particularly

_____

_____

_____

put an end to their torments and lead them forth into everlasting joy.

Eternal rest grant unto them and let perpetual light shine upon them. Amen.

DATE: _____

Today make the Stations of the Cross for the benefit of the Holy Souls in Purgatory.

Morning Prayer for the Poor Souls:

Out of the depths I have cried to Thee O Lord! Lord, hear my voice. Let Thine ears be attentive to the voice of my supplication.
If Thou, O Lord, wilt mark iniquities, Lord, who shall stand it?
For with Thee there is mercy: and by reason of Thy law I have waited on Thee, O Lord! My soul hath relied on His word: my soul hath hoped in the Lord. From the morning watch even until night. Let Israel hope in the Lord. For with the Lord there is mercy; and with Him plentiful Redemption. And He will redeem Israel from all his iniquities.
Eternal rest give unto them, O Lord! And let perpetual light shine upon them. May they rest in peace. Amen.

Evening Prayer for the Poor Souls:

V. Lord, hear my prayer.
R. And let my cry come unto Thee.
Bless, O my God! the repose I am about to take, that, renewing my strength, I may be better enabled to serve Thee. Pour down Thy blessings, O Lord! on my parents, relations, friends, and enemies. Protect the Pope, our Bishop, and all the Pastors of Thy holy Church. Assist the poor and the afflicted, and those who are now in their last agony. Look with an eye of pity on the suffering souls in purgatory, particularly

_____
_____

_____

put an end to their torments and lead them forth into everlasting joy.

Eternal rest grant unto them and let perpetual light shine upon them. Amen.

DATE: _____

Pray today for the souls of all Jewish people who have died.

Morning Prayer for the Poor Souls:

Out of the depths I have cried to Thee O Lord! Lord, hear my voice. Let Thine ears be attentive to the voice of my supplication.
If Thou, O Lord, wilt mark iniquities, Lord, who shall stand it?
For with Thee there is mercy: and by reason of Thy law I have waited on Thee, O Lord! My soul hath relied on His word: my soul hath hoped in the Lord. From the morning watch even until night. Let Israel hope in the Lord. For with the Lord there is mercy; and with Him plentiful Redemption. And He will redeem Israel from all his iniquities.
Eternal rest give unto them, O Lord! And let perpetual light shine upon them. May they rest in peace. Amen.

Evening Prayer for the Poor Souls:

V. Lord, hear my prayer.
R. And let my cry come unto Thee.
Bless, O my God! the repose I am about to take, that, renewing my strength, I may be better enabled to serve Thee. Pour down Thy blessings, O Lord! on my parents, relations, friends, and enemies. Protect the Pope, our Bishop, and all the Pastors of Thy holy Church. Assist the poor and the afflicted, and those who are now in their last agony. Look with an eye of pity on the suffering souls in purgatory, particularly

_____
_____

_____

put an end to their torments and lead them forth into everlasting joy.

Eternal rest grant unto them and let perpetual light shine upon them. Amen.

DATE: _____

Today, pray for the souls of persecutors of Christians who have died.

Morning Prayer for the Poor Souls:

Out of the depths I have cried to Thee O Lord! Lord, hear my voice. Let Thine ears be attentive to the voice of my supplication.
If Thou, O Lord, wilt mark iniquities, Lord, who shall stand it?
For with Thee there is mercy: and by reason of Thy law I have waited on Thee, O Lord! My soul hath relied on His word: my soul hath hoped in the Lord. From the morning watch even until night. Let Israel hope in the Lord. For with the Lord there is mercy; and with Him plentiful Redemption. And He will redeem Israel from all his iniquities.
Eternal rest give unto them, O Lord! And let perpetual light shine upon them. May they rest in peace. Amen.

Evening Prayer for the Poor Souls:

V. Lord, hear my prayer.
R. And let my cry come unto Thee.
Bless, O my God! the repose I am about to take, that, renewing my strength, I may be better enabled to serve Thee. Pour down Thy blessings, O Lord! on my parents, relations, friends, and enemies. Protect the Pope, our Bishop, and all the Pastors of Thy holy Church. Assist the poor and the afflicted, and those who are now in their last agony. Look with an eye of pity on the suffering souls in purgatory, particularly

_____

_____

_____

put an end to their torments and lead them forth into everlasting joy.

Eternal rest grant unto them and let perpetual light shine upon them. Amen.

DATE: _____

Light a blessed candle today in remembrance of the Holy Souls.

Morning Prayer for the Poor Souls:

Out of the depths I have cried to Thee O Lord! Lord, hear my voice. Let Thine ears be attentive to the voice of my supplication.
If Thou, O Lord, wilt mark iniquities, Lord, who shall stand it?
For with Thee there is mercy: and by reason of Thy law I have waited on Thee, O Lord! My soul hath relied on His word: my soul hath hoped in the Lord. From the morning watch even until night. Let Israel hope in the Lord. For with the Lord there is mercy; and with Him plentiful Redemption. And He will redeem Israel from all his iniquities.
Eternal rest give unto them, O Lord! And let perpetual light shine upon them. May they rest in peace. Amen.

Evening Prayer for the Poor Souls:

V. Lord, hear my prayer.
R. And let my cry come unto Thee.
Bless, O my God! the repose I am about to take, that, renewing my strength, I may be better enabled to serve Thee. Pour down Thy blessings, O Lord! on my parents, relations, friends, and enemies. Protect the Pope, our Bishop, and all the Pastors of Thy holy Church. Assist the poor and the afflicted, and those who are now in their last agony. Look with an eye of pity on the suffering souls in purgatory, particularly

_____

_____

_____

put an end to their torments and lead them forth into everlasting joy.

Eternal rest grant unto them and let perpetual light shine upon them. Amen.

DATE: _____

Begin a Novena today for the benefit of the Poor Souls. St. Alphonsus Liguori wrote a powerful one just for the Holy Souls, which may be found online, but any Novena will be appreciated.

Morning Prayer for the Poor Souls:

Out of the depths I have cried to Thee O Lord! Lord, hear my voice. Let Thine ears be attentive to the voice of my supplication.
If Thou, O Lord, wilt mark iniquities, Lord, who shall stand it?
For with Thee there is mercy: and by reason of Thy law I have waited on Thee, O Lord! My soul hath relied on His word: my soul hath hoped in the Lord. From the morning watch even until night. Let Israel hope in the Lord. For with the Lord there is mercy; and with Him plentiful Redemption. And He will redeem Israel from all his iniquities.
Eternal rest give unto them, O Lord! And let perpetual light shine upon them. May they rest in peace. Amen.

Evening Prayer for the Poor Souls:

V. Lord, hear my prayer.
R. And let my cry come unto Thee.
Bless, O my God! the repose I am about to take, that, renewing my strength, I may be better enabled to serve Thee. Pour down Thy blessings, O Lord! on my parents, relations, friends, and enemies. Protect the Pope, our Bishop, and all the Pastors of Thy holy Church. Assist the poor and the afflicted, and those who are now in their last agony. Look with an eye of pity on the suffering souls in purgatory, particularly

_____
_____
_____

put an end to their torments and lead them forth into everlasting joy.

Eternal rest grant unto them and let perpetual light shine upon them. Amen.

DATE: _____

Give alms to the poor today to benefit the souls in Purgatory. We are told that giving alms is of great benefit to suffering souls.

Morning Prayer for the Poor Souls:

Out of the depths I have cried to Thee O Lord! Lord, hear my voice. Let Thine ears be attentive to the voice of my supplication.
If Thou, O Lord, wilt mark iniquities, Lord, who shall stand it?
For with Thee there is mercy: and by reason of Thy law I have waited on Thee, O Lord! My soul hath relied on His word: my soul hath hoped in the Lord. From the morning watch even until night. Let Israel hope in the Lord. For with the Lord there is mercy; and with Him plentiful Redemption. And He will redeem Israel from all his iniquities.
Eternal rest give unto them, O Lord! And let perpetual light shine upon them. May they rest in peace. Amen.

Evening Prayer for the Poor Souls:

V. Lord, hear my prayer.
R. And let my cry come unto Thee.
Bless, O my God! the repose I am about to take, that, renewing my strength, I may be better enabled to serve Thee. Pour down Thy blessings, O Lord! on my parents, relations, friends, and enemies. Protect the Pope, our Bishop, and all the Pastors of Thy holy Church. Assist the poor and the afflicted, and those who are now in their last agony. Look with an eye of pity on the suffering souls in purgatory, particularly

_____

_____

_____

put an end to their torments and lead them forth into everlasting joy.

Eternal rest grant unto them and let perpetual light shine upon them. Amen.

DATE: _____

Read aloud today from the Acts of the Apostles to comfort the Holy Souls. The Good News of Jesus' salvation is of great relief to their suffering.

Morning Prayer for the Poor Souls:

Out of the depths I have cried to Thee O Lord! Lord, hear my voice. Let Thine ears be attentive to the voice of my supplication.
If Thou, O Lord, wilt mark iniquities, Lord, who shall stand it?
For with Thee there is mercy: and by reason of Thy law I have waited on Thee, O Lord! My soul hath relied on His word: my soul hath hoped in the Lord. From the morning watch even until night. Let Israel hope in the Lord. For with the Lord there is mercy; and with Him plentiful Redemption. And He will redeem Israel from all his iniquities.
Eternal rest give unto them, O Lord! And let perpetual light shine upon them. May they rest in peace. Amen.

Evening Prayer for the Poor Souls:

V. Lord, hear my prayer.
R. And let my cry come unto Thee.
Bless, O my God! the repose I am about to take, that, renewing my strength, I may be better enabled to serve Thee. Pour down Thy blessings, O Lord! on my parents, relations, friends, and enemies. Protect the Pope, our Bishop, and all the Pastors of Thy holy Church. Assist the poor and the afflicted, and those who are now in their last agony. Look with an eye of pity on the suffering souls in purgatory, particularly

_____
_____
_____

put an end to their torments and lead them forth into everlasting joy.

Eternal rest grant unto them and let perpetual light shine upon them. Amen.

DATE: _____

Today, ask the saints known as intercessors for the dead to pray with you for their release, including St. Nicholas of Tolentino, St. Gertrude the Great, St. Catherine of Genoa, St. Padre Pio, St. Philip Neri, St. John Macías, St. Faustina Kowalska, St. Joseph and, of course, the Blessed Mother.

Morning Prayer for the Poor Souls:

Out of the depths I have cried to Thee O Lord! Lord, hear my voice. Let Thine ears be attentive to the voice of my supplication.
If Thou, O Lord, wilt mark iniquities, Lord, who shall stand it?
For with Thee there is mercy: and by reason of Thy law I have waited on Thee, O Lord! My soul hath relied on His word: my soul hath hoped in the Lord. From the morning watch even until night. Let Israel hope in the Lord. For with the Lord there is mercy; and with Him plentiful Redemption. And He will redeem Israel from all his iniquities.
Eternal rest give unto them, O Lord! And let perpetual light shine upon them. May they rest in peace. Amen.

Evening Prayer for the Poor Souls:

V. Lord, hear my prayer.
R. And let my cry come unto Thee.
Bless, O my God! the repose I am about to take, that, renewing my strength, I may be better enabled to serve Thee. Pour down Thy blessings, O Lord! on my parents, relations, friends, and enemies. Protect the Pope, our Bishop, and all the Pastors of Thy holy Church. Assist the poor and the afflicted, and those who are now in their last agony. Look with an eye of pity on the suffering souls in purgatory, particularly

_____
_____
_____

put an end to their torments and lead them forth into everlasting joy.

Eternal rest grant unto them and let perpetual light shine upon them. Amen.

The Month of
_____

DATE: _____

Today, have a Mass said for the soul of a family member or friend who has passed away. This can be through your own parish or through an order or national shrine via their website.

Morning Prayer for the Poor Souls:

Out of the depths I have cried to Thee O Lord! Lord, hear my voice. Let Thine ears be attentive to the voice of my supplication.
If Thou, O Lord, wilt mark iniquities, Lord, who shall stand it?
For with Thee there is mercy: and by reason of Thy law I have waited on Thee, O Lord! My soul hath relied on His word: my soul hath hoped in the Lord. From the morning watch even until night. Let Israel hope in the Lord. For with the Lord there is mercy; and with Him plentiful Redemption. And He will redeem Israel from all his iniquities.
Eternal rest give unto them, O Lord! And let perpetual light shine upon them. May they rest in peace. Amen.

Evening Prayer for the Poor Souls:

V. Lord, hear my prayer.
R. And let my cry come unto Thee.
Bless, O my God! the repose I am about to take, that, renewing my strength, I may be better enabled to serve Thee. Pour down Thy blessings, O Lord! on my parents, relations, friends, and enemies. Protect the Pope, our Bishop, and all the Pastors of Thy holy Church. Assist the poor and the afflicted, and those who are now in their last agony. Look with an eye of pity on the suffering souls in purgatory, particularly

_____
_____
_____

put an end to their torments and lead them forth into everlasting joy.

Eternal rest grant unto them and let perpetual light shine upon them. Amen.

DATE:

_____

Pray the Rosary today for the release of souls from Purgatory. Mystic saints have told us that the Blessed Mother herself comes to Purgatory to bring souls with her back to Heaven.

Morning Prayer for the Poor Souls:

Out of the depths I have cried to Thee O Lord! Lord, hear my voice. Let Thine ears be attentive to the voice of my supplication.
If Thou, O Lord, wilt mark iniquities, Lord, who shall stand it?
For with Thee there is mercy: and by reason of Thy law I have waited on Thee, O Lord! My soul hath relied on His word: my soul hath hoped in the Lord. From the morning watch even until night. Let Israel hope in the Lord. For with the Lord there is mercy; and with Him plentiful Redemption. And He will redeem Israel from all his iniquities.
Eternal rest give unto them, O Lord! And let perpetual light shine upon them. May they rest in peace. Amen.

Evening Prayer for the Poor Souls:

V. Lord, hear my prayer.
R. And let my cry come unto Thee.
Bless, O my God! the repose I am about to take, that, renewing my strength, I may be better enabled to serve Thee. Pour down Thy blessings, O Lord! on my parents, relations, friends, and enemies. Protect the Pope, our Bishop, and all the Pastors of Thy holy Church. Assist the poor and the afflicted, and those who are now in their last agony. Look with an eye of pity on the suffering souls in purgatory, particularly

_____
_____
_____

put an end to their torments and lead them forth into everlasting joy.

Eternal rest grant unto them and let perpetual light shine upon them. Amen.

DATE:

_____

Today, ask the Blessed Mother to apply your prayers and works to a poor soul who has no one to pray for them.

Morning Prayer for the Poor Souls:

Out of the depths I have cried to Thee O Lord! Lord, hear my voice. Let Thine ears be attentive to the voice of my supplication.
If Thou, O Lord, wilt mark iniquities, Lord, who shall stand it?
For with Thee there is mercy: and by reason of Thy law I have waited on Thee, O Lord! My soul hath relied on His word: my soul hath hoped in the Lord. From the morning watch even until night. Let Israel hope in the Lord. For with the Lord there is mercy; and with Him plentiful Redemption. And He will redeem Israel from all his iniquities.
Eternal rest give unto them, O Lord! And let perpetual light shine upon them. May they rest in peace. Amen.

Evening Prayer for the Poor Souls:

V. Lord, hear my prayer.
R. And let my cry come unto Thee.
Bless, O my God! the repose I am about to take, that, renewing my strength, I may be better enabled to serve Thee. Pour down Thy blessings, O Lord! on my parents, relations, friends, and enemies. Protect the Pope, our Bishop, and all the Pastors of Thy holy Church. Assist the poor and the afflicted, and those who are now in their last agony. Look with an eye of pity on the suffering souls in purgatory, particularly

_____

_____

_____

put an end to their torments and lead them forth into everlasting joy.

Eternal rest grant unto them and let perpetual light shine upon them. Amen.

DATE:

_____

We all have a spiritual or physical affliction or burden that we suffer with daily. Today, dedicate your ailment-related suffering to the Poor souls.

Morning Prayer for the Poor Souls:

Out of the depths I have cried to Thee O Lord! Lord, hear my voice. Let Thine ears be attentive to the voice of my supplication.
If Thou, O Lord, wilt mark iniquities, Lord, who shall stand it?
For with Thee there is mercy: and by reason of Thy law I have waited on Thee, O Lord! My soul hath relied on His word: my soul hath hoped in the Lord. From the morning watch even until night. Let Israel hope in the Lord. For with the Lord there is mercy; and with Him plentiful Redemption. And He will redeem Israel from all his iniquities.
Eternal rest give unto them, O Lord! And let perpetual light shine upon them. May they rest in peace. Amen.

Evening Prayer for the Poor Souls:

V. Lord, hear my prayer.
R. And let my cry come unto Thee.
Bless, O my God! the repose I am about to take, that, renewing my strength, I may be better enabled to serve Thee. Pour down Thy blessings, O Lord! on my parents, relations, friends, and enemies. Protect the Pope, our Bishop, and all the Pastors of Thy holy Church. Assist the poor and the afflicted, and those who are now in their last agony. Look with an eye of pity on the suffering souls in purgatory, particularly

_____

_____

_____

put an end to their torments and lead them forth into everlasting joy.

Eternal rest grant unto them and let perpetual light shine upon them. Amen.

DATE:
_____

Today, visit or call someone elderly or alone and offer your work of mercy for the souls in Purgatory.

Morning Prayer for the Poor Souls:

Out of the depths I have cried to Thee O Lord! Lord, hear my voice. Let Thine ears be attentive to the voice of my supplication.
If Thou, O Lord, wilt mark iniquities, Lord, who shall stand it?
For with Thee there is mercy: and by reason of Thy law I have waited on Thee, O Lord! My soul hath relied on His word: my soul hath hoped in the Lord. From the morning watch even until night. Let Israel hope in the Lord. For with the Lord there is mercy; and with Him plentiful Redemption. And He will redeem Israel from all his iniquities.
Eternal rest give unto them, O Lord! And let perpetual light shine upon them. May they rest in peace. Amen.

Evening Prayer for the Poor Souls:

V. Lord, hear my prayer.
R. And let my cry come unto Thee.
Bless, O my God! the repose I am about to take, that, renewing my strength, I may be better enabled to serve Thee. Pour down Thy blessings, O Lord! on my parents, relations, friends, and enemies. Protect the Pope, our Bishop, and all the Pastors of Thy holy Church. Assist the poor and the afflicted, and those who are now in their last agony. Look with an eye of pity on the suffering souls in purgatory, particularly

_____
_____
_____

put an end to their torments and lead them forth into everlasting joy.

Eternal rest grant unto them, and let perpetual light shine upon them. Amen.

DATE:

_____

During the course of the day today, pray for those you meet and strangers you see on street, asking God to apply your prayers for them to their future time in Purgatory.

Morning Prayer for the Poor Souls:

Out of the depths I have cried to Thee O Lord! Lord, hear my voice. Let Thine ears be attentive to the voice of my supplication.
If Thou, O Lord, wilt mark iniquities, Lord, who shall stand it?
For with Thee there is mercy: and by reason of Thy law I have waited on Thee, O Lord! My soul hath relied on His word: my soul hath hoped in the Lord. From the morning watch even until night. Let Israel hope in the Lord. For with the Lord there is mercy; and with Him plentiful Redemption. And He will redeem Israel from all his iniquities.
Eternal rest give unto them, O Lord! And let perpetual light shine upon them. May they rest in peace. Amen.

Evening Prayer for the Poor Souls:

V. Lord, hear my prayer.
R. And let my cry come unto Thee.
Bless, O my God! the repose I am about to take, that, renewing my strength, I may be better enabled to serve Thee. Pour down Thy blessings, O Lord! on my parents, relations, friends, and enemies. Protect the Pope, our Bishop, and all the Pastors of Thy holy Church. Assist the poor and the afflicted, and those who are now in their last agony. Look with an eye of pity on the suffering souls in purgatory, particularly

_____
_____
_____

put an end to their torments and lead them forth into everlasting joy.

Eternal rest grant unto them, and let perpetual light shine upon them. Amen.

DATE:
_____

Today, ask the Blessed Mother to use your prayers for someone in Purgatory with no one to pray for them.

Morning Prayer for the Poor Souls:

Out of the depths I have cried to Thee O Lord! Lord, hear my voice. Let Thine ears be attentive to the voice of my supplication.
If Thou, O Lord, wilt mark iniquities, Lord, who shall stand it?
For with Thee there is mercy: and by reason of Thy law I have waited on Thee, O Lord! My soul hath relied on His word: my soul hath hoped in the Lord. From the morning watch even until night. Let Israel hope in the Lord. For with the Lord there is mercy; and with Him plentiful Redemption. And He will redeem Israel from all his iniquities.
Eternal rest give unto them, O Lord! And let perpetual light shine upon them. May they rest in peace. Amen.

Evening Prayer for the Poor Souls:

V. Lord, hear my prayer.
R. And let my cry come unto Thee.
Bless, O my God! the repose I am about to take, that, renewing my strength, I may be better enabled to serve Thee. Pour down Thy blessings, O Lord! on my parents, relations, friends, and enemies. Protect the Pope, our Bishop, and all the Pastors of Thy holy Church. Assist the poor and the afflicted, and those who are now in their last agony. Look with an eye of pity on the suffering souls in purgatory, particularly

_____
_____
_____

put an end to their torments and lead them forth into everlasting joy.

Eternal rest grant unto them, and let perpetual light shine upon them. Amen.

DATE: _____

Today, sprinkle holy water on the carpet of your home or outside your house as a comfort to the Poor Souls.

Morning Prayer for the Poor Souls:

Out of the depths I have cried to Thee O Lord! Lord, hear my voice. Let Thine ears be attentive to the voice of my supplication.
If Thou, O Lord, wilt mark iniquities, Lord, who shall stand it?
For with Thee there is mercy: and by reason of Thy law I have waited on Thee, O Lord! My soul hath relied on His word: my soul hath hoped in the Lord. From the morning watch even until night. Let Israel hope in the Lord. For with the Lord there is mercy; and with Him plentiful Redemption. And He will redeem Israel from all his iniquities.
Eternal rest give unto them, O Lord! And let perpetual light shine upon them. May they rest in peace. Amen.

Evening Prayer for the Poor Souls:

V. Lord, hear my prayer.
R. And let my cry come unto Thee.
Bless, O my God! the repose I am about to take, that, renewing my strength, I may be better enabled to serve Thee. Pour down Thy blessings, O Lord! on my parents, relations, friends, and enemies. Protect the Pope, our Bishop, and all the Pastors of Thy holy Church. Assist the poor and the afflicted, and those who are now in their last agony. Look with an eye of pity on the suffering souls in purgatory, particularly

_____
_____
_____

put an end to their torments and lead them forth into everlasting joy.

Eternal rest grant unto them, and let perpetual light shine upon them. Amen.

DATE:
_____

Today, visit a church if you are able, and pray for the souls who are spending their Purgatorial time there. Catholic mystics have told us that God allows many souls to do so. If you cannot visit a church, think of a local church and pray for any souls who might be there.

Morning Prayer for the Poor Souls:

Out of the depths I have cried to Thee O Lord! Lord, hear my voice. Let Thine ears be attentive to the voice of my supplication.
If Thou, O Lord, wilt mark iniquities, Lord, who shall stand it?
For with Thee there is mercy: and by reason of Thy law I have waited on Thee, O Lord! My soul hath relied on His word: my soul hath hoped in the Lord. From the morning watch even until night. Let Israel hope in the Lord. For with the Lord there is mercy; and with Him plentiful Redemption. And He will redeem Israel from all his iniquities.
Eternal rest give unto them, O Lord! And let perpetual light shine upon them. May they rest in peace. Amen.

Evening Prayer for the Poor Souls:

V. Lord, hear my prayer.
R. And let my cry come unto Thee.
Bless, O my God! the repose I am about to take, that, renewing my strength, I may be better enabled to serve Thee. Pour down Thy blessings, O Lord! on my parents, relations, friends, and enemies. Protect the Pope, our Bishop, and all the Pastors of Thy holy Church. Assist the poor and the afflicted, and those who are now in their last agony. Look with an eye of pity on the suffering souls in purgatory, particularly

_____
_____

put an end to their torments and lead them forth into everlasting joy.

Eternal rest grant unto them, and let perpetual light shine upon them. Amen.

DATE:

_____

Today, visit someone who is sick if you are able, and offer up this work of mercy for the Holy Souls. If you cannot, pray for those in your local hospital or nursing home.

Morning Prayer for the Poor Souls:

Out of the depths I have cried to Thee O Lord! Lord, hear my voice. Let Thine ears be attentive to the voice of my supplication.
If Thou, O Lord, wilt mark iniquities, Lord, who shall stand it?
For with Thee there is mercy: and by reason of Thy law I have waited on Thee, O Lord! My soul hath relied on His word: my soul hath hoped in the Lord. From the morning watch even until night. Let Israel hope in the Lord. For with the Lord there is mercy; and with Him plentiful Redemption. And He will redeem Israel from all his iniquities.
Eternal rest give unto them, O Lord! And let perpetual light shine upon them. May they rest in peace. Amen.

Evening Prayer for the Poor Souls:

V. Lord, hear my prayer.
R. And let my cry come unto Thee.
Bless, O my God! the repose I am about to take, that, renewing my strength, I may be better enabled to serve Thee. Pour down Thy blessings, O Lord! on my parents, relations, friends, and enemies. Protect the Pope, our Bishop, and all the Pastors of Thy holy Church. Assist the poor and the afflicted, and those who are now in their last agony. Look with an eye of pity on the suffering souls in purgatory, particularly

_____

_____

_____

put an end to their torments and lead them forth into everlasting joy.

Eternal rest grant unto them, and let perpetual light shine upon them. Amen.

DATE:

_____

Today pray for the souls of all the atheists who have died.

Morning Prayer for the Poor Souls:

Out of the depths I have cried to Thee O Lord! Lord, hear my voice. Let Thine ears be attentive to the voice of my supplication.
If Thou, O Lord, wilt mark iniquities, Lord, who shall stand it?
For with Thee there is mercy: and by reason of Thy law I have waited on Thee, O Lord! My soul hath relied on His word: my soul hath hoped in the Lord. From the morning watch even until night. Let Israel hope in the Lord. For with the Lord there is mercy; and with Him plentiful Redemption. And He will redeem Israel from all his iniquities.
Eternal rest give unto them, O Lord! And let perpetual light shine upon them. May they rest in peace. Amen.

Evening Prayer for the Poor Souls:

V. Lord, hear my prayer.
R. And let my cry come unto Thee.
Bless, O my God! the repose I am about to take, that, renewing my strength, I may be better enabled to serve Thee. Pour down Thy blessings, O Lord! on my parents, relations, friends, and enemies. Protect the Pope, our Bishop, and all the Pastors of Thy holy Church. Assist the poor and the afflicted, and those who are now in their last agony. Look with an eye of pity on the suffering souls in purgatory, particularly

_____

_____

_____

put an end to their torments and lead them forth into everlasting joy.

Eternal rest grant unto them, and let perpetual light shine upon them. Amen.

DATE:

_____

Today, read the obituaries in your local newspaper and pray for the souls who have died in the past several days.

Morning Prayer for the Poor Souls:

Out of the depths I have cried to Thee O Lord! Lord, hear my voice. Let Thine ears be attentive to the voice of my supplication.
If Thou, O Lord, wilt mark iniquities, Lord, who shall stand it?
For with Thee there is mercy: and by reason of Thy law I have waited on Thee, O Lord! My soul hath relied on His word: my soul hath hoped in the Lord. From the morning watch even until night. Let Israel hope in the Lord. For with the Lord there is mercy; and with Him plentiful Redemption. And He will redeem Israel from all his iniquities.
Eternal rest give unto them, O Lord! And let perpetual light shine upon them. May they rest in peace. Amen.

Evening Prayer for the Poor Souls:

V. Lord, hear my prayer.
R. And let my cry come unto Thee.
Bless, O my God! the repose I am about to take, that, renewing my strength, I may be better enabled to serve Thee. Pour down Thy blessings, O Lord! on my parents, relations, friends, and enemies. Protect the Pope, our Bishop, and all the Pastors of Thy holy Church. Assist the poor and the afflicted, and those who are now in their last agony. Look with an eye of pity on the suffering souls in purgatory, particularly

_____

_____

_____

put an end to their torments and lead them forth into everlasting joy.

Eternal rest grant unto them, and let perpetual light shine upon them. Amen.

DATE:
_____

Spend some time in Eucharistic Adoration today for the Poor Souls. If you cannot travel to a church physically, watch live Adoration on EWTN, YouTube or Facebook.

***Morning Prayer for the Poor Souls*:**

Out of the depths I have cried to Thee O Lord! Lord, hear my voice. Let Thine ears be attentive to the voice of my supplication.
If Thou, O Lord, wilt mark iniquities, Lord, who shall stand it?
For with Thee there is mercy: and by reason of Thy law I have waited on Thee, O Lord! My soul hath relied on His word: my soul hath hoped in the Lord. From the morning watch even until night. Let Israel hope in the Lord. For with the Lord there is mercy; and with Him plentiful Redemption. And He will redeem Israel from all his iniquities.
Eternal rest give unto them, O Lord! And let perpetual light shine upon them. May they rest in peace. Amen.

Evening Prayer for the Poor Souls:

V. Lord, hear my prayer.
R. And let my cry come unto Thee.
Bless, O my God! the repose I am about to take, that, renewing my strength, I may be better enabled to serve Thee. Pour down Thy blessings, O Lord! on my parents, relations, friends, and enemies. Protect the Pope, our Bishop, and all the Pastors of Thy holy Church. Assist the poor and the afflicted, and those who are now in their last agony. Look with an eye of pity on the suffering souls in purgatory, particularly

_____
_____

_____

put an end to their torments and lead them forth into everlasting joy.

Eternal rest grant unto them, and let perpetual light shine upon them. Amen.

DATE:

_____

a drive today to a cemetery and pray for the souls of those interred there. If you cannot physically visit a cemetery, think of a cemetery in your city or town and pray for the souls of those buried there.

Morning Prayer for the Poor Souls:

Out of the depths I have cried to Thee O Lord! Lord, hear my voice. Let Thine ears be attentive to the voice of my supplication.
If Thou, O Lord, wilt mark iniquities, Lord, who shall stand it?
For with Thee there is mercy: and by reason of Thy law I have waited on Thee, O Lord! My soul hath relied on His word: my soul hath hoped in the Lord. From the morning watch even until night. Let Israel hope in the Lord. For with the Lord there is mercy; and with Him plentiful Redemption. And He will redeem Israel from all his iniquities.
Eternal rest give unto them, O Lord! And let perpetual light shine upon them. May they rest in peace. Amen.

Evening Prayer for the Poor Souls:

V. Lord, hear my prayer.
R. And let my cry come unto Thee.
Bless, O my God! the repose I am about to take, that, renewing my strength, I may be better enabled to serve Thee. Pour down Thy blessings, O Lord! on my parents, relations, friends, and enemies. Protect the Pope, our Bishop, and all the Pastors of Thy holy Church. Assist the poor and the afflicted, and those who are now in their last agony. Look with an eye of pity on the suffering souls in purgatory, particularly

_____

_____

_____

put an end to their torments and lead them forth into everlasting joy.

Eternal rest grant unto them, and let perpetual light shine upon them. Amen.

DATE:

_____

Today, play some sacred music to comfort the Poor Souls. Mystic saints have told us that these small gestures provide great relief to their suffering.

Morning Prayer for the Poor Souls:

Out of the depths I have cried to Thee O Lord! Lord, hear my voice. Let Thine ears be attentive to the voice of my supplication.
If Thou, O Lord, wilt mark iniquities, Lord, who shall stand it?
For with Thee there is mercy: and by reason of Thy law I have waited on Thee, O Lord! My soul hath relied on His word: my soul hath hoped in the Lord. From the morning watch even until night. Let Israel hope in the Lord. For with the Lord there is mercy; and with Him plentiful Redemption. And He will redeem Israel from all his iniquities.
Eternal rest give unto them, O Lord! And let perpetual light shine upon them. May they rest in peace. Amen.

Evening Prayer for the Poor Souls:

V. Lord, hear my prayer.
R. And let my cry come unto Thee.
Bless, O my God! the repose I am about to take, that, renewing my strength, I may be better enabled to serve Thee. Pour down Thy blessings, O Lord! on my parents, relations, friends, and enemies. Protect the Pope, our Bishop, and all the Pastors of Thy holy Church. Assist the poor and the afflicted, and those who are now in their last agony. Look with an eye of pity on the suffering souls in purgatory, particularly

_____

_____

_____

put an end to their torments and lead them forth into everlasting joy.

Eternal rest grant unto them, and let perpetual light shine upon them. Amen.

DATE:
_____

Today, make reparation to the Sacred Heart of Jesus for the souls in Purgatory who offended His most precious Heart with the following: Adorable Heart of Jesus, glowing with love for us and inflamed with zeal for our salvation. O Heart that understands the misery to which our sins have brought us, infinitely rich in mercy to heal the wounds of our souls, behold me humbly kneeling before You to express the sorrow that fills my heart for the coldness and indifference with which I have so long returned the numberless benefits which You have bestowed upon me.

Morning Prayer for the Poor Souls:

Out of the depths I have cried to Thee O Lord! Lord, hear my voice. Let Thine ears be attentive to the voice of my supplication. If Thou, O Lord, wilt mark iniquities, Lord, who shall stand it? For with Thee there is mercy: and by reason of Thy law I have waited on Thee, O Lord! My soul hath relied on His word: my soul hath hoped in the Lord. From the morning watch even until night. Let Israel hope in the Lord. For with the Lord there is mercy; and with Him plentiful Redemption. And He will redeem Israel from all his iniquities. Eternal rest give unto them, O Lord! And let perpetual light shine upon them. May they rest in peace. Amen.

Evening Prayer for the Poor Souls:

V. Lord, hear my prayer.
R. And let my cry come unto Thee.
Bless, O my God! the repose I am about to take, that, renewing my strength, I may be better enabled to serve Thee. Pour down Thy blessings, O Lord! on my parents, relations, friends, and enemies. Protect the Pope, our Bishop, and all the Pastors of Thy holy Church. Assist the poor and the afflicted, and those who are now in their last agony. Look with an eye of pity on the suffering souls in purgatory, particularly

_____

put an end to their torments and lead them forth into everlasting joy.

Eternal rest grant unto them, and let perpetual light shine upon them. Amen.

DATE:

_____

Start a Mass Collection jar or envelope today for the Holy Souls. Add money to it as you are able, and when you have enough for a donation, have a Mass said for a soul in Purgatory.

Morning Prayer for the Poor Souls:

Out of the depths I have cried to Thee O Lord! Lord, hear my voice. Let Thine ears be attentive to the voice of my supplication.
If Thou, O Lord, wilt mark iniquities, Lord, who shall stand it?
For with Thee there is mercy: and by reason of Thy law I have waited on Thee, O Lord! My soul hath relied on His word: my soul hath hoped in the Lord. From the morning watch even until night. Let Israel hope in the Lord. For with the Lord there is mercy; and with Him plentiful Redemption. And He will redeem Israel from all his iniquities.
Eternal rest give unto them, O Lord! And let perpetual light shine upon them. May they rest in peace. Amen.

Evening Prayer for the Poor Souls:

V. Lord, hear my prayer.
R. And let my cry come unto Thee.
Bless, O my God! the repose I am about to take, that, renewing my strength, I may be better enabled to serve Thee. Pour down Thy blessings, O Lord! on my parents, relations, friends, and enemies. Protect the Pope, our Bishop, and all the Pastors of Thy holy Church. Assist the poor and the afflicted, and those who are now in their last agony. Look with an eye of pity on the suffering souls in purgatory, particularly

_____
_____
_____

put an end to their torments and lead them forth into everlasting joy.

Eternal rest grant unto them, and let perpetual light shine upon them. Amen.

DATE:
_____

Go without a meal or snack today if possible, for the benefit of the Holy Souls. If you are in ill health, give up a special treat instead.

Morning Prayer for the Poor Souls:

Out of the depths I have cried to Thee O Lord! Lord, hear my voice. Let Thine ears be attentive to the voice of my supplication.
If Thou, O Lord, wilt mark iniquities, Lord, who shall stand it?
For with Thee there is mercy: and by reason of Thy law I have waited on Thee, O Lord! My soul hath relied on His word: my soul hath hoped in the Lord. From the morning watch even until night. Let Israel hope in the Lord. For with the Lord there is mercy; and with Him plentiful Redemption. And He will redeem Israel from all his iniquities.
Eternal rest give unto them, O Lord! And let perpetual light shine upon them. May they rest in peace. Amen.

Evening Prayer for the Poor Souls:

V. Lord, hear my prayer.
R. And let my cry come unto Thee.
Bless, O my God! the repose I am about to take, that, renewing my strength, I may be better enabled to serve Thee. Pour down Thy blessings, O Lord! on my parents, relations, friends, and enemies. Protect the Pope, our Bishop, and all the Pastors of Thy holy Church. Assist the poor and the afflicted, and those who are now in their last agony. Look with an eye of pity on the suffering souls in purgatory, particularly

_____
_____
_____

put an end to their torments and lead them forth into everlasting joy.

Eternal rest grant unto them, and let perpetual light shine upon them. Amen.

DATE:

_____

Today, say a Divine Mercy chaplet for the Poor Souls.

Morning Prayer for the Poor Souls:

Out of the depths I have cried to Thee O Lord! Lord, hear my voice. Let Thine ears be attentive to the voice of my supplication.
If Thou, O Lord, wilt mark iniquities, Lord, who shall stand it?
For with Thee there is mercy: and by reason of Thy law I have waited on Thee, O Lord! My soul hath relied on His word: my soul hath hoped in the Lord. From the morning watch even until night. Let Israel hope in the Lord. For with the Lord there is mercy; and with Him plentiful Redemption. And He will redeem Israel from all his iniquities.
Eternal rest give unto them, O Lord! And let perpetual light shine upon them. May they rest in peace. Amen.

Evening Prayer for the Poor Souls:

V. Lord, hear my prayer.
R. And let my cry come unto Thee.
Bless, O my God! the repose I am about to take, that, renewing my strength, I may be better enabled to serve Thee. Pour down Thy blessings, O Lord! on my parents, relations, friends, and enemies. Protect the Pope, our Bishop, and all the Pastors of Thy holy Church. Assist the poor and the afflicted, and those who are now in their last agony. Look with an eye of pity on the suffering souls in purgatory, particularly

_____
_____
_____

put an end to their torments and lead them forth into everlasting joy.

Eternal rest grant unto them, and let perpetual light shine upon them. Amen.

DATE: _____

Pray today for the souls of priests and religious in Purgatory.

Morning Prayer for the Poor Souls:

Out of the depths I have cried to Thee O Lord! Lord, hear my voice. Let Thine ears be attentive to the voice of my supplication.
If Thou, O Lord, wilt mark iniquities, Lord, who shall stand it?
For with Thee there is mercy: and by reason of Thy law I have waited on Thee, O Lord! My soul hath relied on His word: my soul hath hoped in the Lord. From the morning watch even until night. Let Israel hope in the Lord. For with the Lord there is mercy; and with Him plentiful Redemption. And He will redeem Israel from all his iniquities.
Eternal rest give unto them, O Lord! And let perpetual light shine upon them. May they rest in peace. Amen.

Evening Prayer for the Poor Souls:

V. Lord, hear my prayer.
R. And let my cry come unto Thee.
Bless, O my God! the repose I am about to take, that, renewing my strength, I may be better enabled to serve Thee. Pour down Thy blessings, O Lord! on my parents, relations, friends, and enemies. Protect the Pope, our Bishop, and all the Pastors of Thy holy Church. Assist the poor and the afflicted, and those who are now in their last agony. Look with an eye of pity on the suffering souls in purgatory, particularly

_____

_____

_____

put an end to their torments and lead them forth into everlasting joy.

Eternal rest grant unto them, and let perpetual light shine upon them. Amen.

DATE: _____

While you are going about your day today, remember your friends and colleagues who have passed away over the years, asking God to release them from Purgatory.

Morning Prayer for the Poor Souls:

Out of the depths I have cried to Thee O Lord! Lord, hear my voice. Let Thine ears be attentive to the voice of my supplication.
If Thou, O Lord, wilt mark iniquities, Lord, who shall stand it?
For with Thee there is mercy: and by reason of Thy law I have waited on Thee, O Lord! My soul hath relied on His word: my soul hath hoped in the Lord. From the morning watch even until night. Let Israel hope in the Lord. For with the Lord there is mercy; and with Him plentiful Redemption. And He will redeem Israel from all his iniquities.
Eternal rest give unto them, O Lord! And let perpetual light shine upon them. May they rest in peace. Amen.

Evening Prayer for the Poor Souls:

V. Lord, hear my prayer.
R. And let my cry come unto Thee.
Bless, O my God! the repose I am about to take, that, renewing my strength, I may be better enabled to serve Thee. Pour down Thy blessings, O Lord! on my parents, relations, friends, and enemies. Protect the Pope, our Bishop, and all the Pastors of Thy holy Church. Assist the poor and the afflicted, and those who are now in their last agony. Look with an eye of pity on the suffering souls in purgatory, particularly

put an end to their torments and lead them forth into everlasting joy.

Eternal rest grant unto them, and let perpetual light shine upon them. Amen.

DATE: _____

Pray today for the dead who heard the Gospel but rejected it. May they be spared Hell and be released from Purgatory to be with Jesus.

Morning Prayer for the Poor Souls:

Out of the depths I have cried to Thee O Lord! Lord, hear my voice. Let Thine ears be attentive to the voice of my supplication.
If Thou, O Lord, wilt mark iniquities, Lord, who shall stand it?
For with Thee there is mercy: and by reason of Thy law I have waited on Thee, O Lord! My soul hath relied on His word: my soul hath hoped in the Lord. From the morning watch even until night. Let Israel hope in the Lord. For with the Lord there is mercy; and with Him plentiful Redemption. And He will redeem Israel from all his iniquities.
Eternal rest give unto them, O Lord! And let perpetual light shine upon them. May they rest in peace. Amen.

Evening Prayer for the Poor Souls:

V. Lord, hear my prayer.
R. And let my cry come unto Thee.
Bless, O my God! the repose I am about to take, that, renewing my strength, I may be better enabled to serve Thee. Pour down Thy blessings, O Lord! on my parents, relations, friends, and enemies. Protect the Pope, our Bishop, and all the Pastors of Thy holy Church. Assist the poor and the afflicted, and those who are now in their last agony. Look with an eye of pity on the suffering souls in purgatory, particularly

_____

_____

_____

put an end to their torments and lead them forth into everlasting joy.

Eternal rest grant unto them, and let perpetual light shine upon them. Amen.

DATE: _____

Today, spend some time reading devotional literature aloud for the comfort of the Poor Souls.

Morning Prayer for the Poor Souls:

Out of the depths I have cried to Thee O Lord! Lord, hear my voice. Let Thine ears be attentive to the voice of my supplication.
If Thou, O Lord, wilt mark iniquities, Lord, who shall stand it?
For with Thee there is mercy: and by reason of Thy law I have waited on Thee, O Lord! My soul hath relied on His word: my soul hath hoped in the Lord. From the morning watch even until night. Let Israel hope in the Lord. For with the Lord there is mercy; and with Him plentiful Redemption. And He will redeem Israel from all his iniquities.
Eternal rest give unto them, O Lord! And let perpetual light shine upon them. May they rest in peace. Amen.

Evening Prayer for the Poor Souls:

V. Lord, hear my prayer.
R. And let my cry come unto Thee.
Bless, O my God! the repose I am about to take, that, renewing my strength, I may be better enabled to serve Thee. Pour down Thy blessings, O Lord! on my parents, relations, friends, and enemies. Protect the Pope, our Bishop, and all the Pastors of Thy holy Church. Assist the poor and the afflicted, and those who are now in their last agony. Look with an eye of pity on the suffering souls in purgatory, particularly

_____
_____

_____

put an end to their torments and lead them forth into everlasting joy.

Eternal rest grant unto them, and let perpetual light shine upon them. Amen.

DATE: _____

Today make the Stations of the Cross for the benefit of the Holy Souls in Purgatory.

Morning Prayer for the Poor Souls:

Out of the depths I have cried to Thee O Lord! Lord, hear my voice. Let Thine ears be attentive to the voice of my supplication.
If Thou, O Lord, wilt mark iniquities, Lord, who shall stand it?
For with Thee there is mercy: and by reason of Thy law I have waited on Thee, O Lord! My soul hath relied on His word: my soul hath hoped in the Lord. From the morning watch even until night. Let Israel hope in the Lord. For with the Lord there is mercy; and with Him plentiful Redemption. And He will redeem Israel from all his iniquities.
Eternal rest give unto them, O Lord! And let perpetual light shine upon them. May they rest in peace. Amen.

Evening Prayer for the Poor Souls:

V. Lord, hear my prayer.
R. And let my cry come unto Thee.
Bless, O my God! the repose I am about to take, that, renewing my strength, I may be better enabled to serve Thee. Pour down Thy blessings, O Lord! on my parents, relations, friends, and enemies. Protect the Pope, our Bishop, and all the Pastors of Thy holy Church. Assist the poor and the afflicted, and those who are now in their last agony. Look with an eye of pity on the suffering souls in purgatory, particularly

_____

_____

_____

put an end to their torments and lead them forth into everlasting joy.

Eternal rest grant unto them, and let perpetual light shine upon them. Amen.

DATE: _____

Pray today for the souls of all Jewish people who have died.

Morning Prayer for the Poor Souls:

Out of the depths I have cried to Thee O Lord! Lord, hear my voice. Let Thine ears be attentive to the voice of my supplication.
If Thou, O Lord, wilt mark iniquities, Lord, who shall stand it?
For with Thee there is mercy: and by reason of Thy law I have waited on Thee, O Lord! My soul hath relied on His word: my soul hath hoped in the Lord. From the morning watch even until night. Let Israel hope in the Lord. For with the Lord there is mercy; and with Him plentiful Redemption. And He will redeem Israel from all his iniquities.
Eternal rest give unto them, O Lord! And let perpetual light shine upon them. May they rest in peace. Amen.

Evening Prayer for the Poor Souls:

V. Lord, hear my prayer.
R. And let my cry come unto Thee.
Bless, O my God! the repose I am about to take, that, renewing my strength, I may be better enabled to serve Thee. Pour down Thy blessings, O Lord! on my parents, relations, friends, and enemies. Protect the Pope, our Bishop, and all the Pastors of Thy holy Church. Assist the poor and the afflicted, and those who are now in their last agony. Look with an eye of pity on the suffering souls in purgatory, particularly

_____

_____

_____

put an end to their torments and lead them forth into everlasting joy.

Eternal rest grant unto them and let perpetual light shine upon them. Amen.

DATE: _____

Today, pray for the souls of persecutors of Christians who have died.

Morning Prayer for the Poor Souls:

Out of the depths I have cried to Thee O Lord! Lord, hear my voice. Let Thine ears be attentive to the voice of my supplication.
If Thou, O Lord, wilt mark iniquities, Lord, who shall stand it?
For with Thee there is mercy: and by reason of Thy law I have waited on Thee, O Lord! My soul hath relied on His word: my soul hath hoped in the Lord. From the morning watch even until night. Let Israel hope in the Lord. For with the Lord there is mercy; and with Him plentiful Redemption. And He will redeem Israel from all his iniquities.
Eternal rest give unto them, O Lord! And let perpetual light shine upon them. May they rest in peace. Amen.

Evening Prayer for the Poor Souls:

V. Lord, hear my prayer.
R. And let my cry come unto Thee.
Bless, O my God! the repose I am about to take, that, renewing my strength, I may be better enabled to serve Thee. Pour down Thy blessings, O Lord! on my parents, relations, friends, and enemies. Protect the Pope, our Bishop, and all the Pastors of Thy holy Church. Assist the poor and the afflicted, and those who are now in their last agony. Look with an eye of pity on the suffering souls in purgatory, particularly

_____

_____

_____

put an end to their torments and lead them forth into everlasting joy.

Eternal rest grant unto them, and let perpetual light shine upon them. Amen.

DATE: _____

Light a blessed candle today in remembrance of the Holy Souls.

Morning Prayer for the Poor Souls:

Out of the depths I have cried to Thee O Lord! Lord, hear my voice. Let Thine ears be attentive to the voice of my supplication.
If Thou, O Lord, wilt mark iniquities, Lord, who shall stand it?
For with Thee there is mercy: and by reason of Thy law I have waited on Thee, O Lord! My soul hath relied on His word: my soul hath hoped in the Lord. From the morning watch even until night. Let Israel hope in the Lord. For with the Lord there is mercy; and with Him plentiful Redemption. And He will redeem Israel from all his iniquities.
Eternal rest give unto them, O Lord! And let perpetual light shine upon them. May they rest in peace. Amen.

Evening Prayer for the Poor Souls:

V. Lord, hear my prayer.
R. And let my cry come unto Thee.
Bless, O my God! the repose I am about to take, that, renewing my strength, I may be better enabled to serve Thee. Pour down Thy blessings, O Lord! on my parents, relations, friends, and enemies. Protect the Pope, our Bishop, and all the Pastors of Thy holy Church. Assist the poor and the afflicted, and those who are now in their last agony. Look with an eye of pity on the suffering souls in purgatory, particularly

_____

_____

_____

put an end to their torments and lead them forth into everlasting joy.

Eternal rest grant unto them, and let perpetual light shine upon them. Amen.

DATE: _____

Begin a Novena today for the benefit of the Poor Souls. St. Alphonsus Liguori wrote a powerful one just for the Holy Souls, which may be found online, but any Novena will be appreciated.

Morning Prayer for the Poor Souls:

Out of the depths I have cried to Thee O Lord! Lord, hear my voice. Let Thine ears be attentive to the voice of my supplication.
If Thou, O Lord, wilt mark iniquities, Lord, who shall stand it?
For with Thee there is mercy: and by reason of Thy law I have waited on Thee, O Lord! My soul hath relied on His word: my soul hath hoped in the Lord. From the morning watch even until night. Let Israel hope in the Lord. For with the Lord there is mercy; and with Him plentiful Redemption. And He will redeem Israel from all his iniquities.
Eternal rest give unto them, O Lord! And let perpetual light shine upon them. May they rest in peace. Amen.

Evening Prayer for the Poor Souls:

V. Lord, hear my prayer.
R. And let my cry come unto Thee.
Bless, O my God! the repose I am about to take, that, renewing my strength, I may be better enabled to serve Thee. Pour down Thy blessings, O Lord! on my parents, relations, friends, and enemies. Protect the Pope, our Bishop, and all the Pastors of Thy holy Church. Assist the poor and the afflicted, and those who are now in their last agony. Look with an eye of pity on the suffering souls in purgatory, particularly

_____

_____

_____

put an end to their torments and lead them forth into everlasting joy.

Eternal rest grant unto them, and let perpetual light shine upon them. Amen.

DATE: _____

Give alms to the poor today to benefit the souls in Purgatory. We are told that giving alms is of great benefit to suffering souls.

Morning Prayer for the Poor Souls:

Out of the depths I have cried to Thee O Lord! Lord, hear my voice. Let Thine ears be attentive to the voice of my supplication.
If Thou, O Lord, wilt mark iniquities, Lord, who shall stand it?
For with Thee there is mercy: and by reason of Thy law I have waited on Thee, O Lord! My soul hath relied on His word: my soul hath hoped in the Lord. From the morning watch even until night. Let Israel hope in the Lord. For with the Lord there is mercy; and with Him plentiful Redemption. And He will redeem Israel from all his iniquities.
Eternal rest give unto them, O Lord! And let perpetual light shine upon them. May they rest in peace. Amen.

Evening Prayer for the Poor Souls:

V. Lord, hear my prayer.
R. And let my cry come unto Thee.
Bless, O my God! the repose I am about to take, that, renewing my strength, I may be better enabled to serve Thee. Pour down Thy blessings, O Lord! on my parents, relations, friends, and enemies. Protect the Pope, our Bishop, and all the Pastors of Thy holy Church. Assist the poor and the afflicted, and those who are now in their last agony. Look with an eye of pity on the suffering souls in purgatory, particularly

_____
_____
_____

put an end to their torments and lead them forth into everlasting joy.

Eternal rest grant unto them, and let perpetual light shine upon them. Amen.

DATE: _____

Read aloud today from the Acts of the Apostles to comfort the Holy Souls. The Good News of Jesus' salvation is of great relief to their suffering.

Morning Prayer for the Poor Souls:

Out of the depths I have cried to Thee O Lord! Lord, hear my voice. Let Thine ears be attentive to the voice of my supplication.
If Thou, O Lord, wilt mark iniquities, Lord, who shall stand it?
For with Thee there is mercy: and by reason of Thy law I have waited on Thee, O Lord! My soul hath relied on His word: my soul hath hoped in the Lord. From the morning watch even until night. Let Israel hope in the Lord. For with the Lord there is mercy; and with Him plentiful Redemption. And He will redeem Israel from all his iniquities.
Eternal rest give unto them, O Lord! And let perpetual light shine upon them. May they rest in peace. Amen.

Evening Prayer for the Poor Souls:

V. Lord, hear my prayer.
R. And let my cry come unto Thee.
Bless, O my God! the repose I am about to take, that, renewing my strength, I may be better enabled to serve Thee. Pour down Thy blessings, O Lord! on my parents, relations, friends, and enemies. Protect the Pope, our Bishop, and all the Pastors of Thy holy Church. Assist the poor and the afflicted, and those who are now in their last agony. Look with an eye of pity on the suffering souls in purgatory, particularly

_____

_____

_____

put an end to their torments and lead them forth into everlasting joy.

Eternal rest grant unto them, and let perpetual light shine upon them. Amen.

DATE: _____

Today, ask the saints known as intercessors for the dead to pray with you for their release, including St. Nicholas of Tolentino, St. Gertrude the Great, St. Catherine of Genoa, St. Padre Pio, St. Philip Neri, St. John Macías, St. Faustina Kowalska, St. Joseph and, of course, the Blessed Mother.

Morning Prayer for the Poor Souls:

Out of the depths I have cried to Thee O Lord! Lord, hear my voice. Let Thine ears be attentive to the voice of my supplication.
If Thou, O Lord, wilt mark iniquities, Lord, who shall stand it?
For with Thee there is mercy: and by reason of Thy law I have waited on Thee, O Lord! My soul hath relied on His word: my soul hath hoped in the Lord. From the morning watch even until night. Let Israel hope in the Lord. For with the Lord there is mercy; and with Him plentiful Redemption. And He will redeem Israel from all his iniquities.
Eternal rest give unto them, O Lord! And let perpetual light shine upon them. May they rest in peace. Amen.

Evening Prayer for the Poor Souls:

V. Lord, hear my prayer.
R. And let my cry come unto Thee.
Bless, O my God! the repose I am about to take, that, renewing my strength, I may be better enabled to serve Thee. Pour down Thy blessings, O Lord! on my parents, relations, friends, and enemies. Protect the Pope, our Bishop, and all the Pastors of Thy holy Church. Assist the poor and the afflicted, and those who are now in their last agony. Look with an eye of pity on the suffering souls in purgatory, particularly

_____
_____
_____

put an end to their torments and lead them forth into everlasting joy.

Eternal rest grant unto them and let perpetual light shine upon them. Amen.

DATE: _____

Today, have a Mass said for the soul of a family member or friend who has passed away. This can be through your own parish or through an order or national shrine via their website.

Morning Prayer for the Poor Souls:

Out of the depths I have cried to Thee O Lord! Lord, hear my voice. Let Thine ears be attentive to the voice of my supplication.
If Thou, O Lord, wilt mark iniquities, Lord, who shall stand it?
For with Thee there is mercy: and by reason of Thy law I have waited on Thee, O Lord! My soul hath relied on His word: my soul hath hoped in the Lord. From the morning watch even until night. Let Israel hope in the Lord. For with the Lord there is mercy; and with Him plentiful Redemption. And He will redeem Israel from all his iniquities.
Eternal rest give unto them, O Lord! And let perpetual light shine upon them. May they rest in peace. Amen.

Evening Prayer for the Poor Souls:

V. Lord, hear my prayer.
R. And let my cry come unto Thee.
Bless, O my God! the repose I am about to take, that, renewing my strength, I may be better enabled to serve Thee. Pour down Thy blessings, O Lord! on my parents, relations, friends, and enemies. Protect the Pope, our Bishop, and all the Pastors of Thy holy Church. Assist the poor and the afflicted, and those who are now in their last agony. Look with an eye of pity on the suffering souls in purgatory, particularly

_____
_____
_____

put an end to their torments and lead them forth into everlasting joy.

Eternal rest grant unto them and let perpetual light shine upon them. Amen.

DATE:

_____

Pray the Rosary today for the release of souls from Purgatory. Mystic saints have told us that the Blessed Mother herself comes to Purgatory to bring souls with her back to Heaven.

Morning Prayer for the Poor Souls:

Out of the depths I have cried to Thee O Lord! Lord, hear my voice. Let Thine ears be attentive to the voice of my supplication.
If Thou, O Lord, wilt mark iniquities, Lord, who shall stand it?
For with Thee there is mercy: and by reason of Thy law I have waited on Thee, O Lord! My soul hath relied on His word: my soul hath hoped in the Lord. From the morning watch even until night. Let Israel hope in the Lord. For with the Lord there is mercy; and with Him plentiful Redemption. And He will redeem Israel from all his iniquities.
Eternal rest give unto them, O Lord! And let perpetual light shine upon them. May they rest in peace. Amen.

Evening Prayer for the Poor Souls:

V. Lord, hear my prayer.
R. And let my cry come unto Thee.
Bless, O my God! the repose I am about to take, that, renewing my strength, I may be better enabled to serve Thee. Pour down Thy blessings, O Lord! on my parents, relations, friends, and enemies. Protect the Pope, our Bishop, and all the Pastors of Thy holy Church. Assist the poor and the afflicted, and those who are now in their last agony. Look with an eye of pity on the suffering souls in purgatory, particularly

_____
_____
_____

put an end to their torments and lead them forth into everlasting joy.

Eternal rest grant unto them and let perpetual light shine upon them. Amen.

DATE:

_____

Today, ask the Blessed Mother to apply your prayers and works to a poor soul who has no one to pray for them.

Morning Prayer for the Poor Souls:

Out of the depths I have cried to Thee O Lord! Lord, hear my voice. Let Thine ears be attentive to the voice of my supplication.
If Thou, O Lord, wilt mark iniquities, Lord, who shall stand it?
For with Thee there is mercy: and by reason of Thy law I have waited on Thee, O Lord! My soul hath relied on His word: my soul hath hoped in the Lord. From the morning watch even until night. Let Israel hope in the Lord. For with the Lord there is mercy; and with Him plentiful Redemption. And He will redeem Israel from all his iniquities.
Eternal rest give unto them, O Lord! And let perpetual light shine upon them. May they rest in peace. Amen.

Evening Prayer for the Poor Souls:

V. Lord, hear my prayer.
R. And let my cry come unto Thee.
Bless, O my God! the repose I am about to take, that, renewing my strength, I may be better enabled to serve Thee. Pour down Thy blessings, O Lord! on my parents, relations, friends, and enemies. Protect the Pope, our Bishop, and all the Pastors of Thy holy Church. Assist the poor and the afflicted, and those who are now in their last agony. Look with an eye of pity on the suffering souls in purgatory, particularly

_____
_____
_____

put an end to their torments and lead them forth into everlasting joy.

Eternal rest grant unto them and let perpetual light shine upon them. Amen.

DATE:
_____

We all have a spiritual or physical affliction or burden that we suffer with daily. Today, dedicate your ailment-related suffering to the Poor souls.

Morning Prayer for the Poor Souls:

Out of the depths I have cried to Thee O Lord! Lord, hear my voice. Let Thine ears be attentive to the voice of my supplication.
If Thou, O Lord, wilt mark iniquities, Lord, who shall stand it?
For with Thee there is mercy: and by reason of Thy law I have waited on Thee, O Lord! My soul hath relied on His word: my soul hath hoped in the Lord. From the morning watch even until night. Let Israel hope in the Lord. For with the Lord there is mercy; and with Him plentiful Redemption. And He will redeem Israel from all his iniquities.
Eternal rest give unto them, O Lord! And let perpetual light shine upon them. May they rest in peace. Amen.

Evening Prayer for the Poor Souls:

V. Lord, hear my prayer.
R. And let my cry come unto Thee.
Bless, O my God! the repose I am about to take, that, renewing my strength, I may be better enabled to serve Thee. Pour down Thy blessings, O Lord! on my parents, relations, friends, and enemies. Protect the Pope, our Bishop, and all the Pastors of Thy holy Church. Assist the poor and the afflicted, and those who are now in their last agony. Look with an eye of pity on the suffering souls in purgatory, particularly

_____
_____
_____

put an end to their torments and lead them forth into everlasting joy.

Eternal rest grant unto them and let perpetual light shine upon them. Amen.

DATE:
_____

Today, visit or call someone elderly or alone and offer your work of mercy for the souls in Purgatory.

Morning Prayer for the Poor Souls:

Out of the depths I have cried to Thee O Lord! Lord, hear my voice. Let Thine ears be attentive to the voice of my supplication.
If Thou, O Lord, wilt mark iniquities, Lord, who shall stand it?
For with Thee there is mercy: and by reason of Thy law I have waited on Thee, O Lord! My soul hath relied on His word: my soul hath hoped in the Lord. From the morning watch even until night. Let Israel hope in the Lord. For with the Lord there is mercy; and with Him plentiful Redemption. And He will redeem Israel from all his iniquities.
Eternal rest give unto them, O Lord! And let perpetual light shine upon them. May they rest in peace. Amen.

Evening Prayer for the Poor Souls:

V. Lord, hear my prayer.
R. And let my cry come unto Thee.
Bless, O my God! the repose I am about to take, that, renewing my strength, I may be better enabled to serve Thee. Pour down Thy blessings, O Lord! on my parents, relations, friends, and enemies. Protect the Pope, our Bishop, and all the Pastors of Thy holy Church. Assist the poor and the afflicted, and those who are now in their last agony. Look with an eye of pity on the suffering souls in purgatory, particularly

_____

_____

_____

put an end to their torments and lead them forth into everlasting joy.

Eternal rest grant unto them and let perpetual light shine upon them. Amen.

DATE:

_____

During the course of the day today, pray for those you meet and strangers you see on street, asking God to apply your prayers for them to their future time in Purgatory.

Morning Prayer for the Poor Souls:

Out of the depths I have cried to Thee O Lord! Lord, hear my voice. Let Thine ears be attentive to the voice of my supplication.
If Thou, O Lord, wilt mark iniquities, Lord, who shall stand it?
For with Thee there is mercy: and by reason of Thy law I have waited on Thee, O Lord! My soul hath relied on His word: my soul hath hoped in the Lord. From the morning watch even until night. Let Israel hope in the Lord. For with the Lord there is mercy; and with Him plentiful Redemption. And He will redeem Israel from all his iniquities.
Eternal rest give unto them, O Lord! And let perpetual light shine upon them. May they rest in peace. Amen.

Evening Prayer for the Poor Souls:

V. Lord, hear my prayer.
R. And let my cry come unto Thee.
Bless, O my God! the repose I am about to take, that, renewing my strength, I may be better enabled to serve Thee. Pour down Thy blessings, O Lord! on my parents, relations, friends, and enemies. Protect the Pope, our Bishop, and all the Pastors of Thy holy Church. Assist the poor and the afflicted, and those who are now in their last agony. Look with an eye of pity on the suffering souls in purgatory, particularly

_____
_____

_____

put an end to their torments and lead them forth into everlasting joy.

Eternal rest grant unto them and let perpetual light shine upon them. Amen.

DATE:

_____

Today, ask the Blessed Mother to use your prayers for someone in Purgatory with no one to pray for them.

Morning Prayer for the Poor Souls:

Out of the depths I have cried to Thee O Lord! Lord, hear my voice. Let Thine ears be attentive to the voice of my supplication.
If Thou, O Lord, wilt mark iniquities, Lord, who shall stand it?
For with Thee there is mercy: and by reason of Thy law I have waited on Thee, O Lord! My soul hath relied on His word: my soul hath hoped in the Lord. From the morning watch even until night. Let Israel hope in the Lord. For with the Lord there is mercy; and with Him plentiful Redemption. And He will redeem Israel from all his iniquities.
Eternal rest give unto them, O Lord! And let perpetual light shine upon them. May they rest in peace. Amen.

Evening Prayer for the Poor Souls:

V. Lord, hear my prayer.
R. And let my cry come unto Thee.
Bless, O my God! the repose I am about to take, that, renewing my strength, I may be better enabled to serve Thee. Pour down Thy blessings, O Lord! on my parents, relations, friends, and enemies. Protect the Pope, our Bishop, and all the Pastors of Thy holy Church. Assist the poor and the afflicted, and those who are now in their last agony. Look with an eye of pity on the suffering souls in purgatory, particularly

_____

_____

_____

put an end to their torments and lead them forth into everlasting joy.

Eternal rest grant unto them and let perpetual light shine upon them. Amen.

DATE:
_____

Today, sprinkle holy water on the carpet of your home or outside your house as a comfort to the Poor Souls.

Morning Prayer for the Poor Souls:

Out of the depths I have cried to Thee O Lord! Lord, hear my voice. Let Thine ears be attentive to the voice of my supplication.
If Thou, O Lord, wilt mark iniquities, Lord, who shall stand it?
For with Thee there is mercy: and by reason of Thy law I have waited on Thee, O Lord! My soul hath relied on His word: my soul hath hoped in the Lord. From the morning watch even until night. Let Israel hope in the Lord. For with the Lord there is mercy; and with Him plentiful Redemption. And He will redeem Israel from all his iniquities.
Eternal rest give unto them, O Lord! And let perpetual light shine upon them. May they rest in peace. Amen.

Evening Prayer for the Poor Souls:

V. Lord, hear my prayer.
R. And let my cry come unto Thee.
Bless, O my God! the repose I am about to take, that, renewing my strength, I may be better enabled to serve Thee. Pour down Thy blessings, O Lord! on my parents, relations, friends, and enemies. Protect the Pope, our Bishop, and all the Pastors of Thy holy Church. Assist the poor and the afflicted, and those who are now in their last agony. Look with an eye of pity on the suffering souls in purgatory, particularly

_____
_____

_____

put an end to their torments and lead them forth into everlasting joy.

Eternal rest grant unto them and let perpetual light shine upon them. Amen.

DATE:

_____

Today, visit a church if you are able, and pray for the souls who are spending their Purgatorial time there. Catholic mystics have told us that God allows many souls to do so. If you cannot visit a church, think of a local church and pray for any souls who might be there.

Morning Prayer for the Poor Souls:

Out of the depths I have cried to Thee O Lord! Lord, hear my voice. Let Thine ears be attentive to the voice of my supplication.
If Thou, O Lord, wilt mark iniquities, Lord, who shall stand it?
For with Thee there is mercy: and by reason of Thy law I have waited on Thee, O Lord! My soul hath relied on His word: my soul hath hoped in the Lord. From the morning watch even until night. Let Israel hope in the Lord. For with the Lord there is mercy; and with Him plentiful Redemption. And He will redeem Israel from all his iniquities.
Eternal rest give unto them, O Lord! And let perpetual light shine upon them. May they rest in peace. Amen.

Evening Prayer for the Poor Souls:

V. Lord, hear my prayer.
R. And let my cry come unto Thee.
Bless, O my God! the repose I am about to take, that, renewing my strength, I may be better enabled to serve Thee. Pour down Thy blessings, O Lord! on my parents, relations, friends, and enemies. Protect the Pope, our Bishop, and all the Pastors of Thy holy Church. Assist the poor and the afflicted, and those who are now in their last agony. Look with an eye of pity on the suffering souls in purgatory, particularly

_____

_____

put an end to their torments and lead them forth into everlasting joy.

Eternal rest grant unto them and let perpetual light shine upon them. Amen.

DATE:
_____

Today, visit someone who is sick if you are able, and offer up this work of mercy for the Holy Souls. If you cannot, pray for those in your local hospital or nursing home.

Morning Prayer for the Poor Souls:

Out of the depths I have cried to Thee O Lord! Lord, hear my voice. Let Thine ears be attentive to the voice of my supplication.
If Thou, O Lord, wilt mark iniquities, Lord, who shall stand it?
For with Thee there is mercy: and by reason of Thy law I have waited on Thee, O Lord! My soul hath relied on His word: my soul hath hoped in the Lord. From the morning watch even until night. Let Israel hope in the Lord. For with the Lord there is mercy; and with Him plentiful Redemption. And He will redeem Israel from all his iniquities.
Eternal rest give unto them, O Lord! And let perpetual light shine upon them. May they rest in peace. Amen.

Evening Prayer for the Poor Souls:

V. Lord, hear my prayer.
R. And let my cry come unto Thee.
Bless, O my God! the repose I am about to take, that, renewing my strength, I may be better enabled to serve Thee. Pour down Thy blessings, O Lord! on my parents, relations, friends, and enemies. Protect the Pope, our Bishop, and all the Pastors of Thy holy Church. Assist the poor and the afflicted, and those who are now in their last agony. Look with an eye of pity on the suffering souls in purgatory, particularly

_____

_____

_____

put an end to their torments and lead them forth into everlasting joy.

Eternal rest grant unto them and let perpetual light shine upon them. Amen.

DATE:
_____

Today pray for the souls of all the atheists who have died.

Morning Prayer for the Poor Souls:

Out of the depths I have cried to Thee O Lord! Lord, hear my voice. Let Thine ears be attentive to the voice of my supplication.
If Thou, O Lord, wilt mark iniquities, Lord, who shall stand it?
For with Thee there is mercy: and by reason of Thy law I have waited on Thee, O Lord! My soul hath relied on His word: my soul hath hoped in the Lord. From the morning watch even until night. Let Israel hope in the Lord. For with the Lord there is mercy; and with Him plentiful Redemption. And He will redeem Israel from all his iniquities.
Eternal rest give unto them, O Lord! And let perpetual light shine upon them. May they rest in peace. Amen.

Evening Prayer for the Poor Souls:

V. Lord, hear my prayer.
R. And let my cry come unto Thee.
Bless, O my God! the repose I am about to take, that, renewing my strength, I may be better enabled to serve Thee. Pour down Thy blessings, O Lord! on my parents, relations, friends, and enemies. Protect the Pope, our Bishop, and all the Pastors of Thy holy Church. Assist the poor and the afflicted, and those who are now in their last agony. Look with an eye of pity on the suffering souls in purgatory, particularly

_____
_____
_____

put an end to their torments and lead them forth into everlasting joy.

Eternal rest grant unto them and let perpetual light shine upon them. Amen.

DATE:

_____

Today, read the obituaries in your local newspaper and pray for the souls who have died in the past several days.

Morning Prayer for the Poor Souls:

Out of the depths I have cried to Thee O Lord! Lord, hear my voice. Let Thine ears be attentive to the voice of my supplication.
If Thou, O Lord, wilt mark iniquities, Lord, who shall stand it?
For with Thee there is mercy: and by reason of Thy law I have waited on Thee, O Lord! My soul hath relied on His word: my soul hath hoped in the Lord. From the morning watch even until night. Let Israel hope in the Lord. For with the Lord there is mercy; and with Him plentiful Redemption. And He will redeem Israel from all his iniquities.
Eternal rest give unto them, O Lord! And let perpetual light shine upon them. May they rest in peace. Amen.

Evening Prayer for the Poor Souls:

V. Lord, hear my prayer.
R. And let my cry come unto Thee.
Bless, O my God! the repose I am about to take, that, renewing my strength, I may be better enabled to serve Thee. Pour down Thy blessings, O Lord! on my parents, relations, friends, and enemies. Protect the Pope, our Bishop, and all the Pastors of Thy holy Church. Assist the poor and the afflicted, and those who are now in their last agony. Look with an eye of pity on the suffering souls in purgatory, particularly

_____
_____
_____

put an end to their torments and lead them forth into everlasting joy.

Eternal rest grant unto them and let perpetual light shine upon them. Amen.

DATE:

_____

Spend some time in Eucharistic Adoration today for the Poor Souls. If you cannot travel to a church physically, watch live Adoration on EWTN, YouTube or Facebook.

Morning Prayer for the Poor Souls:

Out of the depths I have cried to Thee O Lord! Lord, hear my voice. Let Thine ears be attentive to the voice of my supplication.
If Thou, O Lord, wilt mark iniquities, Lord, who shall stand it?
For with Thee there is mercy: and by reason of Thy law I have waited on Thee, O Lord! My soul hath relied on His word: my soul hath hoped in the Lord. From the morning watch even until night. Let Israel hope in the Lord. For with the Lord there is mercy; and with Him plentiful Redemption. And He will redeem Israel from all his iniquities.
Eternal rest give unto them, O Lord! And let perpetual light shine upon them. May they rest in peace. Amen.

Evening Prayer for the Poor Souls:

V. Lord, hear my prayer.
R. And let my cry come unto Thee.
Bless, O my God! the repose I am about to take, that, renewing my strength, I may be better enabled to serve Thee. Pour down Thy blessings, O Lord! on my parents, relations, friends, and enemies. Protect the Pope, our Bishop, and all the Pastors of Thy holy Church. Assist the poor and the afflicted, and those who are now in their last agony. Look with an eye of pity on the suffering souls in purgatory, particularly

_____

_____

_____

put an end to their torments and lead them forth into everlasting joy.

Eternal rest grant unto them, and let perpetual light shine upon them. Amen.

DATE:

_____

a drive today to a cemetery and pray for the souls of those interred there. If you cannot physically visit a cemetery, think of a cemetery in your city or town and pray for the souls of those buried there.

Morning Prayer for the Poor Souls:

Out of the depths I have cried to Thee O Lord! Lord, hear my voice. Let Thine ears be attentive to the voice of my supplication.
If Thou, O Lord, wilt mark iniquities, Lord, who shall stand it?
For with Thee there is mercy: and by reason of Thy law I have waited on Thee, O Lord! My soul hath relied on His word: my soul hath hoped in the Lord. From the morning watch even until night. Let Israel hope in the Lord. For with the Lord there is mercy; and with Him plentiful Redemption. And He will redeem Israel from all his iniquities.
Eternal rest give unto them, O Lord! And let perpetual light shine upon them. May they rest in peace. Amen.

Evening Prayer for the Poor Souls:

V. Lord, hear my prayer.
R. And let my cry come unto Thee.
Bless, O my God! the repose I am about to take, that, renewing my strength, I may be better enabled to serve Thee. Pour down Thy blessings, O Lord! on my parents, relations, friends, and enemies. Protect the Pope, our Bishop, and all the Pastors of Thy holy Church. Assist the poor and the afflicted, and those who are now in their last agony. Look with an eye of pity on the suffering souls in purgatory, particularly

_____
_____

_____

put an end to their torments and lead them forth into everlasting joy.

Eternal rest grant unto them, and let perpetual light shine upon them. Amen.

DATE:

_____

Today, play some sacred music to comfort the Poor Souls. Mystic saints have told us that these small gestures provide great relief to their suffering.

Morning Prayer for the Poor Souls:

Out of the depths I have cried to Thee O Lord! Lord, hear my voice. Let Thine ears be attentive to the voice of my supplication.
If Thou, O Lord, wilt mark iniquities, Lord, who shall stand it?
For with Thee there is mercy: and by reason of Thy law I have waited on Thee, O Lord! My soul hath relied on His word: my soul hath hoped in the Lord. From the morning watch even until night. Let Israel hope in the Lord. For with the Lord there is mercy; and with Him plentiful Redemption. And He will redeem Israel from all his iniquities.
Eternal rest give unto them, O Lord! And let perpetual light shine upon them. May they rest in peace. Amen.

Evening Prayer for the Poor Souls:

V. Lord, hear my prayer.
R. And let my cry come unto Thee.
Bless, O my God! the repose I am about to take, that, renewing my strength, I may be better enabled to serve Thee. Pour down Thy blessings, O Lord! on my parents, relations, friends, and enemies. Protect the Pope, our Bishop, and all the Pastors of Thy holy Church. Assist the poor and the afflicted, and those who are now in their last agony. Look with an eye of pity on the suffering souls in purgatory, particularly

_____
_____

_____

put an end to their torments and lead them forth into everlasting joy.

Eternal rest grant unto them, and let perpetual light shine upon them. Amen.

DATE:

_____

Today, make reparation to the Sacred Heart of Jesus for the souls in Purgatory who offended His most precious Heart with the following: Adorable Heart of Jesus, glowing with love for us and inflamed with zeal for our salvation. O Heart that understands the misery to which our sins have brought us, infinitely rich in mercy to heal the wounds of our souls, behold me humbly kneeling before You to express the sorrow that fills my heart for the coldness and indifference with which I have so long returned the numberless benefits which You have bestowed upon me.

Morning Prayer for the Poor Souls:

Out of the depths I have cried to Thee O Lord! Lord, hear my voice. Let Thine ears be attentive to the voice of my supplication. If Thou, O Lord, wilt mark iniquities, Lord, who shall stand it? For with Thee there is mercy: and by reason of Thy law I have waited on Thee, O Lord! My soul hath relied on His word: my soul hath hoped in the Lord. From the morning watch even until night. Let Israel hope in the Lord. For with the Lord there is mercy; and with Him plentiful Redemption. And He will redeem Israel from all his iniquities. Eternal rest give unto them, O Lord! And let perpetual light shine upon them. May they rest in peace. Amen.

Evening Prayer for the Poor Souls:

V. Lord, hear my prayer.
R. And let my cry come unto Thee.
Bless, O my God! the repose I am about to take, that, renewing my strength, I may be better enabled to serve Thee. Pour down Thy blessings, O Lord! on my parents, relations, friends, and enemies. Protect the Pope, our Bishop, and all the Pastors of Thy holy Church. Assist the poor and the afflicted, and those who are now in their last agony. Look with an eye of pity on the suffering souls in purgatory, particularly

_____

put an end to their torments and lead them forth into everlasting joy.

Eternal rest grant unto them, and let perpetual light shine upon them. Amen.

DATE:

_____

Start a Mass Collection jar or envelope today for the Holy Souls. Add money to it as you are able, and when you have enough for a donation, have a Mass said for a soul in Purgatory.

Morning Prayer for the Poor Souls:

Out of the depths I have cried to Thee O Lord! Lord, hear my voice. Let Thine ears be attentive to the voice of my supplication.
If Thou, O Lord, wilt mark iniquities, Lord, who shall stand it?
For with Thee there is mercy: and by reason of Thy law I have waited on Thee, O Lord! My soul hath relied on His word: my soul hath hoped in the Lord. From the morning watch even until night. Let Israel hope in the Lord. For with the Lord there is mercy; and with Him plentiful Redemption. And He will redeem Israel from all his iniquities.
Eternal rest give unto them, O Lord! And let perpetual light shine upon them. May they rest in peace. Amen.

Evening Prayer for the Poor Souls:

V. Lord, hear my prayer.
R. And let my cry come unto Thee.
Bless, O my God! the repose I am about to take, that, renewing my strength, I may be better enabled to serve Thee. Pour down Thy blessings, O Lord! on my parents, relations, friends, and enemies. Protect the Pope, our Bishop, and all the Pastors of Thy holy Church. Assist the poor and the afflicted, and those who are now in their last agony. Look with an eye of pity on the suffering souls in purgatory, particularly

_____
_____

_____

put an end to their torments and lead them forth into everlasting joy.

Eternal rest grant unto them, and let perpetual light shine upon them. Amen.

DATE:
_____

Go without a meal or snack today if possible, for the benefit of the Holy Souls. If you are in ill health, give up a special treat instead.

Morning Prayer for the Poor Souls:

Out of the depths I have cried to Thee O Lord! Lord, hear my voice. Let Thine ears be attentive to the voice of my supplication.
If Thou, O Lord, wilt mark iniquities, Lord, who shall stand it?
For with Thee there is mercy: and by reason of Thy law I have waited on Thee, O Lord! My soul hath relied on His word: my soul hath hoped in the Lord. From the morning watch even until night. Let Israel hope in the Lord. For with the Lord there is mercy; and with Him plentiful Redemption. And He will redeem Israel from all his iniquities.
Eternal rest give unto them, O Lord! And let perpetual light shine upon them. May they rest in peace. Amen.

Evening Prayer for the Poor Souls:

V. Lord, hear my prayer.
R. And let my cry come unto Thee.
Bless, O my God! the repose I am about to take, that, renewing my strength, I may be better enabled to serve Thee. Pour down Thy blessings, O Lord! on my parents, relations, friends, and enemies. Protect the Pope, our Bishop, and all the Pastors of Thy holy Church. Assist the poor and the afflicted, and those who are now in their last agony. Look with an eye of pity on the suffering souls in purgatory, particularly

_____
_____

_____

put an end to their torments and lead them forth into everlasting joy.

Eternal rest grant unto them, and let perpetual light shine upon them. Amen.

DATE:

_____

Today, say a Divine Mercy chaplet for the Poor Souls.

Morning Prayer for the Poor Souls:

Out of the depths I have cried to Thee O Lord! Lord, hear my voice. Let Thine ears be attentive to the voice of my supplication.
If Thou, O Lord, wilt mark iniquities, Lord, who shall stand it?
For with Thee there is mercy: and by reason of Thy law I have waited on Thee, O Lord! My soul hath relied on His word: my soul hath hoped in the Lord. From the morning watch even until night. Let Israel hope in the Lord. For with the Lord there is mercy; and with Him plentiful Redemption. And He will redeem Israel from all his iniquities.
Eternal rest give unto them, O Lord! And let perpetual light shine upon them. May they rest in peace. Amen.

Evening Prayer for the Poor Souls:

V. Lord, hear my prayer.
R. And let my cry come unto Thee.
Bless, O my God! the repose I am about to take, that, renewing my strength, I may be better enabled to serve Thee. Pour down Thy blessings, O Lord! on my parents, relations, friends, and enemies. Protect the Pope, our Bishop, and all the Pastors of Thy holy Church. Assist the poor and the afflicted, and those who are now in their last agony. Look with an eye of pity on the suffering souls in purgatory, particularly

_____

_____

_____

put an end to their torments and lead them forth into everlasting joy.

Eternal rest grant unto them, and let perpetual light shine upon them. Amen.

DATE: _____

Pray today for the souls of priests and religious in Purgatory.

Morning Prayer for the Poor Souls:

Out of the depths I have cried to Thee O Lord! Lord, hear my voice. Let Thine ears be attentive to the voice of my supplication.
If Thou, O Lord, wilt mark iniquities, Lord, who shall stand it?
For with Thee there is mercy: and by reason of Thy law I have waited on Thee, O Lord! My soul hath relied on His word: my soul hath hoped in the Lord. From the morning watch even until night. Let Israel hope in the Lord. For with the Lord there is mercy; and with Him plentiful Redemption. And He will redeem Israel from all his iniquities.
Eternal rest give unto them, O Lord! And let perpetual light shine upon them. May they rest in peace. Amen.

Evening Prayer for the Poor Souls:

V. Lord, hear my prayer.
R. And let my cry come unto Thee.
Bless, O my God! the repose I am about to take, that, renewing my strength, I may be better enabled to serve Thee. Pour down Thy blessings, O Lord! on my parents, relations, friends, and enemies. Protect the Pope, our Bishop, and all the Pastors of Thy holy Church. Assist the poor and the afflicted, and those who are now in their last agony. Look with an eye of pity on the suffering souls in purgatory, particularly

_____
_____
_____

put an end to their torments and lead them forth into everlasting joy.

Eternal rest grant unto them, and let perpetual light shine upon them. Amen.

DATE: _____

While you are going about your day today, remember your friends and colleagues who have passed away over the years, asking God to release them from Purgatory.

Morning Prayer for the Poor Souls:

Out of the depths I have cried to Thee O Lord! Lord, hear my voice. Let Thine ears be attentive to the voice of my supplication.
If Thou, O Lord, wilt mark iniquities, Lord, who shall stand it?
For with Thee there is mercy: and by reason of Thy law I have waited on Thee, O Lord! My soul hath relied on His word: my soul hath hoped in the Lord. From the morning watch even until night. Let Israel hope in the Lord. For with the Lord there is mercy; and with Him plentiful Redemption. And He will redeem Israel from all his iniquities.
Eternal rest give unto them, O Lord! And let perpetual light shine upon them. May they rest in peace. Amen.

Evening Prayer for the Poor Souls:

V. Lord, hear my prayer.
R. And let my cry come unto Thee.
Bless, O my God! the repose I am about to take, that, renewing my strength, I may be better enabled to serve Thee. Pour down Thy blessings, O Lord! on my parents, relations, friends, and enemies. Protect the Pope, our Bishop, and all the Pastors of Thy holy Church. Assist the poor and the afflicted, and those who are now in their last agony. Look with an eye of pity on the suffering souls in purgatory, particularly

put an end to their torments and lead them forth into everlasting joy.

Eternal rest grant unto them, and let perpetual light shine upon them. Amen.

DATE: _____

Pray today for the dead who heard the Gospel but rejected it. May they be spared Hell and be released from Purgatory to be with Jesus.

Morning Prayer for the Poor Souls:

Out of the depths I have cried to Thee O Lord! Lord, hear my voice. Let Thine ears be attentive to the voice of my supplication.
If Thou, O Lord, wilt mark iniquities, Lord, who shall stand it?
For with Thee there is mercy: and by reason of Thy law I have waited on Thee, O Lord! My soul hath relied on His word: my soul hath hoped in the Lord. From the morning watch even until night. Let Israel hope in the Lord. For with the Lord there is mercy; and with Him plentiful Redemption. And He will redeem Israel from all his iniquities.
Eternal rest give unto them, O Lord! And let perpetual light shine upon them. May they rest in peace. Amen.

Evening Prayer for the Poor Souls:

V. Lord, hear my prayer.
R. And let my cry come unto Thee.
Bless, O my God! the repose I am about to take, that, renewing my strength, I may be better enabled to serve Thee. Pour down Thy blessings, O Lord! on my parents, relations, friends, and enemies. Protect the Pope, our Bishop, and all the Pastors of Thy holy Church. Assist the poor and the afflicted, and those who are now in their last agony. Look with an eye of pity on the suffering souls in purgatory, particularly

_____

_____

_____

put an end to their torments and lead them forth into everlasting joy.

Eternal rest grant unto them, and let perpetual light shine upon them. Amen.

DATE: _____

Today, spend some time reading devotional literature aloud for the comfort of the Poor Souls.

Morning Prayer for the Poor Souls:

Out of the depths I have cried to Thee O Lord! Lord, hear my voice. Let Thine ears be attentive to the voice of my supplication.
If Thou, O Lord, wilt mark iniquities, Lord, who shall stand it?
For with Thee there is mercy: and by reason of Thy law I have waited on Thee, O Lord! My soul hath relied on His word: my soul hath hoped in the Lord. From the morning watch even until night. Let Israel hope in the Lord. For with the Lord there is mercy; and with Him plentiful Redemption. And He will redeem Israel from all his iniquities.
Eternal rest give unto them, O Lord! And let perpetual light shine upon them. May they rest in peace. Amen.

Evening Prayer for the Poor Souls:

V. Lord, hear my prayer.
R. And let my cry come unto Thee.
Bless, O my God! the repose I am about to take, that, renewing my strength, I may be better enabled to serve Thee. Pour down Thy blessings, O Lord! on my parents, relations, friends, and enemies. Protect the Pope, our Bishop, and all the Pastors of Thy holy Church. Assist the poor and the afflicted, and those who are now in their last agony. Look with an eye of pity on the suffering souls in purgatory, particularly

_____

_____

put an end to their torments and lead them forth into everlasting joy.

Eternal rest grant unto them, and let perpetual light shine upon them. Amen.

DATE: _____

Today make the Stations of the Cross for the benefit of the Holy Souls in Purgatory.

Morning Prayer for the Poor Souls:

Out of the depths I have cried to Thee O Lord! Lord, hear my voice. Let Thine ears be attentive to the voice of my supplication.
If Thou, O Lord, wilt mark iniquities, Lord, who shall stand it?
For with Thee there is mercy: and by reason of Thy law I have waited on Thee, O Lord! My soul hath relied on His word: my soul hath hoped in the Lord. From the morning watch even until night. Let Israel hope in the Lord. For with the Lord there is mercy; and with Him plentiful Redemption. And He will redeem Israel from all his iniquities.
Eternal rest give unto them, O Lord! And let perpetual light shine upon them. May they rest in peace. Amen.

Evening Prayer for the Poor Souls:

V. Lord, hear my prayer.
R. And let my cry come unto Thee.
Bless, O my God! the repose I am about to take, that, renewing my strength, I may be better enabled to serve Thee. Pour down Thy blessings, O Lord! on my parents, relations, friends, and enemies. Protect the Pope, our Bishop, and all the Pastors of Thy holy Church. Assist the poor and the afflicted, and those who are now in their last agony. Look with an eye of pity on the suffering souls in purgatory, particularly

_____

_____

_____

put an end to their torments and lead them forth into everlasting joy.

Eternal rest grant unto them, and let perpetual light shine upon them. Amen.

DATE: _____

Pray today for the souls of all Jewish people who have died.

Morning Prayer for the Poor Souls:

Out of the depths I have cried to Thee O Lord! Lord, hear my voice. Let Thine ears be attentive to the voice of my supplication.
If Thou, O Lord, wilt mark iniquities, Lord, who shall stand it?
For with Thee there is mercy: and by reason of Thy law I have waited on Thee, O Lord! My soul hath relied on His word: my soul hath hoped in the Lord. From the morning watch even until night. Let Israel hope in the Lord. For with the Lord there is mercy; and with Him plentiful Redemption. And He will redeem Israel from all his iniquities.
Eternal rest give unto them, O Lord! And let perpetual light shine upon them. May they rest in peace. Amen.

Evening Prayer for the Poor Souls:

V. Lord, hear my prayer.
R. And let my cry come unto Thee.
Bless, O my God! the repose I am about to take, that, renewing my strength, I may be better enabled to serve Thee. Pour down Thy blessings, O Lord! on my parents, relations, friends, and enemies. Protect the Pope, our Bishop, and all the Pastors of Thy holy Church. Assist the poor and the afflicted, and those who are now in their last agony. Look with an eye of pity on the suffering souls in purgatory, particularly

_____

_____

_____

put an end to their torments and lead them forth into everlasting joy.

Eternal rest grant unto them, and let perpetual light shine upon them. Amen.

DATE: _____

Today, pray for the souls of persecutors of Christians who have died.

Morning Prayer for the Poor Souls:

Out of the depths I have cried to Thee O Lord! Lord, hear my voice. Let Thine ears be attentive to the voice of my supplication.
If Thou, O Lord, wilt mark iniquities, Lord, who shall stand it?
For with Thee there is mercy: and by reason of Thy law I have waited on Thee, O Lord! My soul hath relied on His word: my soul hath hoped in the Lord. From the morning watch even until night. Let Israel hope in the Lord. For with the Lord there is mercy; and with Him plentiful Redemption. And He will redeem Israel from all his iniquities.
Eternal rest give unto them, O Lord! And let perpetual light shine upon them. May they rest in peace. Amen.

Evening Prayer for the Poor Souls:

V. Lord, hear my prayer.
R. And let my cry come unto Thee.
Bless, O my God! the repose I am about to take, that, renewing my strength, I may be better enabled to serve Thee. Pour down Thy blessings, O Lord! on my parents, relations, friends, and enemies. Protect the Pope, our Bishop, and all the Pastors of Thy holy Church. Assist the poor and the afflicted, and those who are now in their last agony. Look with an eye of pity on the suffering souls in purgatory, particularly

_____
_____

_____

put an end to their torments and lead them forth into everlasting joy.

Eternal rest grant unto them, and let perpetual light shine upon them. Amen.

DATE: _____

Light a blessed candle today in remembrance of the Holy Souls.

Morning Prayer for the Poor Souls:

Out of the depths I have cried to Thee O Lord! Lord, hear my voice. Let Thine ears be attentive to the voice of my supplication.
If Thou, O Lord, wilt mark iniquities, Lord, who shall stand it?
For with Thee there is mercy: and by reason of Thy law I have waited on Thee, O Lord! My soul hath relied on His word: my soul hath hoped in the Lord. From the morning watch even until night. Let Israel hope in the Lord. For with the Lord there is mercy; and with Him plentiful Redemption. And He will redeem Israel from all his iniquities.
Eternal rest give unto them, O Lord! And let perpetual light shine upon them. May they rest in peace. Amen.

Evening Prayer for the Poor Souls:

V. Lord, hear my prayer.
R. And let my cry come unto Thee.
Bless, O my God! the repose I am about to take, that, renewing my strength, I may be better enabled to serve Thee. Pour down Thy blessings, O Lord! on my parents, relations, friends, and enemies. Protect the Pope, our Bishop, and all the Pastors of Thy holy Church. Assist the poor and the afflicted, and those who are now in their last agony. Look with an eye of pity on the suffering souls in purgatory, particularly

_____

_____

_____

put an end to their torments and lead them forth into everlasting joy.

Eternal rest grant unto them, and let perpetual light shine upon them. Amen.

DATE: _____

Begin a Novena today for the benefit of the Poor Souls. St. Alphonsus Liguori wrote a powerful one just for the Holy Souls, which may be found online, but any Novena will be appreciated.

Morning Prayer for the Poor Souls:

Out of the depths I have cried to Thee O Lord! Lord, hear my voice. Let Thine ears be attentive to the voice of my supplication.
If Thou, O Lord, wilt mark iniquities, Lord, who shall stand it?
For with Thee there is mercy: and by reason of Thy law I have waited on Thee, O Lord! My soul hath relied on His word: my soul hath hoped in the Lord. From the morning watch even until night. Let Israel hope in the Lord. For with the Lord there is mercy; and with Him plentiful Redemption. And He will redeem Israel from all his iniquities.
Eternal rest give unto them, O Lord! And let perpetual light shine upon them. May they rest in peace. Amen.

Evening Prayer for the Poor Souls:

V. Lord, hear my prayer.
R. And let my cry come unto Thee.
Bless, O my God! the repose I am about to take, that, renewing my strength, I may be better enabled to serve Thee. Pour down Thy blessings, O Lord! on my parents, relations, friends, and enemies. Protect the Pope, our Bishop, and all the Pastors of Thy holy Church. Assist the poor and the afflicted, and those who are now in their last agony. Look with an eye of pity on the suffering souls in purgatory, particularly

_____
_____

_____

put an end to their torments and lead them forth into everlasting joy.

Eternal rest grant unto them, and let perpetual light shine upon them. Amen.

DATE: _____

Give alms to the poor today to benefit the souls in Purgatory. We are told that giving alms is of great benefit to suffering souls.

Morning Prayer for the Poor Souls:

Out of the depths I have cried to Thee O Lord! Lord, hear my voice. Let Thine ears be attentive to the voice of my supplication.
If Thou, O Lord, wilt mark iniquities, Lord, who shall stand it?
For with Thee there is mercy: and by reason of Thy law I have waited on Thee, O Lord! My soul hath relied on His word: my soul hath hoped in the Lord. From the morning watch even until night. Let Israel hope in the Lord. For with the Lord there is mercy; and with Him plentiful Redemption. And He will redeem Israel from all his iniquities.
Eternal rest give unto them, O Lord! And let perpetual light shine upon them. May they rest in peace. Amen.

Evening Prayer for the Poor Souls:

V. Lord, hear my prayer.
R. And let my cry come unto Thee.
Bless, O my God! the repose I am about to take, that, renewing my strength, I may be better enabled to serve Thee. Pour down Thy blessings, O Lord! on my parents, relations, friends, and enemies. Protect the Pope, our Bishop, and all the Pastors of Thy holy Church. Assist the poor and the afflicted, and those who are now in their last agony. Look with an eye of pity on the suffering souls in purgatory, particularly

_____
_____
_____

put an end to their torments and lead them forth into everlasting joy.

Eternal rest grant unto them, and let perpetual light shine upon them. Amen.

DATE: _____

Read aloud today from the Acts of the Apostles to comfort the Holy Souls. The Good News of Jesus' salvation is of great relief to their suffering.

Morning Prayer for the Poor Souls:

Out of the depths I have cried to Thee O Lord! Lord, hear my voice. Let Thine ears be attentive to the voice of my supplication.
If Thou, O Lord, wilt mark iniquities, Lord, who shall stand it?
For with Thee there is mercy: and by reason of Thy law I have waited on Thee, O Lord! My soul hath relied on His word: my soul hath hoped in the Lord. From the morning watch even until night. Let Israel hope in the Lord. For with the Lord there is mercy; and with Him plentiful Redemption. And He will redeem Israel from all his iniquities.
Eternal rest give unto them, O Lord! And let perpetual light shine upon them. May they rest in peace. Amen.

Evening Prayer for the Poor Souls:

V. Lord, hear my prayer.
R. And let my cry come unto Thee.
Bless, O my God! the repose I am about to take, that, renewing my strength, I may be better enabled to serve Thee. Pour down Thy blessings, O Lord! on my parents, relations, friends, and enemies. Protect the Pope, our Bishop, and all the Pastors of Thy holy Church. Assist the poor and the afflicted, and those who are now in their last agony. Look with an eye of pity on the suffering souls in purgatory, particularly

_____

_____

_____

put an end to their torments and lead them forth into everlasting joy.

Eternal rest grant unto them, and let perpetual light shine upon them. Amen.

DATE: _____

Today, ask the saints known as intercessors for the dead to pray with you for their release, including St. Nicholas of Tolentino, St. Gertrude the Great, St. Catherine of Genoa, St. Padre Pio, St. Philip Neri, St. John Macías, St. Faustina Kowalska, St. Joseph and, of course, the Blessed Mother.

Morning Prayer for the Poor Souls:

Out of the depths I have cried to Thee O Lord! Lord, hear my voice. Let Thine ears be attentive to the voice of my supplication.
If Thou, O Lord, wilt mark iniquities, Lord, who shall stand it?
For with Thee there is mercy: and by reason of Thy law I have waited on Thee, O Lord! My soul hath relied on His word: my soul hath hoped in the Lord. From the morning watch even until night. Let Israel hope in the Lord. For with the Lord there is mercy; and with Him plentiful Redemption. And He will redeem Israel from all his iniquities.
Eternal rest give unto them, O Lord! And let perpetual light shine upon them. May they rest in peace. Amen.

Evening Prayer for the Poor Souls:

V. Lord, hear my prayer.
R. And let my cry come unto Thee.
Bless, O my God! the repose I am about to take, that, renewing my strength, I may be better enabled to serve Thee. Pour down Thy blessings, O Lord! on my parents, relations, friends, and enemies. Protect the Pope, our Bishop, and all the Pastors of Thy holy Church. Assist the poor and the afflicted, and those who are now in their last agony. Look with an eye of pity on the suffering souls in purgatory, particularly

_____
_____
_____

put an end to their torments and lead them forth into everlasting joy.

Eternal rest grant unto them, and let perpetual light shine upon them. Amen.

The Month of
_____

DATE: _____

Today, have a Mass said for the soul of a family member or friend who has passed away. This can be through your own parish or through an order or national shrine via their website.

Morning Prayer for the Poor Souls:

Out of the depths I have cried to Thee O Lord! Lord, hear my voice. Let Thine ears be attentive to the voice of my supplication.
If Thou, O Lord, wilt mark iniquities, Lord, who shall stand it?
For with Thee there is mercy: and by reason of Thy law I have waited on Thee, O Lord! My soul hath relied on His word: my soul hath hoped in the Lord. From the morning watch even until night. Let Israel hope in the Lord. For with the Lord there is mercy; and with Him plentiful Redemption. And He will redeem Israel from all his iniquities.
Eternal rest give unto them, O Lord! And let perpetual light shine upon them. May they rest in peace. Amen.

Evening Prayer for the Poor Souls:

V. Lord, hear my prayer.
R. And let my cry come unto Thee.
Bless, O my God! the repose I am about to take, that, renewing my strength, I may be better enabled to serve Thee. Pour down Thy blessings, O Lord! on my parents, relations, friends, and enemies. Protect the Pope, our Bishop, and all the Pastors of Thy holy Church. Assist the poor and the afflicted, and those who are now in their last agony. Look with an eye of pity on the suffering souls in purgatory, particularly

_____

_____

_____

put an end to their torments and lead them forth into everlasting joy.

Eternal rest grant unto them, and let perpetual light shine upon them. Amen.

DATE:
_____

Pray the Rosary today for the release of souls from Purgatory. Mystic saints have told us that the Blessed Mother herself comes to Purgatory to bring souls with her back to Heaven.

Morning Prayer for the Poor Souls:

Out of the depths I have cried to Thee O Lord! Lord, hear my voice. Let Thine ears be attentive to the voice of my supplication.
If Thou, O Lord, wilt mark iniquities, Lord, who shall stand it?
For with Thee there is mercy: and by reason of Thy law I have waited on Thee, O Lord! My soul hath relied on His word: my soul hath hoped in the Lord. From the morning watch even until night. Let Israel hope in the Lord. For with the Lord there is mercy; and with Him plentiful Redemption. And He will redeem Israel from all his iniquities.
Eternal rest give unto them, O Lord! And let perpetual light shine upon them. May they rest in peace. Amen.

Evening Prayer for the Poor Souls:

V. Lord, hear my prayer.
R. And let my cry come unto Thee.
Bless, O my God! the repose I am about to take, that, renewing my strength, I may be better enabled to serve Thee. Pour down Thy blessings, O Lord! on my parents, relations, friends, and enemies. Protect the Pope, our Bishop, and all the Pastors of Thy holy Church. Assist the poor and the afflicted, and those who are now in their last agony. Look with an eye of pity on the suffering souls in purgatory, particularly

_____
_____
_____

put an end to their torments and lead them forth into everlasting joy.

Eternal rest grant unto them, and let perpetual light shine upon them. Amen.

DATE:

_____

Today, ask the Blessed Mother to apply your prayers and works to a poor soul who has no one to pray for them.

Morning Prayer for the Poor Souls:

Out of the depths I have cried to Thee O Lord! Lord, hear my voice. Let Thine ears be attentive to the voice of my supplication.
If Thou, O Lord, wilt mark iniquities, Lord, who shall stand it?
For with Thee there is mercy: and by reason of Thy law I have waited on Thee, O Lord! My soul hath relied on His word: my soul hath hoped in the Lord. From the morning watch even until night. Let Israel hope in the Lord. For with the Lord there is mercy; and with Him plentiful Redemption. And He will redeem Israel from all his iniquities.
Eternal rest give unto them, O Lord! And let perpetual light shine upon them. May they rest in peace. Amen.

Evening Prayer for the Poor Souls:

V. Lord, hear my prayer.
R. And let my cry come unto Thee.
Bless, O my God! the repose I am about to take, that, renewing my strength, I may be better enabled to serve Thee. Pour down Thy blessings, O Lord! on my parents, relations, friends, and enemies. Protect the Pope, our Bishop, and all the Pastors of Thy holy Church. Assist the poor and the afflicted, and those who are now in their last agony. Look with an eye of pity on the suffering souls in purgatory, particularly

_____
_____
_____

put an end to their torments and lead them forth into everlasting joy.

Eternal rest grant unto them, and let perpetual light shine upon them. Amen.

DATE:

We all have a spiritual or physical affliction or burden that we suffer with daily. Today, dedicate your ailment-related suffering to the Poor souls.

Morning Prayer for the Poor Souls:

Out of the depths I have cried to Thee O Lord! Lord, hear my voice. Let Thine ears be attentive to the voice of my supplication.
If Thou, O Lord, wilt mark iniquities, Lord, who shall stand it?
For with Thee there is mercy: and by reason of Thy law I have waited on Thee, O Lord! My soul hath relied on His word: my soul hath hoped in the Lord. From the morning watch even until night. Let Israel hope in the Lord. For with the Lord there is mercy; and with Him plentiful Redemption. And He will redeem Israel from all his iniquities.
Eternal rest give unto them, O Lord! And let perpetual light shine upon them. May they rest in peace. Amen.

Evening Prayer for the Poor Souls:

V. Lord, hear my prayer.
R. And let my cry come unto Thee.
Bless, O my God! the repose I am about to take, that, renewing my strength, I may be better enabled to serve Thee. Pour down Thy blessings, O Lord! on my parents, relations, friends, and enemies. Protect the Pope, our Bishop, and all the Pastors of Thy holy Church. Assist the poor and the afflicted, and those who are now in their last agony. Look with an eye of pity on the suffering souls in purgatory, particularly

---

---

put an end to their torments and lead them forth into everlasting joy.

Eternal rest grant unto them, and let perpetual light shine upon them. Amen.

DATE:
_____

Today, visit or call someone elderly or alone and offer your work of mercy for the souls in Purgatory.

Morning Prayer for the Poor Souls:

Out of the depths I have cried to Thee O Lord! Lord, hear my voice. Let Thine ears be attentive to the voice of my supplication.
If Thou, O Lord, wilt mark iniquities, Lord, who shall stand it?
For with Thee there is mercy: and by reason of Thy law I have waited on Thee, O Lord! My soul hath relied on His word: my soul hath hoped in the Lord. From the morning watch even until night. Let Israel hope in the Lord. For with the Lord there is mercy; and with Him plentiful Redemption. And He will redeem Israel from all his iniquities.
Eternal rest give unto them, O Lord! And let perpetual light shine upon them. May they rest in peace. Amen.

Evening Prayer for the Poor Souls:

V. Lord, hear my prayer.
R. And let my cry come unto Thee.
Bless, O my God! the repose I am about to take, that, renewing my strength, I may be better enabled to serve Thee. Pour down Thy blessings, O Lord! on my parents, relations, friends, and enemies. Protect the Pope, our Bishop, and all the Pastors of Thy holy Church. Assist the poor and the afflicted, and those who are now in their last agony. Look with an eye of pity on the suffering souls in purgatory, particularly

_____
_____

_____

put an end to their torments and lead them forth into everlasting joy.

Eternal rest grant unto them, and let perpetual light shine upon them. Amen.

DATE:
_____

During the course of the day today, pray for those you meet and strangers you see on street, asking God to apply your prayers for them to their future time in Purgatory.

Morning Prayer for the Poor Souls:

Out of the depths I have cried to Thee O Lord! Lord, hear my voice. Let Thine ears be attentive to the voice of my supplication.
If Thou, O Lord, wilt mark iniquities, Lord, who shall stand it?
For with Thee there is mercy: and by reason of Thy law I have waited on Thee, O Lord! My soul hath relied on His word: my soul hath hoped in the Lord. From the morning watch even until night. Let Israel hope in the Lord. For with the Lord there is mercy; and with Him plentiful Redemption. And He will redeem Israel from all his iniquities.
Eternal rest give unto them, O Lord! And let perpetual light shine upon them. May they rest in peace. Amen.

Evening Prayer for the Poor Souls:

V. Lord, hear my prayer.
R. And let my cry come unto Thee.
Bless, O my God! the repose I am about to take, that, renewing my strength, I may be better enabled to serve Thee. Pour down Thy blessings, O Lord! on my parents, relations, friends, and enemies. Protect the Pope, our Bishop, and all the Pastors of Thy holy Church. Assist the poor and the afflicted, and those who are now in their last agony. Look with an eye of pity on the suffering souls in purgatory, particularly

_____
_____
_____

put an end to their torments and lead them forth into everlasting joy.

Eternal rest grant unto them, and let perpetual light shine upon them. Amen.

DATE:

_____

Today, ask the Blessed Mother to use your prayers for someone in Purgatory with no one to pray for them.

Morning Prayer for the Poor Souls:

Out of the depths I have cried to Thee O Lord! Lord, hear my voice. Let Thine ears be attentive to the voice of my supplication.
If Thou, O Lord, wilt mark iniquities, Lord, who shall stand it?
For with Thee there is mercy: and by reason of Thy law I have waited on Thee, O Lord! My soul hath relied on His word: my soul hath hoped in the Lord. From the morning watch even until night. Let Israel hope in the Lord. For with the Lord there is mercy; and with Him plentiful Redemption. And He will redeem Israel from all his iniquities.
Eternal rest give unto them, O Lord! And let perpetual light shine upon them. May they rest in peace. Amen.

Evening Prayer for the Poor Souls:

V. Lord, hear my prayer.
R. And let my cry come unto Thee.
Bless, O my God! the repose I am about to take, that, renewing my strength, I may be better enabled to serve Thee. Pour down Thy blessings, O Lord! on my parents, relations, friends, and enemies. Protect the Pope, our Bishop, and all the Pastors of Thy holy Church. Assist the poor and the afflicted, and those who are now in their last agony. Look with an eye of pity on the suffering souls in purgatory, particularly

_____

_____

_____

put an end to their torments and lead them forth into everlasting joy.

Eternal rest grant unto them, and let perpetual light shine upon them. Amen.

DATE:

_____

Today, sprinkle holy water on the carpet of your home or outside your house as a comfort to the Poor Souls.

Morning Prayer for the Poor Souls:

Out of the depths I have cried to Thee O Lord! Lord, hear my voice. Let Thine ears be attentive to the voice of my supplication.
If Thou, O Lord, wilt mark iniquities, Lord, who shall stand it?
For with Thee there is mercy: and by reason of Thy law I have waited on Thee, O Lord! My soul hath relied on His word: my soul hath hoped in the Lord. From the morning watch even until night. Let Israel hope in the Lord. For with the Lord there is mercy; and with Him plentiful Redemption. And He will redeem Israel from all his iniquities.
Eternal rest give unto them, O Lord! And let perpetual light shine upon them. May they rest in peace. Amen.

Evening Prayer for the Poor Souls:

V. Lord, hear my prayer.
R. And let my cry come unto Thee.
Bless, O my God! the repose I am about to take, that, renewing my strength, I may be better enabled to serve Thee. Pour down Thy blessings, O Lord! on my parents, relations, friends, and enemies. Protect the Pope, our Bishop, and all the Pastors of Thy holy Church. Assist the poor and the afflicted, and those who are now in their last agony. Look with an eye of pity on the suffering souls in purgatory, particularly

_____

_____

_____

put an end to their torments and lead them forth into everlasting joy.

Eternal rest grant unto them, and let perpetual light shine upon them. Amen.

DATE:
_____

Today, visit a church if you are able, and pray for the souls who are spending their Purgatorial time there. Catholic mystics have told us that God allows many souls to do so. If you cannot visit a church, think of a local church and pray for any souls who might be there.

Morning Prayer for the Poor Souls:

Out of the depths I have cried to Thee O Lord! Lord, hear my voice. Let Thine ears be attentive to the voice of my supplication.
If Thou, O Lord, wilt mark iniquities, Lord, who shall stand it?
For with Thee there is mercy: and by reason of Thy law I have waited on Thee, O Lord! My soul hath relied on His word: my soul hath hoped in the Lord. From the morning watch even until night. Let Israel hope in the Lord. For with the Lord there is mercy; and with Him plentiful Redemption. And He will redeem Israel from all his iniquities.
Eternal rest give unto them, O Lord! And let perpetual light shine upon them. May they rest in peace. Amen.

Evening Prayer for the Poor Souls:

V. Lord, hear my prayer.
R. And let my cry come unto Thee.
Bless, O my God! the repose I am about to take, that, renewing my strength, I may be better enabled to serve Thee. Pour down Thy blessings, O Lord! on my parents, relations, friends, and enemies. Protect the Pope, our Bishop, and all the Pastors of Thy holy Church. Assist the poor and the afflicted, and those who are now in their last agony. Look with an eye of pity on the suffering souls in purgatory, particularly

_____
_____

put an end to their torments and lead them forth into everlasting joy.

Eternal rest grant unto them, and let perpetual light shine upon them. Amen.

DATE:

_____

Today, visit someone who is sick if you are able, and offer up this work of mercy for the Holy Souls. If you cannot, pray for those in your local hospital or nursing home.

Morning Prayer for the Poor Souls:

Out of the depths I have cried to Thee O Lord! Lord, hear my voice. Let Thine ears be attentive to the voice of my supplication.
If Thou, O Lord, wilt mark iniquities, Lord, who shall stand it?
For with Thee there is mercy: and by reason of Thy law I have waited on Thee, O Lord! My soul hath relied on His word: my soul hath hoped in the Lord. From the morning watch even until night. Let Israel hope in the Lord. For with the Lord there is mercy; and with Him plentiful Redemption. And He will redeem Israel from all his iniquities.
Eternal rest give unto them, O Lord! And let perpetual light shine upon them. May they rest in peace. Amen.

Evening Prayer for the Poor Souls:

V. Lord, hear my prayer.
R. And let my cry come unto Thee.
Bless, O my God! the repose I am about to take, that, renewing my strength, I may be better enabled to serve Thee. Pour down Thy blessings, O Lord! on my parents, relations, friends, and enemies. Protect the Pope, our Bishop, and all the Pastors of Thy holy Church. Assist the poor and the afflicted, and those who are now in their last agony. Look with an eye of pity on the suffering souls in purgatory, particularly

_____
_____

_____

put an end to their torments and lead them forth into everlasting joy.

Eternal rest grant unto them, and let perpetual light shine upon them. Amen.

DATE:
_____

Today pray for the souls of all the atheists who have died.

Morning Prayer for the Poor Souls:

Out of the depths I have cried to Thee O Lord! Lord, hear my voice. Let Thine ears be attentive to the voice of my supplication.
If Thou, O Lord, wilt mark iniquities, Lord, who shall stand it?
For with Thee there is mercy: and by reason of Thy law I have waited on Thee, O Lord! My soul hath relied on His word: my soul hath hoped in the Lord. From the morning watch even until night. Let Israel hope in the Lord. For with the Lord there is mercy; and with Him plentiful Redemption. And He will redeem Israel from all his iniquities.
Eternal rest give unto them, O Lord! And let perpetual light shine upon them. May they rest in peace. Amen.

Evening Prayer for the Poor Souls:

V. Lord, hear my prayer.
R. And let my cry come unto Thee.
Bless, O my God! the repose I am about to take, that, renewing my strength, I may be better enabled to serve Thee. Pour down Thy blessings, O Lord! on my parents, relations, friends, and enemies. Protect the Pope, our Bishop, and all the Pastors of Thy holy Church. Assist the poor and the afflicted, and those who are now in their last agony. Look with an eye of pity on the suffering souls in purgatory, particularly

_____
_____

_____

put an end to their torments and lead them forth into everlasting joy.

Eternal rest grant unto them, and let perpetual light shine upon them. Amen.

DATE:
_____

Today, read the obituaries in your local newspaper and pray for the souls who have died in the past several days.

Morning Prayer for the Poor Souls:

Out of the depths I have cried to Thee O Lord! Lord, hear my voice. Let Thine ears be attentive to the voice of my supplication.
If Thou, O Lord, wilt mark iniquities, Lord, who shall stand it?
For with Thee there is mercy: and by reason of Thy law I have waited on Thee, O Lord! My soul hath relied on His word: my soul hath hoped in the Lord. From the morning watch even until night. Let Israel hope in the Lord. For with the Lord there is mercy; and with Him plentiful Redemption. And He will redeem Israel from all his iniquities.
Eternal rest give unto them, O Lord! And let perpetual light shine upon them. May they rest in peace. Amen.

Evening Prayer for the Poor Souls:

V. Lord, hear my prayer.
R. And let my cry come unto Thee.
Bless, O my God! the repose I am about to take, that, renewing my strength, I may be better enabled to serve Thee. Pour down Thy blessings, O Lord! on my parents, relations, friends, and enemies. Protect the Pope, our Bishop, and all the Pastors of Thy holy Church. Assist the poor and the afflicted, and those who are now in their last agony. Look with an eye of pity on the suffering souls in purgatory, particularly

_____
_____
_____

put an end to their torments and lead them forth into everlasting joy.

Eternal rest grant unto them, and let perpetual light shine upon them. Amen.

DATE:

_____

Spend some time in Eucharistic Adoration today for the Poor Souls. If you cannot travel to a church physically, watch live Adoration on EWTN, YouTube or Facebook.

Morning Prayer for the Poor Souls:

Out of the depths I have cried to Thee O Lord! Lord, hear my voice. Let Thine ears be attentive to the voice of my supplication.
If Thou, O Lord, wilt mark iniquities, Lord, who shall stand it?
For with Thee there is mercy: and by reason of Thy law I have waited on Thee, O Lord! My soul hath relied on His word: my soul hath hoped in the Lord. From the morning watch even until night. Let Israel hope in the Lord. For with the Lord there is mercy; and with Him plentiful Redemption. And He will redeem Israel from all his iniquities.
Eternal rest give unto them, O Lord! And let perpetual light shine upon them. May they rest in peace. Amen.

Evening Prayer for the Poor Souls:

V. Lord, hear my prayer.
R. And let my cry come unto Thee.
Bless, O my God! the repose I am about to take, that, renewing my strength, I may be better enabled to serve Thee. Pour down Thy blessings, O Lord! on my parents, relations, friends, and enemies. Protect the Pope, our Bishop, and all the Pastors of Thy holy Church. Assist the poor and the afflicted, and those who are now in their last agony. Look with an eye of pity on the suffering souls in purgatory, particularly

_____
_____

_____

put an end to their torments and lead them forth into everlasting joy.

Eternal rest grant unto them, and let perpetual light shine upon them. Amen.

DATE:

_____

a drive today to a cemetery and pray for the souls of those interred there. If you cannot physically visit a cemetery, think of a cemetery in your city or town and pray for the souls of those buried there.

Morning Prayer for the Poor Souls:

Out of the depths I have cried to Thee O Lord! Lord, hear my voice. Let Thine ears be attentive to the voice of my supplication.
If Thou, O Lord, wilt mark iniquities, Lord, who shall stand it?
For with Thee there is mercy: and by reason of Thy law I have waited on Thee, O Lord! My soul hath relied on His word: my soul hath hoped in the Lord. From the morning watch even until night. Let Israel hope in the Lord. For with the Lord there is mercy; and with Him plentiful Redemption. And He will redeem Israel from all his iniquities.
Eternal rest give unto them, O Lord! And let perpetual light shine upon them. May they rest in peace. Amen.

Evening Prayer for the Poor Souls:

V. Lord, hear my prayer.
R. And let my cry come unto Thee.
Bless, O my God! the repose I am about to take, that, renewing my strength, I may be better enabled to serve Thee. Pour down Thy blessings, O Lord! on my parents, relations, friends, and enemies. Protect the Pope, our Bishop, and all the Pastors of Thy holy Church. Assist the poor and the afflicted, and those who are now in their last agony. Look with an eye of pity on the suffering souls in purgatory, particularly

_____

_____

_____

put an end to their torments and lead them forth into everlasting joy.

Eternal rest grant unto them, and let perpetual light shine upon them. Amen.

DATE:
_____

Today, play some sacred music to comfort the Poor Souls. Mystic saints have told us that these small gestures provide great relief to their suffering.

Morning Prayer for the Poor Souls:

Out of the depths I have cried to Thee O Lord! Lord, hear my voice. Let Thine ears be attentive to the voice of my supplication.
If Thou, O Lord, wilt mark iniquities, Lord, who shall stand it?
For with Thee there is mercy: and by reason of Thy law I have waited on Thee, O Lord! My soul hath relied on His word: my soul hath hoped in the Lord. From the morning watch even until night. Let Israel hope in the Lord. For with the Lord there is mercy; and with Him plentiful Redemption. And He will redeem Israel from all his iniquities.
Eternal rest give unto them, O Lord! And let perpetual light shine upon them. May they rest in peace. Amen.

Evening Prayer for the Poor Souls:

V. Lord, hear my prayer.
R. And let my cry come unto Thee.
Bless, O my God! the repose I am about to take, that, renewing my strength, I may be better enabled to serve Thee. Pour down Thy blessings, O Lord! on my parents, relations, friends, and enemies. Protect the Pope, our Bishop, and all the Pastors of Thy holy Church. Assist the poor and the afflicted, and those who are now in their last agony. Look with an eye of pity on the suffering souls in purgatory, particularly

_____
_____

_____

put an end to their torments and lead them forth into everlasting joy.

Eternal rest grant unto them, and let perpetual light shine upon them. Amen.

DATE:
_____

Today, make reparation to the Sacred Heart of Jesus for the souls in Purgatory who offended His most precious Heart with the following: Adorable Heart of Jesus, glowing with love for us and inflamed with zeal for our salvation. O Heart that understands the misery to which our sins have brought us, infinitely rich in mercy to heal the wounds of our souls, behold me humbly kneeling before You to express the sorrow that fills my heart for the coldness and indifference with which I have so long returned the numberless benefits which You have bestowed upon me.

Morning Prayer for the Poor Souls:

Out of the depths I have cried to Thee O Lord! Lord, hear my voice. Let Thine ears be attentive to the voice of my supplication. If Thou, O Lord, wilt mark iniquities, Lord, who shall stand it? For with Thee there is mercy: and by reason of Thy law I have waited on Thee, O Lord! My soul hath relied on His word: my soul hath hoped in the Lord. From the morning watch even until night. Let Israel hope in the Lord. For with the Lord there is mercy; and with Him plentiful Redemption. And He will redeem Israel from all his iniquities. Eternal rest give unto them, O Lord! And let perpetual light shine upon them. May they rest in peace. Amen.

Evening Prayer for the Poor Souls:

V. Lord, hear my prayer.
R. And let my cry come unto Thee.
Bless, O my God! the repose I am about to take, that, renewing my strength, I may be better enabled to serve Thee. Pour down Thy blessings, O Lord! on my parents, relations, friends, and enemies. Protect the Pope, our Bishop, and all the Pastors of Thy holy Church. Assist the poor and the afflicted, and those who are now in their last agony. Look with an eye of pity on the suffering souls in purgatory, particularly

_____

put an end to their torments and lead them forth into everlasting joy.

Eternal rest grant unto them, and let perpetual light shine upon them. Amen.

DATE:

_____

Start a Mass Collection jar or envelope today for the Holy Souls. Add money to it as you are able, and when you have enough for a donation, have a Mass said for a soul in Purgatory.

Morning Prayer for the Poor Souls:

Out of the depths I have cried to Thee O Lord! Lord, hear my voice. Let Thine ears be attentive to the voice of my supplication.
If Thou, O Lord, wilt mark iniquities, Lord, who shall stand it?
For with Thee there is mercy: and by reason of Thy law I have waited on Thee, O Lord! My soul hath relied on His word: my soul hath hoped in the Lord. From the morning watch even until night. Let Israel hope in the Lord. For with the Lord there is mercy; and with Him plentiful Redemption. And He will redeem Israel from all his iniquities.
Eternal rest give unto them, O Lord! And let perpetual light shine upon them. May they rest in peace. Amen.

Evening Prayer for the Poor Souls:

V. Lord, hear my prayer.
R. And let my cry come unto Thee.
Bless, O my God! the repose I am about to take, that, renewing my strength, I may be better enabled to serve Thee. Pour down Thy blessings, O Lord! on my parents, relations, friends, and enemies. Protect the Pope, our Bishop, and all the Pastors of Thy holy Church. Assist the poor and the afflicted, and those who are now in their last agony. Look with an eye of pity on the suffering souls in purgatory, particularly

_____
_____
_____

put an end to their torments and lead them forth into everlasting joy.

Eternal rest grant unto them, and let perpetual light shine upon them. Amen.

DATE:

_____

Go without a meal or snack today if possible, for the benefit of the Holy Souls. If you are in ill health, give up a special treat instead.

Morning Prayer for the Poor Souls:

Out of the depths I have cried to Thee O Lord! Lord, hear my voice. Let Thine ears be attentive to the voice of my supplication.
If Thou, O Lord, wilt mark iniquities, Lord, who shall stand it?
For with Thee there is mercy: and by reason of Thy law I have waited on Thee, O Lord! My soul hath relied on His word: my soul hath hoped in the Lord. From the morning watch even until night. Let Israel hope in the Lord. For with the Lord there is mercy; and with Him plentiful Redemption. And He will redeem Israel from all his iniquities.
Eternal rest give unto them, O Lord! And let perpetual light shine upon them. May they rest in peace. Amen.

Evening Prayer for the Poor Souls:

V. Lord, hear my prayer.
R. And let my cry come unto Thee.
Bless, O my God! the repose I am about to take, that, renewing my strength, I may be better enabled to serve Thee. Pour down Thy blessings, O Lord! on my parents, relations, friends, and enemies. Protect the Pope, our Bishop, and all the Pastors of Thy holy Church. Assist the poor and the afflicted, and those who are now in their last agony. Look with an eye of pity on the suffering souls in purgatory, particularly

_____
_____
_____

put an end to their torments and lead them forth into everlasting joy.

Eternal rest grant unto them, and let perpetual light shine upon them. Amen.

DATE:

_____

Today, say a Divine Mercy chaplet for the Poor Souls.

Morning Prayer for the Poor Souls:

Out of the depths I have cried to Thee O Lord! Lord, hear my voice. Let Thine ears be attentive to the voice of my supplication.
If Thou, O Lord, wilt mark iniquities, Lord, who shall stand it?
For with Thee there is mercy: and by reason of Thy law I have waited on Thee, O Lord! My soul hath relied on His word: my soul hath hoped in the Lord. From the morning watch even until night. Let Israel hope in the Lord. For with the Lord there is mercy; and with Him plentiful Redemption. And He will redeem Israel from all his iniquities.
Eternal rest give unto them, O Lord! And let perpetual light shine upon them. May they rest in peace. Amen.

Evening Prayer for the Poor Souls:

V. Lord, hear my prayer.
R. And let my cry come unto Thee.
Bless, O my God! the repose I am about to take, that, renewing my strength, I may be better enabled to serve Thee. Pour down Thy blessings, O Lord! on my parents, relations, friends, and enemies. Protect the Pope, our Bishop, and all the Pastors of Thy holy Church. Assist the poor and the afflicted, and those who are now in their last agony. Look with an eye of pity on the suffering souls in purgatory, particularly

_____

_____

_____

put an end to their torments and lead them forth into everlasting joy.

Eternal rest grant unto them, and let perpetual light shine upon them. Amen.

DATE: _____

Pray today for the souls of priests and religious in Purgatory.

Morning Prayer for the Poor Souls:

Out of the depths I have cried to Thee O Lord! Lord, hear my voice. Let Thine ears be attentive to the voice of my supplication.
If Thou, O Lord, wilt mark iniquities, Lord, who shall stand it?
For with Thee there is mercy: and by reason of Thy law I have waited on Thee, O Lord! My soul hath relied on His word: my soul hath hoped in the Lord. From the morning watch even until night. Let Israel hope in the Lord. For with the Lord there is mercy; and with Him plentiful Redemption. And He will redeem Israel from all his iniquities.
Eternal rest give unto them, O Lord! And let perpetual light shine upon them. May they rest in peace. Amen.

Evening Prayer for the Poor Souls:

V. Lord, hear my prayer.
R. And let my cry come unto Thee.
Bless, O my God! the repose I am about to take, that, renewing my strength, I may be better enabled to serve Thee. Pour down Thy blessings, O Lord! on my parents, relations, friends, and enemies. Protect the Pope, our Bishop, and all the Pastors of Thy holy Church. Assist the poor and the afflicted, and those who are now in their last agony. Look with an eye of pity on the suffering souls in purgatory, particularly

_____

_____

_____

put an end to their torments and lead them forth into everlasting joy.

Eternal rest grant unto them, and let perpetual light shine upon them. Amen.

DATE: _____

While you are going about your day today, remember your friends and colleagues who have passed away over the years, asking God to release them from Purgatory.

Morning Prayer for the Poor Souls:

Out of the depths I have cried to Thee O Lord! Lord, hear my voice. Let Thine ears be attentive to the voice of my supplication.
If Thou, O Lord, wilt mark iniquities, Lord, who shall stand it?
For with Thee there is mercy: and by reason of Thy law I have waited on Thee, O Lord! My soul hath relied on His word: my soul hath hoped in the Lord. From the morning watch even until night. Let Israel hope in the Lord. For with the Lord there is mercy; and with Him plentiful Redemption. And He will redeem Israel from all his iniquities.
Eternal rest give unto them, O Lord! And let perpetual light shine upon them. May they rest in peace. Amen.

Evening Prayer for the Poor Souls:

V. Lord, hear my prayer.
R. And let my cry come unto Thee.
Bless, O my God! the repose I am about to take, that, renewing my strength, I may be better enabled to serve Thee. Pour down Thy blessings, O Lord! on my parents, relations, friends, and enemies. Protect the Pope, our Bishop, and all the Pastors of Thy holy Church. Assist the poor and the afflicted, and those who are now in their last agony. Look with an eye of pity on the suffering souls in purgatory, particularly

put an end to their torments and lead them forth into everlasting joy.

Eternal rest grant unto them, and let perpetual light shine upon them. Amen.

DATE: _____

Pray today for the dead who heard the Gospel but rejected it. May they be spared Hell and be released from Purgatory to be with Jesus.

Morning Prayer for the Poor Souls:

Out of the depths I have cried to Thee O Lord! Lord, hear my voice. Let Thine ears be attentive to the voice of my supplication.
If Thou, O Lord, wilt mark iniquities, Lord, who shall stand it?
For with Thee there is mercy: and by reason of Thy law I have waited on Thee, O Lord! My soul hath relied on His word: my soul hath hoped in the Lord. From the morning watch even until night. Let Israel hope in the Lord. For with the Lord there is mercy; and with Him plentiful Redemption. And He will redeem Israel from all his iniquities.
Eternal rest give unto them, O Lord! And let perpetual light shine upon them. May they rest in peace. Amen.

Evening Prayer for the Poor Souls:

V. Lord, hear my prayer.
R. And let my cry come unto Thee.
Bless, O my God! the repose I am about to take, that, renewing my strength, I may be better enabled to serve Thee. Pour down Thy blessings, O Lord! on my parents, relations, friends, and enemies. Protect the Pope, our Bishop, and all the Pastors of Thy holy Church. Assist the poor and the afflicted, and those who are now in their last agony. Look with an eye of pity on the suffering souls in purgatory, particularly

_____

_____

_____

put an end to their torments and lead them forth into everlasting joy.

Eternal rest grant unto them, and let perpetual light shine upon them. Amen.

DATE: _____

Today, spend some time reading devotional literature aloud for the comfort of the Poor Souls.

Morning Prayer for the Poor Souls:

Out of the depths I have cried to Thee O Lord! Lord, hear my voice. Let Thine ears be attentive to the voice of my supplication.
If Thou, O Lord, wilt mark iniquities, Lord, who shall stand it?
For with Thee there is mercy: and by reason of Thy law I have waited on Thee, O Lord! My soul hath relied on His word: my soul hath hoped in the Lord. From the morning watch even until night. Let Israel hope in the Lord.
For with the Lord there is mercy; and with Him plentiful Redemption. And He will redeem Israel from all his iniquities.
Eternal rest give unto them, O Lord! And let perpetual light shine upon them. May they rest in peace. Amen.

Evening Prayer for the Poor Souls:

V. Lord, hear my prayer.
R. And let my cry come unto Thee.
Bless, O my God! the repose I am about to take, that, renewing my strength, I may be better enabled to serve Thee. Pour down Thy blessings, O Lord! on my parents, relations, friends, and enemies. Protect the Pope, our Bishop, and all the Pastors of Thy holy Church. Assist the poor and the afflicted, and those who are now in their last agony. Look with an eye of pity on the suffering souls in purgatory, particularly

_____

_____

_____

put an end to their torments and lead them forth into everlasting joy.

Eternal rest grant unto them, and let perpetual light shine upon them. Amen.

DATE: _____

Today make the Stations of the Cross for the benefit of the Holy Souls in Purgatory.

Morning Prayer for the Poor Souls:

Out of the depths I have cried to Thee O Lord! Lord, hear my voice. Let Thine ears be attentive to the voice of my supplication.
If Thou, O Lord, wilt mark iniquities, Lord, who shall stand it?
For with Thee there is mercy: and by reason of Thy law I have waited on Thee, O Lord! My soul hath relied on His word: my soul hath hoped in the Lord. From the morning watch even until night. Let Israel hope in the Lord. For with the Lord there is mercy; and with Him plentiful Redemption. And He will redeem Israel from all his iniquities.
Eternal rest give unto them, O Lord! And let perpetual light shine upon them. May they rest in peace. Amen.

Evening Prayer for the Poor Souls:

V. Lord, hear my prayer.
R. And let my cry come unto Thee.
Bless, O my God! the repose I am about to take, that, renewing my strength, I may be better enabled to serve Thee. Pour down Thy blessings, O Lord! on my parents, relations, friends, and enemies. Protect the Pope, our Bishop, and all the Pastors of Thy holy Church. Assist the poor and the afflicted, and those who are now in their last agony. Look with an eye of pity on the suffering souls in purgatory, particularly

_____

_____

_____

put an end to their torments and lead them forth into everlasting joy.

Eternal rest grant unto them, and let perpetual light shine upon them. Amen.

DATE: _____

Pray today for the souls of all Jewish people who have died.

Morning Prayer for the Poor Souls:

Out of the depths I have cried to Thee O Lord! Lord, hear my voice. Let Thine ears be attentive to the voice of my supplication.
If Thou, O Lord, wilt mark iniquities, Lord, who shall stand it?
For with Thee there is mercy: and by reason of Thy law I have waited on Thee, O Lord! My soul hath relied on His word: my soul hath hoped in the Lord. From the morning watch even until night. Let Israel hope in the Lord. For with the Lord there is mercy; and with Him plentiful Redemption. And He will redeem Israel from all his iniquities.
Eternal rest give unto them, O Lord! And let perpetual light shine upon them. May they rest in peace. Amen.

Evening Prayer for the Poor Souls:

V. Lord, hear my prayer.
R. And let my cry come unto Thee.
Bless, O my God! the repose I am about to take, that, renewing my strength, I may be better enabled to serve Thee. Pour down Thy blessings, O Lord! on my parents, relations, friends, and enemies. Protect the Pope, our Bishop, and all the Pastors of Thy holy Church. Assist the poor and the afflicted, and those who are now in their last agony. Look with an eye of pity on the suffering souls in purgatory, particularly

_____

_____

_____

put an end to their torments and lead them forth into everlasting joy.

Eternal rest grant unto them, and let perpetual light shine upon them. Amen.

DATE: _____

Today, pray for the souls of persecutors of Christians who have died.

Morning Prayer for the Poor Souls:

Out of the depths I have cried to Thee O Lord! Lord, hear my voice. Let Thine ears be attentive to the voice of my supplication.
If Thou, O Lord, wilt mark iniquities, Lord, who shall stand it?
For with Thee there is mercy: and by reason of Thy law I have waited on Thee, O Lord! My soul hath relied on His word: my soul hath hoped in the Lord. From the morning watch even until night. Let Israel hope in the Lord. For with the Lord there is mercy; and with Him plentiful Redemption. And He will redeem Israel from all his iniquities.
Eternal rest give unto them, O Lord! And let perpetual light shine upon them. May they rest in peace. Amen.

Evening Prayer for the Poor Souls:

V. Lord, hear my prayer.
R. And let my cry come unto Thee.
Bless, O my God! the repose I am about to take, that, renewing my strength, I may be better enabled to serve Thee. Pour down Thy blessings, O Lord! on my parents, relations, friends, and enemies. Protect the Pope, our Bishop, and all the Pastors of Thy holy Church. Assist the poor and the afflicted, and those who are now in their last agony. Look with an eye of pity on the suffering souls in purgatory, particularly

_____

_____

_____

put an end to their torments and lead them forth into everlasting joy.

Eternal rest grant unto them, and let perpetual light shine upon them. Amen.

DATE: _____

Light a blessed candle today in remembrance of the Holy Souls.

Morning Prayer for the Poor Souls:

Out of the depths I have cried to Thee O Lord! Lord, hear my voice. Let Thine ears be attentive to the voice of my supplication.
If Thou, O Lord, wilt mark iniquities, Lord, who shall stand it?
For with Thee there is mercy: and by reason of Thy law I have waited on Thee, O Lord! My soul hath relied on His word: my soul hath hoped in the Lord. From the morning watch even until night. Let Israel hope in the Lord. For with the Lord there is mercy; and with Him plentiful Redemption. And He will redeem Israel from all his iniquities.
Eternal rest give unto them, O Lord! And let perpetual light shine upon them. May they rest in peace. Amen.

Evening Prayer for the Poor Souls:

V. Lord, hear my prayer.
R. And let my cry come unto Thee.
Bless, O my God! the repose I am about to take, that, renewing my strength, I may be better enabled to serve Thee. Pour down Thy blessings, O Lord! on my parents, relations, friends, and enemies. Protect the Pope, our Bishop, and all the Pastors of Thy holy Church. Assist the poor and the afflicted, and those who are now in their last agony. Look with an eye of pity on the suffering souls in purgatory, particularly

_____

_____

_____

put an end to their torments and lead them forth into everlasting joy.

Eternal rest grant unto them, and let perpetual light shine upon them. Amen.

DATE: _____

Begin a Novena today for the benefit of the Poor Souls. St. Alphonsus Liguori wrote a powerful one just for the Holy Souls, which may be found online, but any Novena will be appreciated.

Morning Prayer for the Poor Souls:

Out of the depths I have cried to Thee O Lord! Lord, hear my voice. Let Thine ears be attentive to the voice of my supplication.
If Thou, O Lord, wilt mark iniquities, Lord, who shall stand it?
For with Thee there is mercy: and by reason of Thy law I have waited on Thee, O Lord! My soul hath relied on His word: my soul hath hoped in the Lord. From the morning watch even until night. Let Israel hope in the Lord. For with the Lord there is mercy; and with Him plentiful Redemption. And He will redeem Israel from all his iniquities.
Eternal rest give unto them, O Lord! And let perpetual light shine upon them. May they rest in peace. Amen.

Evening Prayer for the Poor Souls:

V. Lord, hear my prayer.
R. And let my cry come unto Thee.
Bless, O my God! the repose I am about to take, that, renewing my strength, I may be better enabled to serve Thee. Pour down Thy blessings, O Lord! on my parents, relations, friends, and enemies. Protect the Pope, our Bishop, and all the Pastors of Thy holy Church. Assist the poor and the afflicted, and those who are now in their last agony. Look with an eye of pity on the suffering souls in purgatory, particularly

_____

_____

_____

put an end to their torments and lead them forth into everlasting joy.

Eternal rest grant unto them, and let perpetual light shine upon them. Amen.

DATE: _____

Give alms to the poor today to benefit the souls in Purgatory. We are told that giving alms is of great benefit to suffering souls.

Morning Prayer for the Poor Souls:

Out of the depths I have cried to Thee O Lord! Lord, hear my voice. Let Thine ears be attentive to the voice of my supplication.
If Thou, O Lord, wilt mark iniquities, Lord, who shall stand it?
For with Thee there is mercy: and by reason of Thy law I have waited on Thee, O Lord! My soul hath relied on His word: my soul hath hoped in the Lord. From the morning watch even until night. Let Israel hope in the Lord. For with the Lord there is mercy; and with Him plentiful Redemption. And He will redeem Israel from all his iniquities.
Eternal rest give unto them, O Lord! And let perpetual light shine upon them. May they rest in peace. Amen.

Evening Prayer for the Poor Souls:

V. Lord, hear my prayer.
R. And let my cry come unto Thee.
Bless, O my God! the repose I am about to take, that, renewing my strength, I may be better enabled to serve Thee. Pour down Thy blessings, O Lord! on my parents, relations, friends, and enemies. Protect the Pope, our Bishop, and all the Pastors of Thy holy Church. Assist the poor and the afflicted, and those who are now in their last agony. Look with an eye of pity on the suffering souls in purgatory, particularly

_____

_____

_____

put an end to their torments and lead them forth into everlasting joy.

Eternal rest grant unto them, and let perpetual light shine upon them. Amen.

DATE: _____

Read aloud today from the Acts of the Apostles to comfort the Holy Souls. The Good News of Jesus' salvation is of great relief to their suffering.

Morning Prayer for the Poor Souls:

Out of the depths I have cried to Thee O Lord! Lord, hear my voice. Let Thine ears be attentive to the voice of my supplication.
If Thou, O Lord, wilt mark iniquities, Lord, who shall stand it?
For with Thee there is mercy: and by reason of Thy law I have waited on Thee, O Lord! My soul hath relied on His word: my soul hath hoped in the Lord. From the morning watch even until night. Let Israel hope in the Lord. For with the Lord there is mercy; and with Him plentiful Redemption. And He will redeem Israel from all his iniquities.
Eternal rest give unto them, O Lord! And let perpetual light shine upon them. May they rest in peace. Amen.

Evening Prayer for the Poor Souls:

V. Lord, hear my prayer.
R. And let my cry come unto Thee.
Bless, O my God! the repose I am about to take, that, renewing my strength, I may be better enabled to serve Thee. Pour down Thy blessings, O Lord! on my parents, relations, friends, and enemies. Protect the Pope, our Bishop, and all the Pastors of Thy holy Church. Assist the poor and the afflicted, and those who are now in their last agony. Look with an eye of pity on the suffering souls in purgatory, particularly

_____

_____

_____

put an end to their torments and lead them forth into everlasting joy.

Eternal rest grant unto them and let perpetual light shine upon them. Amen.

DATE: _____

Today, ask the saints known as intercessors for the dead to pray with you for their release, including St. Nicholas of Tolentino, St. Gertrude the Great, St. Catherine of Genoa, St. Padre Pio, St. Philip Neri, St. John Macías, St. Faustina Kowalska, St. Joseph and, of course, the Blessed Mother.

Morning Prayer for the Poor Souls:

Out of the depths I have cried to Thee O Lord! Lord, hear my voice. Let Thine ears be attentive to the voice of my supplication.
If Thou, O Lord, wilt mark iniquities, Lord, who shall stand it?
For with Thee there is mercy: and by reason of Thy law I have waited on Thee, O Lord! My soul hath relied on His word: my soul hath hoped in the Lord. From the morning watch even until night. Let Israel hope in the Lord. For with the Lord there is mercy; and with Him plentiful Redemption. And He will redeem Israel from all his iniquities.
Eternal rest give unto them, O Lord! And let perpetual light shine upon them. May they rest in peace. Amen.

Evening Prayer for the Poor Souls:

V. Lord, hear my prayer.
R. And let my cry come unto Thee.
Bless, O my God! the repose I am about to take, that, renewing my strength, I may be better enabled to serve Thee. Pour down Thy blessings, O Lord! on my parents, relations, friends, and enemies. Protect the Pope, our Bishop, and all the Pastors of Thy holy Church. Assist the poor and the afflicted, and those who are now in their last agony. Look with an eye of pity on the suffering souls in purgatory, particularly

_____

_____

_____

put an end to their torments and lead them forth into everlasting joy.

Eternal rest grant unto them and let perpetual light shine upon them. Amen.

Father,
source of forgiveness and salvation for all mankind,
hear our prayer.
By the prayers of the ever-virgin Mary,
may our friends, relatives, and benefactors
who have gone from this world
come to share eternal happiness with all your saints.
We ask this through our Lord Jesus Christ, your Son,
who lives and reigns with you and the Holy Spirit,
God, for ever and ever.
Amen.

-from the Office of the Dead

NOTES

NOTES

NOTES

NOTES

NOTES

NOTES

NOTES

Printed in Great Britain
by Amazon